In Search of God

In Search of God

The Meaning and Message of the Everlasting Names

TRYGGVE N. D. METTINGER

Translated by
FREDERICK H. CRYER

Fortress Press   Philadelphia

Quotations from J. C. L. Gibson's translations of the Ugaritic texts, *Canaanite Myths and Legends* (Edinburgh: T & T Clark, 1978), are used by permission.

Translated from the Swedish *Gudsbeteckningar och gudsbild i Gamla Testamentet.* Copyright © 1987 by Tryggve N. D. Mettinger and Bokförlaget Libris Örebro.

Published with the aid of grants from the Swedish Council for Research in the Humanities and the Social Sciences.

Maps 1, 2, 3, 4, and Figure 9 by Per Helin.

Figures 8, 10, 11, 12, and 13 by Andrzej Szlagor.

Biblical quotations, unless otherwise noted, are from the Revised Standard Version of the Bible, copyright 1946, 1952, © 1971, 1973 by the Division of Christian Education of the National Council of the Churches of Christ in the U.S.A., and are used by permission.

ENGLISH TRANSLATION COPYRIGHT © 1988 BY FORTRESS PRESS

Library of Congress Cataloging-in-Publication Data

Mettinger, Tryggve N. D.
  In search of God.

  Translation of: Gudsbeteckningar och gudsbild i
Gamla Testamentet.
  Bibliography: p.
  Includes index.
  1. God—Name—Biblical teaching. 2. Bible.
O.T.—Criticism, interpretation, etc. I. Title.
BS1192.6.M5813 1988   231   88–45335
ISBN 0–8006–0892–5

3438E88   Printed in the United States of America   1–892

Contents

Contents

Contents

Illustrations

Preface

O Lord GOD, thou hast only begun to
show thy servant thy greatness and thy
mighty hand. (Deut 3:24)

The question of God is being posed today with ever-increasing
sharpness. The study of the biblical idea of God has thus assumed
renewed importance. The present work is accordingly a contribution
to this effort. The analysis of the biblical understanding of God presented here is based upon a study of the divine names in the Old
Testament, and it records the results of my research into such divine
designations as "YHWH," "YHWH Sabaoth," "the King," and others.
These names appear to be the key to a better understanding of the
idea of God contained in the Hebrew Bible.

My intention here is to offer an exegetical treatment of the most
representative divine names, with a view to revealing the underlying
theological conceptions which are associated with the various names.
This is done on the basis of a *philological* and *historical* investigation
of each name.

Someone once compared biblical revelation to a two-storied house.
The street floor represents that part of the revelation of which its tradents (i.e., the prophets and authors) were cognizant. The key to the
understanding of this "level" of revelation is therefore the historical-
grammatical study of the texts. By way of contrast, the upper floor
represents God's overarching intentions, which may conceivably go far
beyond what an individual prophet may have consciously intended in
a given historical situation (cf., e.g., Isa 7:14 and Matt 1:22ff.). This
aspect of revelation does not reside within the realm of the historically
tangible; it is not accessible to the scholar. As a Christian I believe that
the key to its right understanding is provided by the Holy Spirit.

Naturally, in this work we shall confine ourselves to "the street-
floor of revelation"; we shall accordingly make use of the tools of

historical-grammatical study. Such efforts, too, are an important part of what has been called "the ministry of the Word" (Acts 6:4). In so doing, however, we must acknowledge our limitations: we must realize that, time and again, in a given situation it may be possible to view matters in a different perspective.

The general plan of the book is as follows. Chapter 1 presents some general observations as to the role played by both mortal and divine names in the biblical world. Chapter 2 then deals with the most holy divine name "YHWH," which the Old Testament especially associates with Moses and the exodus. Without a doubt this is the most important divine name in the Bible. There subsequently follow in more or less historical sequence a series of chapters (3—8) dealing with the more important divine names which were used in the interval between the patriarchs and the Babylonian captivity. In the study of "the God of the Fathers" and of "El Shaddai" (Chapter 3), our focus is on material in the Book of Genesis. This is followed by a quick sketch of the relations between Israelite faith and Canaanite religion (Chapter 4). Chapter 4 will form the background for our study of "the living God" (Chapter 5), "the King" (Chapter 6), and "YHWH Sabaoth" (Chapter 7). In the last two instances texts in the Psalter and in the Book of Isaiah will be the foci of our attention. Finally, the various names employed by the exilic Prophet of Consolation, especially "the Redeemer" and "the Creator," will be studied (Chapter 8). Chapter 9, forming an epilogue, treats the attempts in the Book of Job to wrestle with the question of God; here we shall not be concerned with the various divine names, but we shall observe how the divine speeches are associated with the ideas which are peculiar to one of the most important divine names in the OT.

We are concerned with the divine names and the understanding of God in the Hebrew Bible. In a number of cases, however, we find reason to deal with New Testament materials as well.

Some practical remarks are also in order here. The considerable interest I encountered when I lectured on the topics of this work encouraged me to present the results of my exegetical studies in a way which will be accessible also to the nonspecialist in biblical exegesis. I have therefore attempted to be intelligible not only to biblical scholars and students but also to those engaged in the pursuit of other branches of religion and theology and to parish clergy who weekly confront biblical texts. It is also my hope that this will encourage future interdisciplinary studies.

For the nonspecialist there is a glossary of terms (pp. 220-23) which contains short explanations of a number of terms normally used by the professional exegete.

Two special features of the book merit comment: the illustrations and the excurses. As for the *illustrations,* some are maps for the convenience of the reader. Others are carefully selected representations of ancient Near Eastern art. The latter are part of my scientific approach: to use not only texts but also iconographical material in order to shed light on the ideas discussed. Thus a number of the illustrations form the starting points for my argument and accordingly deserve attention.

The *excurses* contain material of various types: surveys of concordance materials, reviews of important scholarly debates, or detailed discussions of complex problems. College, university, and seminary teachers will find ample material here that lends itself to classroom discussions, research for essays, and other pedagogical exercises.

It should be clear that knowledge of the biblical languages provides a royal highway into the texts. Nevertheless, I have not ventured to assume that every potential reader can easily follow detailed argumentation about Semitic philology. For this reason chapter sections containing a discussion of philological problems are usually set in small type, so that those wishing to follow the main thread of the argument may skip over the detailed discussion. The chapter in this work which might conceivably offer the reader the greatest difficulty is that which deals with the name "YHWH" (Chapter 2); those who might find it a tough nut to crack may wish to save it for last.

Unless otherwise indicated, the biblical quotations follow the Revised Standard Version (RSV). When the reference to a biblical passage is marked with an asterisk (*), as, for example, Exod 3:14*, the author is responsible for the translation in question. It may be a case in which some particular point in the text is not sufficiently expressed in our usual translations. Citations of chapter and verse follow the RSV, while Hebrew transcription follows the system employed by the *Journal of Biblical Literature.* Variant capitulation and versification in the Hebrew text is indicated by brackets [ ] following the normal RSV reference.

This book has grown out of research and lecture activity undertaken at the University of Lund, Sweden, and at Princeton Theological Seminary, New Jersey, where I lectured as a guest professor for a

Preface

semester on the biblical divine names. I now want to thank Professor J.J.M. Roberts of Princeton Theological Seminary, who took the initiative to invite me to lecture and so gave an impetus to the writing of this book. Many students, colleagues, co-workers, and friends on both sides of the Atlantic have generously contributed their tips, views, and intellectual stimuli. To all of them I am grateful. The help I have received has meant a great deal on the practical plane, and has provided much of the pleasure I have experienced in the course of writing this work. The publication of this work was made possible by a grant from *The Swedish Council for Research in the Humanities and Social Sciences.* My colleague in New Testament at the University of Lund, Professor Birger Gerhardsson, read the entire manuscript for the Council and made a number of valuable suggestions. The English translation was done by Frederick H. Cryer, presently teaching at the Ruhr-University, Bochum, West Germany. I am most grateful to Mr. Cryer for having applied both his linguistic and his exegetical expertise to this task. Michael S. Cheney, M.Div., Th.M., and Dr. Gunnlauger A. Jónsson shared with me the burden of proofreading. I also owe my thanks to the staff of Fortress Press for their patience, cooperation, and skill.

One final word: this work should be read with one's Bible at hand. If, in following this rule, the reader should happen to experience some share of the joy of discovery which often arises in the course of immediate contact with the biblical texts, then I have not entirely failed in my aims.

University of Lund, Sweden
May, 1988

Tryggve N.D. Mettinger

1
The Divine Names:
Milestones in Salvation History

Who are you, God? When in the course of human events we should ask, "Who is that person really?" about someone whose identity we do not know, the first thing we are usually told is his or her name. Only subsequently are we informed as to the individual details that comprise the portrait of the individual in question. A name establishes and manifests a person's identity.

This is also the case when human beings encounter the God of Israel. This encounter has taken place at widely separate times and in completely different sorts of situations. In the course of life's many challenges, human beings have been privileged to discern new features in the face of the Eternal. Such milestones in the history of salvation have sometimes been distinguished by God's self-revelation under a new name. In Gen 17:1 God approaches a man (Abraham) for the first time in the Bible with the words, "I am El Shaddai," a divine name which is traditionally translated "God Almighty." Later God reveals himself to Moses and announces,

> I am YHWH. I appeared to Abraham, to Isaac, and to Jacob, as God Almighty, but by my name YHWH I did not make myself known to them. (Exod 6:2-3)

There are a number of viable approaches to the study of the Old Testament understanding of God. I have chosen to use the various divine names as the landmarks of this expedition into the Bible; from their vantage points we take our stand and make our observations. My study will naturally need to be supplemented by others. But it should become clear that my approach will lead us to new heights and new vistas.

In defining our task, we do so on the basis of the insight that the divine names are symbols. These symbols speak of God but do so in terms of categories drawn from the world of human experience. The

1

divine names share the usual peculiarities of metaphorical language. The philosopher Max Black has called attention to the way metaphors function as filters.[1] Black uses as an example the sentence "man is a wolf," and points out that such a metaphorical statement is not meaningful to a person who is ignorant about wolves. Nor, he adds, is it sufficient to know the standard dictionary meaning of the word "wolf." The presupposition for correct understanding of the statement is that the reader is familiar with the system of associated commonplaces that the word "wolf" projects onto "man." In this way, "man" is characterized as an aggressive and crafty beast of prey. Thus the wolf metaphor functions as a filter, which momentarily structures and colors our perceptions of "man." Moreover, other conceivable human features—tenderness, thoughtfulness, or dedication—are excluded by the choice of the metaphor in question. The metaphor selects, suppresses, highlights, and organizes features of the principal subject by implying statements about it that we normally apply to the subsidiary subject.

As for the biblical divine names, this means that we are confronted with a twofold task: (1) to attempt to determine the linguistic contents of each name and (2) to define the system of associated commonplaces that is associated with each name, which we shall do by studying the name in question in its broad, cultural context. Our ultimate aim will always be to contribute to a better understanding of the more important of the ideas of God associated with each divine name. Here I use the expression "ideas of God," by which I understand the Israelite's conceptions of God's qualities, activities, and field of action (i.e., whether God is active in nature or in history, in the life of the individual or of the nation, and so forth).[2]

THE DIVINE NAMES AS
ORGANIZING PRINCIPLE

Who are you, God? This, in essence, is our question. Therefore we will attempt to demonstrate the various answers that the divine names in the Old Testament make possible. The names thus serve as an organizing principle for our investigation. Does this way of working correspond to the question we have posed and the materials with which we shall be dealing?

We will not enter into a theoretical discussion of the serious methodological issues that have been raised in modern accounts of

Old Testament theology and the religion of Israel. Instead, I shall briefly discuss Claus Westermann's contribution to this debate in *What Does the Old Testament Say about God?* (1979).[3]

In brief, Westermann notes that accounts of Old Testament theology frequently focus on terms such as election, covenant, salvation, reconciliation, and eschatology. These terms, he notes, are nouns and, additionally, reifications of abstract concepts. Westermann's main objection to such a procedure is that in pursuing such abstractions the scholar thereby distances herself or himself from the language of the Old Testament. In the majority of cases, the words in question represent the reflections of later ages on matters which in the Bible are depicted in a far more concrete and earthy language.

Westermann recommends an alternative approach: instead of speaking of salvation as a condition, for example, the scholar ought to investigate the verb structures (e.g., the verb *yāša*ʿ, which is the usual Hebrew word signifying "to save"). In this fashion, or so Westermann believes, the scholar will not be operating with a static condition, but with a dynamic event.

Application of this method has made Westermann conscious of two foci in the great ellipse that describes the Old Testament conceptions of God: (1) In one focus we find *the saving God,* a concept that has to do with instantaneous divine intervention coming "out of the blue" (i.e., the "senkrecht von Oben" of Karl Barth). God is active in the history of salvation of his chosen people. (2) In the other focus we find *the blessing God,* who is active in creation. This has nothing to do with dramatic salvation-historical intervention, but with God's constant and unflagging blessing which at every instant connects the creation with its source and which may be considered to function "horizontally," within the very course of events. The harvests of the fields and the offspring populating the patriarchal tent are daily signs of the reality of the blessing God. This understanding of God is to be found in the wisdom literature and the Psalms; whereas the reader of the Bible encounters the saving God in the historical books, above all in Exodus and the Deuteronomistic History (Deuteronomy—2 Kings). (See Fig. 1.)

Westermann's account is a healthy reaction to the narrowness that has long characterized the study of Old Testament theology: scholars have been entirely too fixated on the saving God. The salvation-historical perspective has been dominant. Westermann has given us a useful reminder that the God of the Bible is more than a saving God.

Westermann has also touched a nerve when he points to the curse of abstraction that has plagued Old Testament theologies in modern times. Confronted with the threat of slowly drowning in the ocean of disparate data contained in the texts, the scholar all too often attempts to summarize and generalize, thus ending up with somewhat anemic abstractions.

In short, Westermann's contribution has its value. Working from different points of departure, other scholars have correspondingly helped to call our attention to other features of the Old Testament understanding of God. Among my reasons for choosing the divine names as the focus of this study is the fact that this slippery problem has been largely ignored in modern Old Testament research. The decision to approach the question of the Israelite understanding of God via the divine names helps us to face two important challenges to which one simply must submit if one seriously intends to work with the biblical understanding of God.

The first challenge is this: to take the texts' own formulations seriously, rather than to seize the life preserver of our theological abstractions. When we work with the divine designations, we are dealing with linguistic items that are elements in the God-language of the Hebrew Bible itself. In other words, we are moving on the plane of the Hebrew language. Nor is this all. We are dealing with names, and for the ancient Israelite, names were loaded with content.

The second challenge is this: resolutely to place oneself in the midst of the history in which the biblical actors found themselves when they

FIGURE 1

TWO ASPECTS OF THE OLD TESTAMENT
UNDERSTANDING OF GOD

The Blessing God	The Saving God
God confers his blessing on generation after generation, from the creation and onwards.	God's intervention in history, as in the exodus miracle
The Psalms and wisdom literature (Proverbs, Ecclesiastes, Job)	The OT historical books

The German biblical scholar Claus Westermann distinguishes between two main aspects of the Old Testament understanding of God.

4

bore their witness to God. Our attention should not only be directed to linguistic details but also to historical situations. The Old Testament never provides us with any comprehensive summary account of the various aspects of God's being that might be apprehended in the abstract and outside of all time, isolated from the situational details of historical eventuality. The reader of the Old Testament must simply accept that he or she is confronted with an entire portrait gallery of understandings of God; the texts relate how God encountered humankind in a variety of concrete situations. New historical situations made the people of God aware of new characteristics of the visage of the hidden God. This observation brings us to an important point: the reciprocal interaction between situation and theology. The theology of ancient Israel, understood in a qualified sense as her conceptions of God, emerged in response to the ever-changing challenges of human existence.

The biblical texts bear powerful witness to the conviction that in the midst of all mutability there is one constant factor in the history of revelation: it was one and the same God who spoke to Abraham, Moses, Isaiah, and Ezekiel (cf. Exod 3:6; 6:3). This, however, did not signify that Isaiah's understanding of God was identical with that of the patriarchs. We shall shortly observe in what ways the patriarchs' understanding of God corresponded to important features of their situational existence. They were, of course, wandering herdsmen. Isaiah, by contrast, was an aristocratic prophet from seventh-century Jerusalem; he was at home both at court and among the upper circles of the temple. It is hardly surprising that God reveals himself to Isaiah in a way that corresponds to the latter's frame of reference. Nor, for that matter, is it surprising that this prophet describes how he has seen God sitting "upon a throne, high and lifted up," and shouts that he has beheld "the King, YHWH Sabaoth" (Isa 6:5).

It is of course a historical fact that ancient Israel's divine designations changed over the centuries. It may be inferred that these changes were in some way related to developments in Israel's faith. In turn this insight requires that any serious attempt to study the Old Testament divine names will inevitably make us aware of an important aspect of ancient Israelite faith—its historical dynamic. Thus our eyes are opened to the diversity of the Old Testament world. The method we have chosen saves us from a fixation on any single aspect of the Israelite view of God. The divine reality is so great that it can and must be expressed in continually emerging, new systems of symbols.

5

When one considers the profits to be derived from a study of the divine names versus other conceivable strategies for the investigation of the Israelite understanding of God, it is quite astonishing how small a role such studies have played in the research into Old Testament theology in general and the understanding of the Israelite view of God in particular.

A complete listing of the various Old Testament divine designations would be a long one. Without further ado, such names as YHWH ("the Lord"), El Shaddai ("God Almighty"), Elohim ("God"), and YHWH Sabaoth ("YHWH of Hosts") come to mind, as do such epithets as "the living God," "the Holy One," "the Most High," and "the Redeemer." This book will deal with only a selection of the many divine designations.[4] Some of the designations will be bypassed. Rightly or wrongly, I have chosen not to deal with such names as Elohim, Eloah, and a number of others. Some of these names are so vague and amorphous that they have little to offer to an investigation of this kind, while others are so rarely attested that they cannot be considered to have been representative.

THE SIGNIFICANCE OF NAMES
IN THE BIBLICAL WORLD

First, we want to consider how human names in general and the names of God in particular functioned in the biblical world. We perceive a number of features immediately which indicate that in that world names were things of great moment.

NAME AND REALITY

In the conceptual world of ancient Semitic culture, name and reality were interrelated. The introduction to the Babylonian creation epic, *Enuma Elish*, describes the conditions that obtained before the creation of heaven and earth. In this connection the Akkadian text describes how things were before they had been "named."[5] Name and existence belong together.

We find something similar in the biblical paradise narrative:

> So out of the ground the Lord God formed every beast of the field and every bird of the air, and brought them to the man to see what he would call them; and whatever the man called every living creature, that was its name. (Gen 2:19)

In this connection Dean McBride is astute when he maintains that this act of name-giving is an important complement to God's original act of creation; it is the means by which all life is ordered, subdivided, and defined into recognizable quantities.[6]

NAME AND PERSONALITY

In the modern Western world we tend to regard names as simply labels that have been stuck onto things, that is, as trivial tools that help to identify individuals and distinguish them from each other. In the world of the Hebrew Bible, however, we find evidence of the notion of a more profound connection between the name and its bearer.[7]

In 1 Samuel 25 there is the tale of the man Nabal.[8] He arrogantly rejects an application by David and his men for victuals. Nabal's wife realizes how foolish this is and says to David,

> Let not my lord regard this ill-natured fellow, Nabal; for as his name is, so is he; Nabal is his name, and folly is with him. (1 Sam 25:25)

Nabal's parents had presumably given him a name that meant "the noble one"; however, the same adjective, *nābāl*, may also carry the opposite signification, "the senseless one," "the fool." It is this play on words which is the point of the reference in our narrative; what is typical of Nabal is well expressed in his name. Another example is to be found in the patriarchal narratives, where Esau remarks of his unscrupulous brother,

> Is he not rightly named Jacob? For he has supplanted me these two times. He took away my birthright; and behold, now he has taken away my blessing. (Gen 27:36)

A reliable research tradition holds that the name Jacob means "may God protect" or "may God preserve," and that it was probably pronounced as an act of well wishing by parents over their newborn infant.[9] Esau, however, has associated the name with a different Semitic root, namely, *ʿāqab,* meaning "to deceive," so that the name "Jacob" serves as a trenchant expression of the person's most prominent characteristic, his treacherousness. This may help us to understand why Jacob is accorded a new name and is no longer "Jacob," but "Israel." Jacob's nocturnal experience of God at the Jabbok seems to have entailed so vast a change in his nature that he was no longer the same as before (Gen 32:28).

7

It is against the background of such connections between name and personality—connections that are difficult to define, but nevertheless tangible—that we are able to understand a pair of different expressions. One of these occurs in a conversation between God and Moses in which the former says, "I know you by name" (Exod 33:17; cf. v 12). When, in our contemporary usage, we refer to knowing someone by name, we intend thereby a fairly superficial acquaintance. By way of contrast, the biblical way of speaking refers to something more profound: God knows who Moses really is and God has a personal knowledge of Moses' character.

The second expression is the well-known phrase "for his name's sake." The psalmist says, "He leads me on right paths for his name's sake" (Ps 23:3). There is also the prophetic expression "For my name's sake I defer my anger" (e.g., Isa 48:9, cf. Jer 14:7). This phrase seems to deal with the question of God's real nature. Because God is the way he actually is, because God is God, therefore he leads his own on the right path, is patient, forgives sins, and so on. What is interesting about all this for our purposes is that the Bible expresses these realities by referring to God's name.

The connection envisaged here between the name and the person also provides us with the reason why the name sometimes takes the place of its bearer in the Old Testament, as for example, in Isaiah and the Psalter:

> Behold, the name of the Lord comes from far,
> burning with his anger, and in thick rising smoke.
> (Isa 30:27)

> The Lord answer you in the day of trouble!
> The name of the God of Jacob protect you!
> (Ps 20:1)

NAME AND PRESENCE

So far we have spoken of the associations between name and reality, and between name and personality. Now we must say something about the connection between name and presence.[10] The "presence" in question is that of God; we are speaking of divine self-revelations, the so-called theophanies (see Glossary).

In the ancient "Altar Law" in the Book of the Covenant, there is a statement whose original Hebrew text is difficult to interpret. In my opinion it is to be read as follows:

8

> In every place where I proclaim my name I shall come to you and bless you. (Exod 20:24*[11])

In other words, God proclaims his name in the sanctuary and thus manifests his presence (cf. Deut 4:7).

In the Old Testament we find a number of texts which may with some qualification be said to describe a theophany, a divine self-revelation. These descriptions contain two characteristic features. First, they usually refer to the "coming" of the deity (from Sinai, Paran, and so forth). The verb of motion implies that God is approaching. Second, we are told of natural manifestations in connection with the advent of God: the earth shakes, the mountains tremble and run like melted wax. Such a text as Judges 5:4–5 (cf. also, e.g., Pss 18:8–16; 68:8–9; 97:1–6; Micah 1:3–4) belongs to the peculiar genre of theophany descriptions. Scholars like Artur Weiser[12] and others have maintained that the theophany was ritually realized in the course of worship in the temple of Solomon. Such ritual activity would harmonize well with the dramatic character of the liturgy. In addition to the torches and blasts of the trumpet which, or so we may imagine, may have been ritual requisites of the theophany (cf. Exod 19:16 and 20:18), it is also conceivable that the proclamation of the divine name formed the crucial moment and signified God's presence in a special way. The proclamation may have been performed by the high priest or by a prophet who was an active participant in the cultic service.

Of course, this possibility is and will remain hypothetical. It is a fact, however, that the proclamation of the divine name plays a significant role in texts that may be related to the theophanies. For example, in Exod 33:18–23 Moses requests to be allowed to see the glory of God. The Lord accedes to this request by "passing by" (note the verb of motion) the place where Moses is standing. As far as we can tell, Moses is not allowed to behold God's "glory" (*kābôd*), nor is he allowed to glimpse God's "face" (*pānîm*). Ensconced in a cleft of the rock and protected by God's hand, Moses can scarcely see any of the divine majesty that sweeps by him. But he does hear! And what he hears is clearly stated: he hears God pronounce his name, YHWH, for him. When God pronounces his name (*šēm*), the divine presence is made manifest (v 19, cf. 34:5–6).

In this examination of the special ideas associated with names in ancient Israel, one needs to take into account the use of naming in a special legal ritual context.

PRONOUNCING NAMES AS A LEGAL ACT

When we buy or sell property, normally the transaction in question is the object of binding written documentation. By contrast, we find instead that in ancient Israel the proclamation of the name of the new owner played an important role. For example, when a field changed hands there was a proclamation of the name in the presence of witnesses: the money changed hands and the name of the new owner was called out over the field in question, thereby completing the transaction.

Kurt Galling has shown that this custom explains a number of often misunderstood passages in the Old Testament.[13] Thus, for example, we read in Ps 49:11 [12] concerning the ungodly that "they call out their names over [new] property," that is, they take possession of more and more. This juridical language recurs in numerous passages. In Isa 4:1, for example, the Hebrew text relates that seven women say to one and the same man, "May thy name be called over us." The same juridical language is also used theologically, as, for example, when we are told that the name of the Lord is proclaimed over someone or something. The notion that Jeremiah was named after God's name, as the translations of Jer 15:16 frequently suggest, is clearly unreasonable. What the text actually talks about in this passage is the fact that "your name has been named over me, O YHWH, God of Hosts." The prophet is referring to the fact that he is subject to the property rights of God; he is the slave of the Lord! Similarly, we read in Jer 14:9*, "Yet thou, O Lord, dwellest in the midst of us, and thy name has been called over us." Also, on the occasion of the dedication of the temple, Solomon says that "your name has been called over this house which I have built" (1 Kings 8:43*). Finally, in Amos 9:12 it is "the people" over whom the name of God has been called.

It is an obvious point, but one worth reiterating, that the Old Testament was the Bible of Jesus; the New Testament would lack its proper context if it could not be interpreted in the light of the writings of the earlier covenant. In the course of this study we shall make a number of excursions into the New Testament. Already here, however, I must refer to a specific New Testament passage, namely, the Letter of James 2:7, where we read: "Is it not they [i.e., the rich] who blaspheme the honorable name which was invoked over you?" The expression harks back to the Old Testament proclamation of the name of ownership on the occasion of a transaction, and it apparently refers to the fact that Jesus' name was proclaimed over those who were baptized. Whoever was baptized in the name of Jesus had entered into a new relationship; he or she had become Jesus' property.[14]

SUMMARY

So far we have attempted to examine the associations that in ancient Israel were attached to human names in general and to God's name in particular. We noted the connection between name and reality: the naming of the animals perfected the creation. We then examined the connection between name and personality: the name expresses the essence of the person. Third, we studied some passages that illustrate the important role played by the divine name as a manifestation of God's presence. Finally, we noted the use of the proclamation of names in the context of a legal ritual.

The relation between a name and its bearer is difficult to define. On the one hand, names seem to have served as symbolic attributes of their tradents. On the other, the connection between a name and its bearer is so intimate that it is hard to speak of a name as a quantity that can be clearly separated from the individual who bears it. A person's name tends to be her or his alter ego and reflects her or his nature, power, and reality.

We are now ready to begin our study. First, however, we must remember that God remains the hidden God. The God who in the Old Testament has contacts with mortals remains, nevertheless, always God, and in sacredness God will remain unfathomable. The Old Testament knows of only one response to the divine self-revelation: the worship and fear of the Lord. Anyone seeking contact with God must be prepared to respect God's incognito.

Basically, we are caught up with the tension between the finite and the infinite. It is essential to acknowledge that there are limits to our human reason and our earthly language. Ultimately, we are reminded of the church father, Gregorius, who held that to try to grasp the hidden God through a study of this God's names is like trying to contain the ocean in the palm of one's hand.

EXCURSUS 1
CAN A NAME BE LINGUISTICALLY SIGNIFICANT?

In this book we shall study the "meaning" of some of the more important divine names in the Bible. What do we actually intend when we speak of the "meaning" of a word? Modern linguistic science has stressed that there is no direct relationship between a word and the thing it stands for. There is no law that requires us to call a car a "car"; in Swedish the word is "bil," in German, "Auto," and so forth. In the nature of things, the relationship in question is arbitrary, random.

There is a fundamental distinction between "reference" and "sense" in connection with words. Imagine that the police arrest a criminal named Svensson, who, however, denies all culpability during interrogation. As he goes off shift, one of the policemen utters the following statement: "Svensson is going to prove a hard *nut* for us to crack." In this sentence the word *nut* refers to Svensson; this is the "reference" or "denotation" of the word. At the same time, though, the word awakens among those who hear it associations with the small fruits with hard shells which we call "nuts." Thus the word has a certain associative content, which we term its "connotation." It is therefore proper to speak of both a word's "denotation" and its "connotation."

Linguists who have worked with proper names usually emphasize that such names have referential, denotative meaning, but no connotative meaning. In the circle of our acquaintances, we know who is meant by "Margaret" or "Peter"; the names have reference value. On the other hand, we do not ordinarily place any special significance on the names themselves. Only those of us with some special interest in language associate these names with the Greek words for "pearl" and "rock," respectively. And it is only in quite exceptional circumstances that a proper name becomes a concept (consider such names as "Quisling" or "Adonis," both of which have become appellatives).

In Hebrew the situation is somewhat different. For instance, the root meaning of a given Hebrew word is often apparent, no matter how the word is inflected. Thus in the majority of cases the Israelite proper names were fully intelligible to the Israelites. Moreover, they contained more than merely reference content. As a rule they are likely to have had a connotative meaning as well, although it is naturally questionable to what extent this meaning was actualized in any given speech situation. Names like Melchizedek, Isaiah, and Jehoshaphat were understandable by any adult Israelite. It is easy (and was easy then, too) to separate them into their linguistic component parts and thus to determine their meaning. A modern student can see, even after a single semester's Hebrew instruction, that these names mean "king of righteousness," "the Lord saves," and "the Lord judges," respectively.

The same applies to the Hebrew divine names, which means that it is a legitimate undertaking to attempt to determine their linguistic derivation and etymology. Moreover, it is a reasonable supposition that the etymology of a divine name held certain associative possibilities for the Israelites.

Of course it would be a serious error to imagine that in each given speech situation each of the divine names awakened certain definite associations. This was hardly the case. The names are surely most often used in their simple referential sense, as convenient ways to designate the deity. On the other hand, there are a number of situations in which the divine name in question was laden with a deeper significance. No one can read Exod 3:13–15 without realizing that the entire context constitutes an exploration into the secrets of the name YHWH. Nor can it be coincidence that the name Sabaoth is used of God in the description of the call of Isaiah (Isa. 6).

An additional factor must not be overlooked. As with people, so with words: the childhood milieu can be of inestimable importance for the whole of life. As to certain of the divine names, it is apparently the case that the milieu in which they first came into use stamped their character once and for all (see my study of "Sabaoth", pp. 123–57).

Literature: Sawyer [1967]; Barr [1969]; Holmqvist ([1971]: 64–109), Lyons ([1977]: 215–23); Stamm [1980]; Kjær-Hansen ([1982]: 100–105).

2
The God Who Says "I AM": The Riddle of the Name YHWH

Samuel Josef Agnon, the Israeli winner of the Nobel prize for literature, tells us about a Torah scribe named Raphael, whose profession
it was to make handwritten copies of the sacred scrolls. Every time
Raphael came to a place in the text where the original contained the
divine name YHWH, he left a lacuna in his own copy instead. It was
only when he had carried out special rites of purification that he
filled in the gaps. This tortuous procedure might seem strange to a
modern Westerner; nevertheless, it provides ample witness to the
unique importance of the name YHWH among the biblical divine
names.[1] The name YHWH is the most sacred of them all. It is this
Name the apostle Paul refers to when he speaks of "the name which
is above every name" (Phil 2:9). With its 6,828 attestations, YHWH is
also by far the most commonly used of the Old Testament divine
names.

Our investigation of the name YHWH will proceed as follows. First,
we shall deal with the *historical question* of the origin of the Name.
Next, we shall grapple with the *philological question* of the linguistic
content of this divine Name. Third, we shall tackle the *theological question* as to which theological associations the Name may have evoked in
ancient Israel. Naturally, all three approaches are interconnected in a
profound way. I offer a simplification in the interests of clarity. Before
doing so, however, we must attempt to illuminate some introductory
questions. These include the sacredness of the divine Name and the
use of substitute words, and also the question of the general character
of the major relevant texts (Exod 3 and 6).

A HOLY NAME

WHY DO WE FIND "THE LORD" IN BIBLICAL TRANSLATIONS?

As the Jews began to regard the name *YHWH* to be laden with particular sacredness, they gradually ceased to pronounce it. The very pronunciation of the Name became doubtful, and to this day scholars are not completely sure how it was pronounced. We cannot date this process with precision, but it must have taken place during the period between the Old and New Testaments. Here we will review some evidence as to the sacred status of the divine Name.

In the Book of Leviticus we find an account of a fight between two Israelites (Lev 24:10–16). During the struggle, one of the parties "blasphemed the Name, and cursed." The gravity of the crime is indicated by the punishment that it merited; the man in question was condemned according to the divinely sanctioned principles of sacral law:

> He who blasphemes the name of the Lord shall be put to death; all the congregation shall stone him; the sojourner as well as the native, when he blasphemes the Name, shall be put to death. (Lev 24:16)

The ever-increasing consciousness of the sacredness of the Name is attested to by the tendency to use the less numinous "Elohim" instead of "YHWH" to refer to God. This tendency is fully evident already in the parallels in the Books of Chronicles to the Books of Kings and in a special group of psalms (Pss 42—83).[2]

The Dead Sea Scrolls also provide us with several striking examples of the special treatment of the Name. In certain texts the Name has not been written in the then-contemporary, standard square script, but in the earlier alphabet (the epigraphical one). The effect is the same as if in the midst of a modern piece of printing, we suddenly wrote a particular term in Gothic script. It sometimes also occurs in these texts that the Name is completely left out and is represented instead by four dots, one for each letter in the holy Name.[3]

In the Mishna (see the Glossary), the "tradition of the elders," we read about the class of sinners who have forfeited their right to a share in the age to come. Among these are said to be those who deny the resurrection of the dead, as well as those who claim that the Law did not come from heaven. Among them also, however, are those who pronounce the Name (cf. *m. Sanhedrin* 10:1). This collection of legal traditions brings us down to the first centuries of the Common Era.

But what practice did one follow then in the synagogue, for example, when in the course of reading a text aloud one came to the name YHWH? Of course, one had to replace it with another, less "loaded" name. In fact the replacement was the Hebrew *ʾădōnāy*, which means "Lord." In other words, every time one found "YHWH" in the text, one read "Adonay" instead, which explains why we find the term "the Lord" in modern biblical translations in passages where the Hebrew text simply contains the divine Name.[4]

To eliminate the risk of false readings, the Jews gradually began to vocalize the "YHWH" of the Hebrew text with the vowels of the word "Adonay." This occurred under the aegis of the Masoretes (see Glossary), who were active in the period between 500 and 1000 C.E. It is important to recognize that the vowels one finds in YHWH in the Hebrew Bible tell us nothing at all about the pronunciation of the Name, as they belong to a different word entirely, namely, to "Adonay." Nevertheless, some scholars once read the consonants of "YHWH" together with the vowels of "Adonay" and arrived at the name "Jehovah," a reading which attained considerable popularity until the end of the nineteenth century (see Fig. 2). It is quite certain, however, that the ancient Israelites never used this term of their God; formally it is like a genetic hybrid, as artificial as the words "eledile" and "crocophant."

Two important features of the word *ʾădōnāy* should be noted here. In Hebrew the usual word for "lord" is *ʾādôn*. The form *ʾădōnāy* has been interpreted as

FIGURE 2
"JEHOVAH": AN IMPOSSIBLE DIVINE NAME

JeHoVaH

ʾadonay

"YHWH" is the name we find in the appropriate texts in the Hebrew Bible. "Adonay," however, was read in its place, as "YHWH" was too sacred to utter. In acknowledgment of this fact, the vowels belonging to "Adonay" were assigned to the consonants in "YHWH." However, it was never intended that the consonants of "YHWH" should be read together with the vowels of "Adonay." When this nevertheless occurred during the Middle Ages, the result was "Jehovah," an artificial form bearing no relation to the name of the God of Israel in biblical times.

an intensive form signifying "lord of all" (Eissfeldt [1973]:col. 67), although this view remains controversial. Furthermore, here and there in the Old Testament we run across both of these words used as divine designations, though in contexts in which they are unquestionably not replacements for the most holy divine Name (e.g., Deut 10:17; Josh 3:13; Isa 3:1, 15; Micah 1:2). This usage may well have ancient Canaanite roots (cf. Loretz [1980A]).

We have observed how YHWH in the course of time came to be regarded as too holy to be pronounced and how it was replaced in practice with "Adonay," "the Lord." This reluctance to use the Name is also evidenced in some of Jesus' words in the New Testament. Jesus allows the prodigal son to say, "Father, I have sinned against heaven and before you" (Luke 15:21), a phrase in which the Name has been replaced by the word "heaven." The phrase about seeing the Son of man sitting "at the right hand of Power" (Matt 26:64) is another example. Still yet another way of avoiding the use of the Name was the use of circumlocutions in the passive voice (e.g., Matt 7:7).[5]

At this point a digression on the use of the Greek term "Kyrios" in reference to Jesus is appropriate.[6] The word itself means "Lord." It is of utmost importance for the understanding of New Testament christology that this use of "Kyrios" be seen against its Old Testament background, since this background points from "Kyrios" to "Adonay" and ultimately to the most sacred Name (see Fig. 3).

FIGURE 3

FROM YHWH TO ADONAY TO KYRIOS

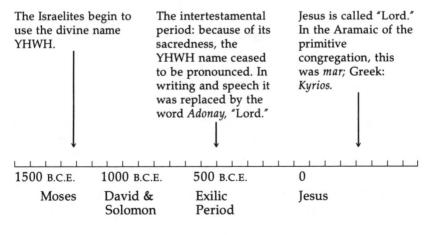

The Israelites begin to use the divine name YHWH.

The intertestamental period: because of its sacredness, the YHWH name ceased to be pronounced. In writing and speech it was replaced by the word *Adonay*, "Lord."

Jesus is called "Lord." In the Aramaic of the primitive congregation, this was *mar*; Greek: *Kyrios.*

1500 B.C.E.	1000 B.C.E.	500 B.C.E.	0
Moses	David & Solomon	Exilic Period	Jesus

A key text in this connection is Phil 2:5–11. The section of Philippians has been characterized as either a hymn about Christ or a poetico-rhetorical didactic piece. The section consists of three strophes: In the first Christ's preexistence is described—his life together with the Father (v 6). In the second we are told of Christ's incarnation, human life, and ultimate death (vv 7–8). In the third strophe (vv 9–11) Christ's exaltation is proclaimed and, moreover, in a way that is important for our purposes:

> Therefore God has highly exalted him
> and bestowed on him the name which is above every name,
> that at the name of Jesus every knee should bow,
> in heaven and on earth and under the earth,
> and every tongue confess that Jesus Christ is *Kyrios,*
> to the glory of God the Father.
>
> (Phil 2:9–11)

Here the writer has not been content to use the normal Greek verb signifying "to elevate" or "to exalt," *hypsoō*; rather, he has chosen the form with the prefix *hyper-*, an intensifier with which we are familiar from such words as "hyper-intelligent," "hyper-active," or the like. We are further told that Christ has received "the name which is above every name" (v 9), a remark that is clarified by the note that every tongue will confess "that Jesus Christ is Lord (*Kyrios*)" (v 11). The confession reveals that Jesus receives that which, according to v 6, he had renounced: equality with God. Jesus is installed in YHWH's own domain.

That Jesus is *Kyrios* (i.e., Lord) is one of the earliest Christian confessions: "Because, if you confess with your lips that Jesus is Lord and believe in your heart that God raised him from the dead, you will be saved" (Rom 10:9; cf. 1 Cor 12:3).[7] It is, furthermore, exciting to observe that we can follow this confession of Jesus as Lord back to the oldest Judeo-Christian milieu in Palestine, to the primeval congregation. The thread which leads us there is the "Maranatha" expression (see Excursus 2).[8]

Summary. Among the Old Testament names of God, the name YHWH enjoys a unique position. In the course of time, this name came to be regarded as so sacred that people virtually stopped pronouncing it. The replacement word "Adonay," meaning "the Lord," was used instead. This explains why the various modern translations contain expressions like "the Lord," "der Herr," "le Seigneur," and so forth in the passages in the Old Testament where we find the most

18

holy Name in the Hebrew text. It should be clear that this way of "reproducing" the divine Name only serves to emphasize its mystery further. The secret remains!

EXCURSUS 2
WHAT IS IMPLIED BY THE "MARANATHA" EXPRESSION?

The word *Kyrios* is Greek for "lord," and the confession of Jesus as Lord was surely pointedly aimed at the competing claims that were expressed in the formula *Kyrios kaisar,* "the Emperor is lord." But does this not suggest that the application of *Kyrios* to Jesus is best understood against a Hellenistic background rather than seen in relation to the use of "Adonay," "Lord," as the Old Testament substitution for the divine Name?

We ignore for the moment the possibility that we have alternatives that do not exclude one another. We happen to possess one reliable indication that already the primitive Christian congregation in Jerusalem prayed to Jesus as "Lord." The language which was mostly employed in Palestine in Jesus' day was Aramaic, and the New Testament still preserves a handful of Aramaic expressions. Here one thinks of "Ephphatha" in Mark 7:34 and "abba" in Mark 14:36, among others. Yet another such Aramaic expression is "maranatha."

The expression "maranatha" occurs in 1 Cor 16:22 and in *The Teaching of the Twelve Apostles,* or *Didache* (10:6). In antiquity Greek manuscripts were written in so-called *scriptio continua,* that is, with no spaces between the individual words. The term "maranatha" actually consists of two words, although the border between them is uncertain. The first element is the Aramaic term for "our Lord"; the second is apparently a form of the Aramaic verb "to come." Some scholars have proposed the division *maran atha,* "our Lord is coming" (reading the Aramaic verb in the perfect tense). Others prefer the division *marana tha,* "come, our Lord!" (imperative of the verb). The latter alternative is supported by the unambiguous formulation in Greek in Rev 22:20. We cannot, however, rule out the possibility that the expression "maranatha" once served as both a prayer and a confession.

It is not only the Aramaic clothing of the phrase that is noteworthy. The antiquity of the expression is also guaranteed by the sort of context in which it occurs. In all three passages in which the expression is recorded (1 Cor 16:22; Rev 22:20; and *Didache* 10:6) there are implied references to Holy Communion. This allows us to suppose that the maranatha expression was used in conjunction with the Lord's Supper (*kyriakon deipnon,* 1 Cor 11:20), perhaps from the very beginning, since in the course of communion the celebrants looked forward to the Lord's return, and no doubt did so from the very establishment of the rite. Thus the maranatha expression bears witness to the fact that Jesus was designated "Lord" already in the very oldest Jewish-Christian milieu.

Literature: Cullmann ([1959]: 208–15); Hahn ([1974]: 100–112); Fitzmeyer ([1981]: 218–35).

The Two Key Texts in Exodus

The Book of Exodus contains two passages that speak of the revelation of the divine Name to Moses. Thus we shall direct our attention to both of these texts and note what information they have to offer.[9] The section in Exodus 3 has usually been regarded as belonging to the Elohistic layer of tradition (esp. vv 9–15), while the text in Exodus 6 (vv 2–9) is usually assigned to the Priestly stream of tradition (see the Glossary). On a single important issue these two texts offer a unanimous witness: both of them associate the revelation of the divine Name YHWH with the time of Moses. In Exodus 6 we read,

> I am the Lord. I appeared to Abraham, to Isaac, and to Jacob, as "God Almighty" ['ēl šadday], but by my name "the Lord" [YHWH] I did not make myself known to them. (Exod 6:2–3)

In the patriarchal age, God had presented himself under other names, such as El Shaddai; but from the time of Moses and later he was known as YHWH.

Corresponding information is offered in Exodus 3, which is the Old Testament proof text for the name of YHWH. The God who, in vv 14–15 reveals his new name (YHWH) to Moses, also emphasizes the continuity backwards to the days of "the fathers": "I am the God of your father, the God of Abraham, the God of Isaac, and the God of Jacob" (Exod 3:6). Subsequently we read,

> Say this to the people of Israel, "The Lord, the God of your fathers, the God of Abraham, the God of Isaac, and the God of Jacob, has sent me to you": this is my name for ever, and thus I am to be remembered throughout all generations. (Exod 3:15)

Taken together, the witness of these two texts is unambiguous: the Name which God revealed to Moses was new to the Hebrew tribes. The patriarchs had not worshiped God under this Name.

This conclusion, that the revelation of the name YHWH was a milestone in the history of Israelite religion, is also supported from another direction. Some evidence is provided by the history of Hebrew name giving. Among the many Israelite names, we find a large group in which the name YHWH is a component element. These are such names as Jo-tham, Jo-el, Jo-nathan, and so forth, in which the first syllable is part of the divine Name. We also know of such names as Obad-iah, Gedal-iah, Uzz-iah, Eli-jah, and so forth, in which the divine Name is the concluding element. In the patriarchal narratives there is not a single name of this sort in which the Name is a constitutive element, as we would have expected if the patriarchs had actually known this divine Name. The first unambiguous occurrence of this Name takes place with "Joshua."[10] (See Fig. 4.)

The texts in Exodus 3 and 6 deserve to be taken seriously when they tell us that the revelation of the name YHWH introduced a new major chapter in the history of the people of God. The same witness is borne by the Book of Hosea: "I am YHWH your God from the land of Egypt" (Hosea 13:4; cf. 12:9).

Now we will take a closer look at our two texts. Exodus 3 speaks of the revelation by fire to Moses on the mount of God, far off in the desert. Of particular importance is the structure of the text, since the revelation of YHWH has a special place and function in the wider context. The text as a whole consists of Exod 2:23—4:17; its background is the slavery of the Israelites in Egypt. In an expression deriving from the legal sphere—the cry of the injured party in the legal assembly—we hear concerning the Israelites that "their cry under bondage came up to God" (2:23). And God reacts:

> I have seen the affliction of my people who are in Egypt, and have heard their cry because of their taskmasters; I know their sufferings. (Exod 3:7)

To the victims of injustice God says emphatically, "I have seen. I have heard. I know." But God does more than just speak; he acts accordingly (cf., e.g., Judges 3:9–10; 3:15). The rest of Exodus deals

FIGURE 4

FROM THE PATRIARCHAL ERA TO THE
TIME OF MOSES:
THE YHWH NAME COMES INTO USE

"The God of your father, the God of Abraham, the God of Isaac, and the God of Jacob" (Exod 3:6)	The YHWH name comes into use in the time of Moses
"God the Almighty," Hebrew *El Shaddai* (Exod 6:2–3)	

The Patriarchal Era	The Age of Moses

The YHWH name first came into use in the days of Moses. Other divine designations were employed previously. The texts clearly refer to a number of stages in this development.

21

with this divine intervention, with the liberation of the Hebrew slaves. Exodus 3 is itself the introduction to this drama.

Many readers probably regard this chapter as dealing primarily with the revelation of the divine Name. A careful reading of the text, however, shows that its real theme is the call of Moses; it is this theme that makes up the macrocontext, in which the revelation of the divine Name is only a contributory motif.

In the Old Testament we find two different types of call narratives.[11] The first of these, represented by Isaiah 6 and Ezekiel 1—3, is characterized by a vision of God seated upon his throne; God speaks, and the one who is called accepts his commission without objection.

The second type of call narrative is distinguished by a dialogue between God and the one who is called. Here the latter protests against his commission; texts of this genre include the accounts of God's calling of Moses (Exodus 3), Gideon (Judges 6:11–18), Saul (1 Sam 9:1—10:16), and Jeremiah (Jer 1:4–19). To take but a single example, the Jeremiah text clearly exhibits the four elements that characterize such narratives: God states the commission (vv 4–5); the recipient of the call protests (v 6: "I am only a youth"); God dispels the protest with a promise (v 8: "I am with you"); the promise itself is confirmed by a sign (vv 11–12: the vision of the almond tree).

Matters are similar in the description of the call of Moses (Exod 3). Here, too, we find the four features: commission, protest, promise, and sign. God's commissioning of Moses to lead the exodus is announced in v 10. Moses objects; with the self-centeredness typical of call recipients, he points to his lack of qualifications to carry out the task in question (v 11: "Who am I that I should go to Pharaoh?"). In answer to this objection God states his promise: "I will be with you" (v 12). It is not a question of Moses' fitness for the task; someone will be with him and aid him. The confirmatory sign is suggested in v 12.

In the description of the call of Moses, the protest of the recipient is unusual in that Moses varies his objections and tries first one and then another evasion to avoid his task. In the continuation of the text (Exod 4:1–17), we find three new objections, each of which is countered by God in due turn: "But behold, they will not believe me" (v 1), "I am not eloquent" (v 10), and "send, I pray, some other person" (v 13).

It is within the framework of this dialogue that Moses poses the question of God's name:

If I come to the people of Israel and say to them, "The God of your fathers has sent me to you," and they ask me, "What is his name?" what shall I say to them? (Exod 3:13)

To this the text has a double answer:

Say this to the people of Israel, "I AM [*'ehyeh*] has sent me to you." (Exod 3:14)

Say this to the people of Israel, "The Lord [*YHWH*], the God of your fathers . . . has sent me to you." (Exod 3:15)

In other words, the revelation of the divine Name is part of a text bearing the typical narrative course of the call narrative, one which here takes the form of a trial of strength between God and Moses. *Here the divine Name is announced as the final legitimation of Moses' commission.*

The narrative has an inherent logic which must not be overlooked. When Moses' first protest ("Who am I?") is countered with the promise "I will be with you," everything depends on the identity of the one who stands behind the promise: the one who says his "I AM," the one called YHWH. Here, as always, the worth of a promise depends on who is behind it.

In other words, here the divine Name functions as something of a legitimating password. This usage may be compared with that in the other of our two main texts, Exod 6:2–9. In this text we repeatedly encounter the expression "I am YHWH." When strangers meet, it is usual to introduce one another. In the same way the words "I am YHWH" seem to have the character of a divine self-presentation.[12]

The formula itself is to be found at the very beginning of the text (v 2), after which it recurs in vv 6–8. These verses deal with the divine message that Moses is to proclaim to Israel: the promise of liberation from slavery. Everything depends upon the one who is behind the promise, and this piece of information is announced no fewer than three times. At the beginning, in the middle, and at the end of the section we find the words "I am YHWH." This formula points to the reality behind the promises concerning the people's future: God is behind the promise and will redeem it personally. *Here the formula containing the Name serves as a guarantee that the promise will one day be realized.* The similarity with what we have seen to be the case in Exodus 3 is tangible.

IN HISTORICAL PERSPECTIVE:
SOME INDICATIONS OF THE ORIGIN
OF THE NAME

The evidence suggests that it was first in the time of Moses that the Hebrew tribes began to employ "YHWH" as the name of their God. The Elohistic (Exod 3) and the Priestly (Exod 6) traditions agree on this point. The occurrence of personal names containing a YHWH element also points in this direction. The various trails all point back to Moses. Can a historical investigation take us farther than this? A number of scholars have made the attempt. These efforts resulted in the so-called Kenite-Midianite Hypothesis, which maintains that the Name had a pre-Israelite and pre-Mosaic history among certain Semitic tribes in eastern Sinai. The theory won considerable popularity after a work by Karl Budde around the turn of the century.[13] Further evidence has accumulated since then, leaving us with pieces of a puzzle.

The first piece of the puzzle is to be found in a group of Old Testament poetic texts which suggest that YHWH once had a "home" somewhere beyond the borders of Palestine, although the texts in question do not point to an exact geographical locality. In poetic language they describe how YHWH "comes out" of a particular area, a region that we may infer to have lain in the territory south of Palestine, since the texts speak of YHWH's emergence from Sinai, Seir, Paran, and so forth (see map 1).[14]

> YHWH came from *Sinai,* and dawned from *Seir* upon them.
> He shone forth from *Mount Paran* and came from *Meribath Kadesh.*
> (Deut 33:2*)

> YHWH, when thou didst go forth from *Seir,*
> when thou didst march from *the region of Edom,*
> the earth trembled, and the heavens dropped . . .
> The mountains quaked before YHWH, the Lord of *Sinai,*
> before YHWH, the God of Israel.
> (Judg 5:4–5*; cf. Ps 68:7–8, 17–18)

> God came from *Teman,* the Holy One from *Mount Paran.*
> (Hab 3:3)

We also know of a *YHWH of Teman* on the basis of inscriptions found at Kuntillet Ajrud, situated to the south of Kadesh in northeastern Sinai; they may be dated to around 800 B.C.E.[15]

These formulations have one feature in common: they speak of how YHWH emerges from a region somewhere to the south of Palestine

MAP 1
THE LOCATION OF BIBLICAL SINAI

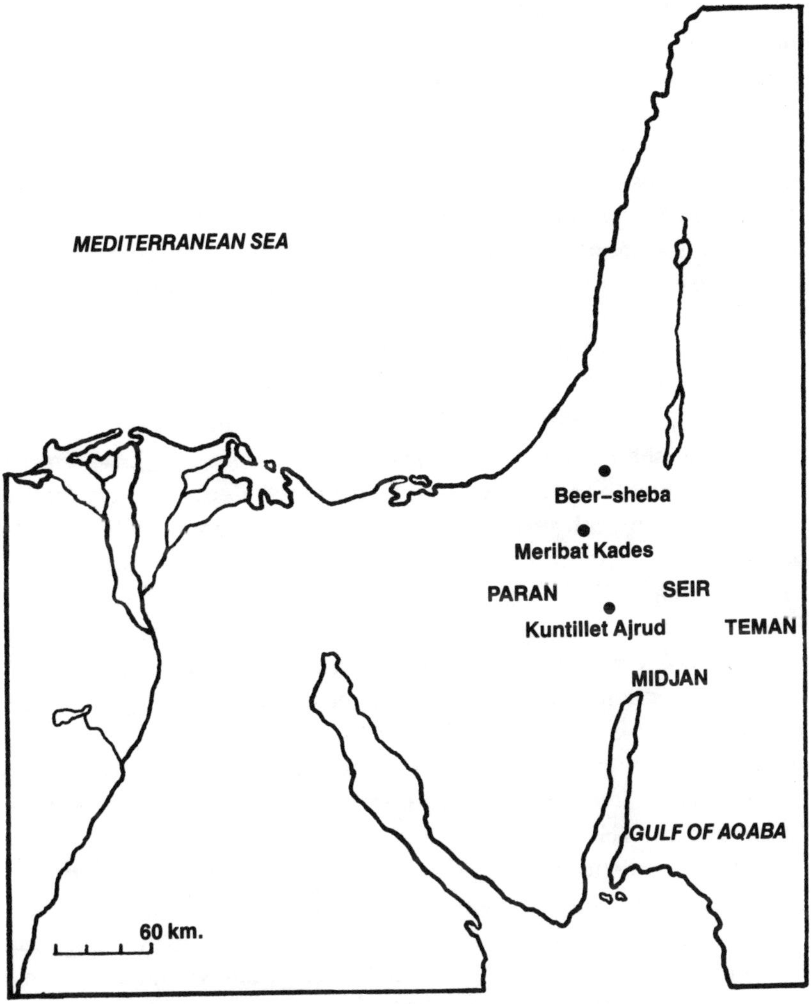

MEDITERRANEAN SEA

• Beer-sheba

• Meribat Kades

PARAN   SEIR

• Kuntillet Ajrud   TEMAN

MIDJAN

GULF OF AQABA

60 km.

We do not know where biblical Sinai was located. In the OT, Sinai is mentioned in texts which describe how YHWH "comes out" from such sites as Seir, Paran, and Teman. All of these sites have been identified by scholars; they are situated in the region north of the Gulf of Aqaba. Perhaps it is in this region that biblical Sinai is to be sought.

proper. We do not know for certain just where the biblical Sinai was located. As for the other localities mentioned above, the extant information about them points to a sizable area around the northern tip of the Gulf of Aqaba.

In other words, the texts describing how YHWH comes out from Seir and other places point to the region between the Dead Sea and the Gulf of Aqaba. Another piece of the puzzle, admittedly difficult to place, seems to suggest the same region. The material evidence in question is extrabiblical: it consists of two texts that were carved on the walls of a couple of temples in ancient Nubia, the modern Sudan. These texts contain what may be the earliest attestations of the biblical Name. The earlier of the two temples derives from Pharaoh Amenophis III, ca. 1400 B.C.E. while the other dates from the days of Ramses II, ca. 1250 B.C.E.

These texts mention the "Shasu bedouins" (which is actually redundant, as the Egyptian word "*š3sw*" means "bedouins"), whom the respective pharaohs are supposed to have defeated, either in reality or by magic. In both texts we find a name that immediately attracts our attention: "*Yhw* in the land of the Shasu bedouins."[16] In one of the lists we also find a reference to a certain "Seir in the land of the Shasu bedouins." In these texts both *Yhw* and Seir are apparently the names of territories or else tribal groups. The occurrence of "Seir" in this connection prompts the not unreasonable conclusion that the *Yhw* we find mentioned here is also to be located in approximately the same region: in the area north of the Gulf of Aqaba.[17] And it was in this very region that the biblical texts referred to above locate the "homeland" of YHWH!

From a linguistic point of view there can be no objection to any connection between the name of the Hebrew God and the *Yhw*-region, which was located in the reaches controlled by the Shasu bedouins.[18] Nor does the fact that in the one case we have the name of a deity and in the other the name of a geographical region present any decisive obstacle. Among the Semites of antiquity there are several examples in which a particular name (e.g., Ashur) designated both the god and the land where that god was worshiped.

The data about a *Yhw* territory and the texts describing how YHWH emerges from his "home" in the south are complemented by yet another piece of the puzzle. The Bible itself relates that Moses received his revelation of the divine Name after having fled to the Land of Midian (Exod 2:15), where he married the daughter of the priest of the

Midianites (Exod 2:16, 21; 3:1; 18:1).[19] According to a different tradition, Moses' wife was of Kainite, or Kenite, origin (Judges 1:16; 4:11). This apparent ambiguity, however, does not occasion any real difficulty, since the Midianites and the Kenites were closely related tribes (note how Enoch is associated with both groups in Gen 4:17 and 25:4).

But where was the Midianite territory? Some geographers have located Midian in Arabia southeast of the Gulf of Aqaba; however, the only precise information in the Old Testament relevant to the subject points in a different direction. A passage in the Books of Kings relates how a young Edomite prince named Hadad flees from Edom (southeast of the Dead Sea) to Egypt. During his journey he passes through first Midian and then Paran (1 Kings 11:18). This means that Midian is to be located in the immediate vicinity of the depression of the Arabah, which runs from the southern tip of the Dead Sea to the northern end of the Gulf of Aqaba. The implications of this are clear: Midian was situated in the same great region that we previously pointed to as YHWH's "homeland," namely, the region in which also the *Yhw* area of the Egyptian inscriptions was located.

In short, it is in the land of Midian that the Bible locates the important encounter between Moses and the God whom Israel was to worship under the name YHWH (Exod 3:1).

Later in the Book of Exodus we read about a meeting between the Hebrew leaders and Moses' father-in-law, Jethro. In conjunction with this encounter, we read of a common sacrifice and a common meal (Exod 18:12). It is unquestionably tempting to regard the common sacrifice as an expression of religious connections between the Hebrews and the Midianites, and to regard the common meal as a covenant ritual, that is, as a way of manifesting religious ties between the two peoples (cf. Gen 26:30; 31:46, 54).[20] In this connection it would also be appropriate to recall the later enmity between the Hebrews and the Midianites; indeed, the texts speak of a regular holy war waged against Midian (Numbers 31; Judges 6—8; Isa 9:4). This fact emphasizes further the source value of the information about an early association between the first great leaders of the Hebrews and the Midianites. In possessing such information we undoubtedly have traditio-historical foundation, material that cannot be dismissed as the literary fictions of later centuries.

Summary. We have studied the Egyptian information about a *Yhw* area in the land of the Shasu bedouins. We have also noted the way certain biblical texts speak of how YHWH emerges from a region somewhere in the south—from Sinai, Seir, Teman, or Paran. And we have seen the way the revelation of the Name is localized to the Midianite territories. Each item taken in isolation would be difficult to evaluate and comprehend; taken together, however, these three pieces of the puzzle form a meaningful pattern. Here the biblical and extrabiblical data agree strikingly and support the conclusion that the peculiar divine Name revered by the Israelites existed prior to the time of Moses (the thirteenth century B.C.E.) among bedouin tribes in eastern Sinai and the region north of the Gulf of Aqaba. Indeed, it is possible that the two Egyptian temple lists provide us with the most ancient attestations of this mysterious Name. If this reasoning is correct, then it is hardly astonishing that already while in Egypt prior to the Exodus the Hebrews knew themselves to be specially bound to a sanctuary in the desert regions (Exod 3:18; 5:1–5; 7:16). Within this context, the information about the revelation of the name YHWH to Moses in the land of Midian (Exod 3:1) fits well.

IN PHILOLOGICAL PERSPECTIVE

It is now necessary to discuss an intricate question: is it possible on the basis of philological criteria to arrive at reasonable conclusions as to the significance of the divine Name? In so doing we are treading a path that is strewn with the rubble of now-abandoned theories. In passing, we also note the contours of developing hypotheses. The following report on the field of problems connected with the name YHWH will be confined to the most important issues. With the aid of the specialized literature cited in the notes, the reader will be able to explore the field as much as he or she likes.[21]

WHAT DID THE NAME LOOK LIKE, AND HOW WAS IT PRONOUNCED?

It is a frustrating but nevertheless ineluctable fact that it is only late in antiquity that we have any direct indications as to how the Name was pronounced. There are some indications in favor of the pronunciation "Yahweh." In the writings of Clement of Alexandria we find the Greek transcriptions *Iaoue* and *Iaouai,* and in those of Theodoret of Cyrrhus we find the forms *Iabe* and *Iabai.*[22] Everything suggests that these authors were familiar with the pronunciation "Yahweh." For some time in the modern period scholars have contended that the Name really was pronounced in this fashion. Moreover, the

"Yahweh" pronunciation fits well with the grammatical patterns of the ancient Semitic languages.[23]

Martin Rose has offered some precise observations, but his main thesis is not tenable.[24] Rose maintains that the original form of the Name was *YHW,* pronounced "Yahw" (with consonantal *w*).[25] He further claims that the long form *YHWH,* pronounced "Yahweh," was introduced by King Josiah in the seventh century B.C.E. The expression in Exod 3:14, which ties the Name to the verb "to be" ("I am who I am") is supposed to have been a product of the same period. Rose is here in agreement with many other scholars who have held that this verse seems to be a late addition to the text (Rose, pp. 34 and 39). A late redaction of all the Old Testament texts would then ultimately be responsible for the change from *YHW* to *YHWH.*

Recent inscriptional finds from the far pre-Josianic period, however, raise serious difficulties for this hypothesis. In these finds, the longer name form *YHWH* occurs in at least two contexts. One occurrence is from a burial inscription from Khirbet el-Qom in southern Judah; the find is generally dated to the eighth century.[26] Other occurrences have appeared in inscriptions from Kuntillet Ajrud, south of Kadesh in northeastern Sinai; these may be dated to around 800 B.C.E.[27]

Rose has emphasized the central role of the divine Name in the movement that supported Josiah's religious reformation in the 620s B.C.E. On the other hand, he has not succeeded in demonstrating that Josiah was responsible for any novelties with respect to the question of the form of the divine Name. We must still assume that the Name was pronounced "Yahweh."[28]

WHAT DOES THE NAME MEAN?

Is the content of the Name accessible to us? The research into this question in the past century has followed some circuitous routes.

One explanation maintained that from the beginning the Name was a cultic shout consisting of two elements: *(a)* an emphatic word *ya,* which we know from the Arabic; plus *(b)* the old Semitic pronoun *huwa* (i.e., "he"). Thus the divine Name was held to signify "O, he!"[29] A number of more or less formulaic passages have been held to lend credence to this theory (e.g., Isa 43:10, 13; Deut 32:39).

Other theories have been based on comparisons with Arabic verbal roots.[30] In Arabic there is a verb consisting of the consonants *h-w-y,* meaning "to fall," or "to throw." Thus the divine Name was assumed to mean "He [who] makes [the lightning] fall." Another theory connected the Name with yet another sense of the same Arabic root, namely, "to love." This led to an interpretation of the Name as "He [who] loves devotedly."

Signs Pointing to the Verb for "To Be"

We have concluded that the divine Name probably had a prehistory among certain Midianite tribes in the Sinai region. The fascinating question as to what the Name may have conveyed at this time naturally lies beyond the horizon of the scholar. The Semitic languages are generally closely related to one another. Thus we do not have to assume that the Name received a new meaning in the context of Hebrew tradition; it is possible that it had one and the same meaning from the very beginning. The difficulty here, however, is that we know virtually nothing about the Midianite language. Thus we will focus on one main question: which linguistic associations were attached to the divine Name within the Hebrew tradition of ancient Israel?

The most significant piece of Old Testament evidence for answering this question appears in Exod 3:14:

> God said to Moses, "I am who I am." And he said, "Say this to the people of Israel, 'Ehyeh [I AM] has sent me to you.'" (Exod 3:14)

It should be obvious that this divine "I AM" provides something of a commentary on the divine name YHWH, which is communicated in the following verse:

> God also said to Moses, "Say this to the people of Israel, *YHWH,* the God of your fathers, . . . has sent me to you: this is my name for ever, and thus I am to be remembered throughout all generations.'" (Exod 3:15)

This tradition is also evident in Hosea 1:9, although this is clearer in the Hebrew text (*wĕ'ānōkî lō' 'ehyeh lākem*) than in many modern translations, which generally render it something like "nor will I belong to you." It is fully justifiable to render the passage "I will no longer be Ehyeh [I AM] for you."[31]

How do matters look from a purely linguistic point of view? Is it philologically permissible to derive the divine Name from a common Semitic verb for "to be"? The answer is an unqualified yes. The first letter of the divine Name need not necessarily belong to the root of the word; it could just as easily be a preformative element used in the formation of the "imperfect" tense. The root itself would then be *h-w-h* (or *h-w-y*). In Hebrew of course the verb "to be" normally has a *y* as its second consonant—*h-y-h*. Of course this is not the case with the divine Name, where we find a *w* as the second consonant.

How is this discrepancy to be explained? By the assumption that the form of the root underlying the divine Name derives from an evolutionary stage in the development of the language which antedates standard Hebrew. In the Bible itself there is evidence for this earlier form in the ancient words of Isaac's blessing upon Esau (Gen 27:29). Moreover, the corresponding verb in Akkadian, Amorite, and Aramaic has a medial *w*.

In short, the biblical text provides us with some indications that the verb "to be" is the key to the divine Name. It is a fact that scholars who have intensively studied the comparative materials from the most ancient Semitic languages in the interests of clarifying the matter of the divine Name have associated it with the verb "to be" (e.g., Wolfram von Soden, Roland de Vaux, and H.-P. Müller).[32]

The conclusion that the divine Name is to be derived from the verb "to be" is just a step on the way. The Hebrew verbs are construed in a number of different conjugations, all of which express different nuances of their root meanings. Each verb has a basic stem, in which its simple and unmodified meaning is expressed. But it also has a causative conjugation or stem form (the Hiphil). Figure 5 gives just a few examples:

FIGURE 5
HEBREW VERBS: BASIC AND
CAUSATIVE FORMS

Basic form (so-called Qal)		Causative (so-called Hiphil)	
yābô'	come	*yābî'*	to cause someone to come, to bring in
yāqûm	stand	*yāqîm*	to cause someone to stand
yēšēb	sit	*yôšîb*	to let sit, let dwell

Most Hebrew verbs have not only a basic form, but a causative one as well, which designates causation. The YHWH name is derived from the verb "to be," but does it come from the basic form or from the causative one?

In grammatical terms the form of the verb "to be" that is attested in the divine Name may be understood as either reflecting the basic stem or the causative stem.[33] In particular, a number of American scholars have emphasized the interpretation of the form *Yahweh* as a causative; Cross and Freedman have done so energetically.[34] If this should prove correct, then the Name would signify "he [who] causes something to exist," or "he [who] creates." Thus the divine Name might be an early expression of the worship of God as Creator. This interpretation has been emphasized among those scholars who prefer to regard YHWH ṣĕbāʾôt as an original grammatical unity signifying "He [who] creates heavenly hosts."

The conclusion according to which the divine Name is a causative formulation that designates God as Creator is, however, scarcely convincing. Why? There are three main objections to this hypothesis:

- It is usually assumed that the concept of creation first assumed theological centrality during the exile, although it was certainly known long before. Had it therefore been the basis of the divine Name, one would have expected it to have been central to Israel's thought at a far earlier stage. Moreover, the Old Testament uses other verbs for "to create" (e.g., bārāʾ, qānâ, etc.).
- In the Hebrew of the Old Testament the verb hāyâ, "to be," is attested 3,561 times. Accordingly, if the divine Name was actually a causative form, then it must be accounted as peculiar. With the exception of the divine Name there is not a single example in which this verb is construed in the causative stem.
- The obvious wordplay on the divine Name which we find in Exod 3:14 is formulated from the basic stem of the verb (ʾehyeh). The attempts that modern scholars have made to correct this text into a causative form are not at all convincing. This means that the text itself points to an interpretation of the divine Name as a form of the basic stem.

One conclusion is clear: we must eliminate the theory according to which the divine Name was a form of the causative stem of the verb signifying "to be." By process of elimination we arrive at the likelihood that the Name is a form of the basic stem of this verb. This conclusion is supported by Exod 3:14. In this event, what does the Name mean? Quite simply, "He is."

The Name was probably pronounced "Yahweh." Grammatical considerations would have led us to expect a different vocalization of the preformative syllable. However, the form ya- may be understood as an archaism, that is, a survival from an earlier stage in the history of the language.[35] This characteristic should be noted, for it now appears that the Name has two significant features indicative of its great antiquity: the vowel of the preformative syllable and the *waw* of the root.

A variety of forms of the divine Name are featured as elements in Hebrew personal names. Thus as preformative syllables we encounter both *yô-* and *yĕhô-* : Jonathan, Jehonathan, Joshaphat, Jehoshaphat. As afformative elements we find the forms *-yāh* and *-yāhû*: Uzzijah, Uzziyahu, Elijah, Elijahu. These names are largely unproblematical as derivations of the independent divine name YHWH from the basic stem of the verb "to be."

The Biblical Interpretation of the Divine Name in Exodus 3:14

Exodus 3:13–15 is the only passage in the Old Testament which offers a formal explanation of the divine Name. It was here that we found the clue that pointed to the verb "to be" as the basic element upon which the divine Name was constructed. In answer to Moses' question in verse 13 as to God's name, we find two parallel answers. Moses is to say to the Israelites:

1. "I AM [Hebrew *'ehyeh*]" has sent me to you. (v 14)
2. YHWH . . . has sent me to you. (v 15)

These formulations have an internal logic that should not be overlooked. God's name is YHWH, "He Is." When God speaks and reveals the deeper significance of the Name, he is not speaking of himself as "He Is" in the third person. Instead, God quite naturally says "I Am" (v 14). Moses, however, cannot properly say this; he must say "He Is" instead (v 15).

This short text also contains a formulation that seems to be provocative and that has been the object of divergent analyses. This is the phrase "I am who I am," in Hebrew *'ehyeh 'ăšer 'ehyeh* (v 14). Our translation represents but one of the various possible interpretations.

From a linguistic point of view there are three ways of understanding this passage.[36] (For a summary, see p. 36.)

1. "I am who I am." The passage has in this case been regarded as an example of a well-known stylistic figure in biblical Hebrew which consists of the repeated use of the same root.[37] The figure in question serves mainly to endow an expression with a suspicion of haziness. Note the following instances:

"Send the one you will send" (i.e., send anyone but me). (Exod 4:13*)

"And they went where they went" (i.e., they wandered about). (1 Sam 23:13*)

"Dwell where you will dwell" (i.e., dwell wherever you choose). (2 Kings 8:1*)

33

If we understand our text in the light of these examples, the expression takes on the quality of an evasion; that is, God appears to sidestep Moses' question.

2. "I am the one who is"; "I am the existing one." Scholars who embrace this interpretation[38] have emphasized that the expression consists of a main clause (*'ehyeh*) and a relative clause (*'ăšer 'ehyeh*). According to the rules of Hebrew grammar, if the main clause is couched in the first or second person, the relative clause is to be construed in the same person. In this case, the literal English rendering would accordingly be "I am the one who *am*," reading "am" instead of "is." There are similar passages in the Old Testament (e.g., Gen 15:7; Exod 20:2; Lev 20:24; 1 Kings 13:14; 1 Chron 21:17).

The Hebrew relative clause *'ăšer 'ehyeh* is in the first person. Following the rule just mentioned, scholars have translated the phrase in the third person and thus have read, "I am the one who is [i.e., who exists]." The Septuagint (LXX) has understood the passage in this sense, thus reading *egō eimi hō ōn*. Note also the renderings in the Wisdom of Solomon 13:1 and the *Manual of Discipline* in the Dead Sea Scrolls (IQS XI.4). Understood in this way, the phrase says something about the nature of God.

3. A third approach insists that the word *'ehyeh* later in the verse (Exod 3:14) functions as a name for God: "'I AM' has sent me to you." Scholars have asked whether we do not have the same sort of statement in the disputed formulation in verse 14a. There are two different variants of this interpretation. One was proposed by an American scholar in 1939, and the other by a Belgian researcher in 1976:

"Ehyeh [I Am]" is who I am. (W.A. Irwin [1939])
"Ehyeh [I Am]," because I am. (J. Schoneveld [1976])

This approach has played no significant part in the scientific discussion of the passage in question, but the first variant has been incorporated into the New English Bible.

How are we to evaluate these three views? An adequate explanation of any passage must answer at least to the demands of grammar and context. Here are my observations.

1. The first interpretation, "I am who I am," encounters no difficulties from the point of view of grammar. The question is, however, whether the proposed evasive reply fits the context. Of course, there

are passages in the Old Testament in which God refuses to reveal his Name, for example, in the account of Jacob's struggle at the Jabbok (Gen 32:29–30). This also occurs when Samson's father inquires after the divine Name (Judges 13:17–18). But these passages do not provide good parallels to our text dealing with Moses, as God actually does reveal his name YHWH (Exod 3:15) and even offers some explanatory wordplay (v 14).

2. The second interpretation, "I am the one who is," "I am the existing one," would in the context of our passage represent a qualified theological statement about the nature of God. Scholars have criticized this interpretation for transforming the text into an existential statement of a sort that would fit better into Greek philosophy than into the Old Testament. Such criticisms, however, hardly apply,[39] since the Hebrew verb *hāyâ*, "to be," possesses numerous nuances and need not be interpreted in a philosophical sense. Bertil Albrektson,[40] however, has formulated a more penetrating criticism of this view, which points out that the interpretation in question does not correspond to ordinary Hebrew usage in the construction of the phrase. In the main clause, we should have expected something like *'ănî hû'*, "I am he (who is)" (cf. Isa 52:6). Albrektson, accordingly, favors the interpretation "I am who I am."

Nevertheless, Dennis McCarthy[41] was prepared to accept the proposed reading in spite of Albrektson's objection. McCarthy argued that Albrektson may be correct from the point of view of ordinary Hebrew grammar; "I am the one who is" should actually be *'ănî hû' 'ăšer 'ehyeh*. However, McCarthy maintains that the desire to emphasize the connection between the divine Name and the verb "to be," *hāyâ*, has won out over the demands of ordinary grammar and so compelled the use of the unusual form which entails the repetition of *'ehyeh*, thus producing the present text: *'ehyeh 'ăšer 'ehyeh*.

3. In spite of McCarthy's elegant attempt to have it both ways, one ought to pay attention to the third possibility: that the first *'ehyeh* in our mysterious expression is simply a name declaration. In particular, I appreciate the analysis offered by Schoneveld (above). The strength of his interpretation is that it fits into the context of Exod 3:13–15. Here Moses first asks what he is to answer his tribal kinsmen when they inquire as to the name of the God who has revealed himself to him (v 13). God's reply to this is then, "*Ehyeh!* Because I am." In other words, this "Ehyeh" is more or less the divine name placed in God's own mouth, whereas mortal man is to call God *YHWH*, "He Is."

This interpretation also has the advantage that it in no way does violence to the Hebrew language. Such a passage with a parallel structure is already to be found in Gen 31:49. We here have a name explanation, that is, a so-called name etiology consisting of two elements: *(a)* the name is presented and *(b)* an explanation is proposed that is introduced by "because," *'ǎšer*.[42] In question is the cairn (i.e., the stone marker) intended to cement the covenant between Jacob and Laban. The site is supposed to have been called Mizpah, "for (*'ǎšer*) he said, 'The Lord watch between you and me'" (cf. also Gen 22:14). An identical structure is present in Exod 3:14, consisting of *(a)* the name, here *Ehyeh* (i.e., "I Am") and *(b)* the explanation, here consisting of the phrase *'ǎšer 'ehyeh* (i.e., "because I am"). In other words, there are some clear reasons for accepting Schoneveld's analysis.

Summary. I draw these conclusions about the philological problems connected with the divine Name:

1. The Hebrew divine name *YHWH* is to be understood as a form of the verb *hāyâ*, "to be." More precisely, we have a form of the main stem of this verb; it means "He Is." Two factors point to the considerable antiquity of this form of the Name: the stem contains *w* and the preformative element was probably vocalized *ya*. Could these be reminiscences of a Midianite prehistory?

2. We have discussed the more important interpretations of Exod 3:14 and rejected translations along the lines of "I am who I am" and "I am the existing one." The passage is instead to be rendered, "[My name shall be] *Ehyeh* [I AM], because I am."

WAS THE DIVINE NAME KNOWN OUTSIDE OF ISRAEL?

Scholars have repeatedly declared that the divine Name of the Israelites existed outside of Israel and long before the time of Moses.

On January 13, 1902, the eminent Assyriologist Friedrich Delitzsch, the son of the conservative and learned exegete Franz Delitzsch, held the first of his famous lectures on the subject of *Babel und Bibel*. Delitzsch's lecture was an attempt to demonstrate point for point that the Old Testament was dependent on the ancient cuneiform cultures to the east. A furor erupted when Delitzsch announced that the Mosaic divine Name had been discovered in documents dating from the time of Hammurabi—from around 1700 B.C.E. He noted in particular the Babylonian personal name *Ja-ú-um-ilum*, which he held meant "YHWH is God."[43] The lecture occasioned a storm of protest; Delitzsch was later to describe how he received fifteen piles of newspaper clippings and

MAP 2
THE EASTERN MEDITERRANEAN WITH EBLA

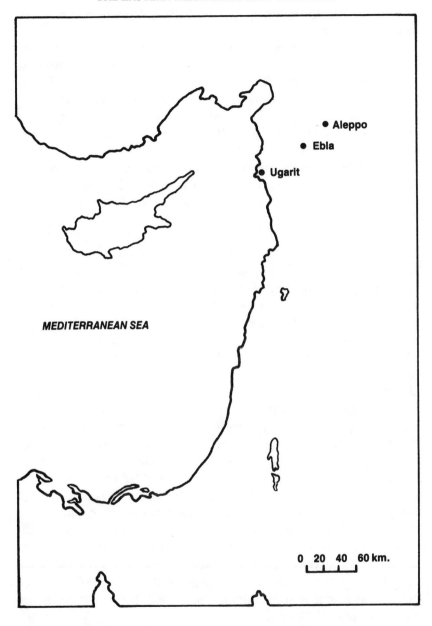

Aleppo

Ebla

Ugarit

MEDITERRANEAN SEA

0 20 40 60 km.

Archaeologists have discovered the ancient city of Ebla, in northern Syria. The YHWH name is also unattested there, although the site has yielded an interesting linguistic parallel.

journal articles, all containing protests from pious circles in and outside of Germany.

Of course the protests against Delitzsch were not uniformly motivated by scholarly considerations. What interests us in this connection, though, is the fact that Delitzsch's colleagues among the Assyriologists were soon able to demonstrate that he was mistaken. In the case of the personal name in question, the element *jāum* is a pronoun signifying "my"; thus the name itself means "God is mine" and has nothing to do with the Israelite divine Name.[44]

Much more interesting material has recently come to our attention from ancient Ebla, in northern Syria (see Map 2). Archaeologists have been excavating the site since the middle of the 1960s. There they discovered the remains of an ancient city which once flourished in the centuries just prior and subsequent to 2000 B.C.E. In 1975 the most remarkable find was made since the discovery of the Dead Sea Scrolls. In two small chambers an archive was discovered containing approximately 16,000 clay tablets inscribed in cuneiform, but in a language that may be called Eblaite and whose exact position within the family of Semitic languages is still being debated.

The finds at Ebla have shed new and surprising light on the biblical divine Name. In 1981, H.-P. Müller, a biblical scholar and orientalist, issued an important contribution to the discussion.[45] He was able to demonstrate that the verb "to be" serves as a divine designation in certain of the personal names from Ebla. One such Eblaite personal name is *sumi-ji(h)ja*. Here the second element is "He Is" (or "He Was"). The name itself means "offspring of 'He Is.'" Müller understands such names as "names of thanksgiving." They do not refer to the existence of the god in question versus his nonexistence; instead, they point to the way the god in question "was present [and helped]," for example, by means of the birth of the child. Müller thinks that the designation "He Is/Was" is a replacement for another, "real" divine name; thus he maintains that the element in question has a "substitutive function." Conceivably, we might extend Müller's reasoning and by analogy hold that the biblical divine Name was a similar substitute, a replacement for an earlier divine name like El or El Shaddai.

Müller's discovery is important because it gives added weight to the interpretation of the Hebrew divine Name as derived from the verb "to be." According to Müller, this view is now philologically unassailable (1981: 323).

Müller's observation does not mean that we now have evidence for the name YHWH in the Ebla texts; he himself notes that this is not the case. What we have discovered is a particular way of speaking of a deity which implies that the conceptual motif underlying Exod 3:14 is truly ancient (1981: 322).

Thus we can draw conclusions concerning a biblical verse which has often been classified as a late addition to the text. The verse in question fits into its textual context well, especially if we accept Schoneveld's interpretation. We have also learned that the expressive content itself has a striking parallel in a far earlier Semitic culture, namely, that of ancient Ebla.

There is another small piece of the puzzle available to the reader, although it is a difficult piece to interpret and possibly an insignificant detail. During the centuries around the beginning of our era, the Nabateans dwelled in the regions east of the Dead Sea and in Sinai; they were an Arabic people and spoke an Aramaic dialect. The Nabatean inscriptions from Sinai include the personal name 'bd-'hyw, perhaps to be read as "servant of 'I Am.'"[46] If this reading is correct, then it is thought-provoking that we encounter the Nabatean "I Am" as a divine designation in Sinai, in the same province where the divine name YHWH is revealed to Moses. After all, it was here that Moses met his Midianite father-in-law, and it was at a sacred mountain in these reaches that the divine Name was revealed.

Are there any indications of any connection between the Nabateans and the Midianite tribes whom Moses encountered? The materials do not permit any certain conclusions, but there is one detail deserving close attention. We know the Nabateans' famous capital by the name of Petra. The name is, of course, a Greek word (meaning "rock"), and we may assume that it was not the Nabateans' own name for the site. The Jewish historian Flavius Josephus helps us when he mentions that the Nabateans themselves called their city Rechem, after its founder (*Antiquities* IV.7.1).[47] Josephus mentions this datum in the context of a discussion of Num 31:8, a passage that regards "Rechem" as the name of a Midianite king. Thus, there may in fact be some historical connection between the Nabatean personal name that means "Servant of 'I Am'" and the divine Name that Moses received while herding the sheep of his father-in-law, the priest of Midian!

Summary. Here is what we can conclude about the existence of the name YHWH before the time of Moses:

1. There is some biblical evidence to the effect that the divine Name had its origins in eastern Sinai. These consist of statements about YHWH coming from the south as well as the tradition about Moses' connections with the Midianite tribes.

2. Egyptian inscriptions contain references to a *"Yhw* in the land of the Shasu bedouins," that is, a geographical name that might be identical with the name we later encounter as the Mosaic divine Name.

3. Personal names are attested at ancient Ebla that contain a divine designation consisting of a form of the verb "to be." This offers us a fascinating parallel to the Israelite divine Name, although the fact does not entitle us to conclude that the God of the Israelites was worshiped already at Ebla. Other important material is offered in the form of a Nabatean name from Sinai (!) that seems to contain the verb "to be" in the first person singular.

More than this we cannot say, though it should be clear that as of yet we have no unambiguous attestation of the name YHWH from the time prior to Moses.

IN THEOLOGICAL PERSPECTIVE

"I AM" AND "HE IS":
WHAT CONTENT IS IMPLIED BY THE VERB "TO BE"?

If the argument presented above is correct, then the Hebrew divine Name is a substantivization of the expression "He Is." It is remarkable that in this way we have arrived at a name that was originally a verb form. One thinks unavoidably of Humpty Dumpty's characterization of the classes of words that go to make up language: "They've a temper, some of them—particularly verbs: they're the proudest—adjectives you can do anything with, but not verbs." (Lewis Carroll, *Through the Looking Glass*). Among the ancient Hebrews we find a verb form employed as a name for the Hebrew God. This is almost unique in the history of religions.[48]

Since the Hebrew verb "to be" (*hāyâ*) has a number of different nuances, it is appropriate to ask which is intended in this context. We shall not assign a special content to each of the 6,828 attestations of the name YHWH in the Old Testament. It is, after all, only conscious reflection that associates the Name with the verb "to be," but the texts only rarely reflect such an awareness of the content of the Name. But it is a reasonable supposition that the first Hebrews who heard the Name and used it also attached special associations to it; it is with these associations that we are now concerned. Moreover, we must acknowledge that the semantic possibilities of the

Name were latent; they could, but in a given situation need not necessarily, have been actualized.

Two competent Assyriologists, von Soden and Müller, studied the divine Name and attempted to interpret it on the basis of Near Eastern personal names that refer to the being of the god. In these "names of thanksgiving" we are not dealing with the question of the existence or non-existence of the god at hand, but with attempts by believers to demonstrate their gratitude that the god has shown himself to be present and helpful (e.g., in the birth of a child). Thus such names entail a retrospective view; the child's name accordingly contains a reference concerning a given god to the effect that "he was [present and helped]."[49]

Seen against this background, we could perhaps affirm that the biblical divine Name expresses *the conviction of God's active and helpful presence,* not as an expression about the past, but rather as a statement of confidence about the present and future: *"He Is [here and is now helping]."* This is undoubtedly a content that could be considered to have been relevant to the oppressed group of Hebrew slaves. It was presumably this sort of content that the Hebrews found in the divine Name during the Mosaic period.

If these speculations are correct, then the tradition in Exodus 3 does not deal with the question of God's existence or non-existence. Exegetical studies, of course, abound with assurances that the ancient Israelites were not interested in the question of God's existence in this sense. In the writings of some scholars one even glimpses the notion that the Israelites were simply unable to make sophisticated philosophical distinctions between existence and non-existence. The next step we take, however, will lead us to question this skepticism, in part because traditions about the divine Name continued and had vitality in later generations.

The text in Exodus 3 bears some traces of the persons who carried on the tradition of the divine Name.[50] They were members of the so-called "D-circles," *who were active in the time after Josiah's reformation in 622* B.C.E. (on the term "D-circles," see the Glossary). There is reason to ask: *at this time* in the history of Israel's faith, what did an Israelite hear in the name forms *Ehyeh* ("I AM") and *YHWH* ("He Is")? I believe that by then the Israelites had achieved a more profound understanding of the content of these names. In the D-literature (see the Glossary) the insight was formulated with programmatic sharpness that Israel's God was the only god.[51] Here we find the formulation of the theme that "there is no other!"

> Know therefore this day, and lay it to your heart, that YHWH is God in heaven above and on the earth beneath; there is no other. (Deut 4:39; cf. v 35)

> . . . that all the peoples of the earth may know that YHWH is God; there is no other. (1 Kings 8:60)

We later find the same idea in the writings of the exilic Prophet of Consolation (Isa 45:21-22).

What will this then have entailed for the understanding of Exodus 3? It is likely that at this stage, when Israel had arrived at a definitional monotheism (i.e., a monotheism in the sense of denying the existence of other gods), the pregnant expressions in 3:14-15 will probably have been taken to signify *a proclamation that the Lord is the only God who exists.*

In spite of suggestions to the contrary, such a use of the verb *hāyâ* to designate existence fully agrees with what we otherwise know of the Hebrew language. Here I offer some examples in which we observe that the verb "to be" is negated, signifying that a distinction was clearly perceived between existence and non-existence:[52]

> No lion shall be [*lō' hāyâ*] there. (Isa 35:9)

> Would that I had died before any eye had seen me,
> and were as though I had not been [*lō' hāyâ*]. (Job 10:18-19)

> . . . but better than both is he who has not yet been [*lō' hāyâ*]. (Eccl 4:3)

> There are others who are unremembered:
> They are dead, and it is as though they had never existed [*lō' hāyâ*]. (Sir 44:9)

Summary. What conclusions may we draw about the content of "I Am" and "He Is" in Exod 3:14-15? It is of course a matter of which associations the two formulations actually conjured up; in this connection, one must take account of the time factors involved.

1. *At the oldest stage of the tradition,* it is likely that one heard in the "He Is" of the divine Name an assurance of God's active and aiding presence; note, for example, the statement in Exod 3:12: "I will be with you" (Hebrew *'ehyeh 'immāk*). It would be reasonable to see in v 12 a play on the name "I Am," which God himself utters in v 14. Thus the theological content of the divine Name comes surprisingly close to the divine promise that is so frequently uttered in the patriarchal narratives: "I shall be with you."

2. *At the later phase of the tradition,* around the time of the exile, there are reasons to believe that the divine "I Am" was regarded as a qualified existential statement. At this time it was recognized that the divine name "He Is" had the character of a confession to the one true God: He Is—He, and no other!

THE NEW TESTAMENT:
WHEN JESUS SAYS "I AM"

Some central aspects of the New Testament first become intelligible once one has viewed them against their Old Testament background. So, for example, we have already seen how the use of the designation *Kyrios* ("Lord") of Jesus in certain passages has to be understood against the background of *Adonay* ("Lord") as the replacement for the most holy divine Name in the Jewish milieu of the New Testament. This established a line which runs from YHWH to Adonay to Kyrios.

There is, however, yet another important line to observe, one that leads from the text dealing with the revelation of the Name and its divine proclamation, "I AM" (Exod 3:14), to the "I AM" utterances of Jesus in the New Testament. I am not thinking of expressions like "I am the light of the world," but of those in which "I AM" is absolute, alone, and without any complement. Note the examples in which the absolute "I AM" serves as a New Testament equivalent to the divine proclamation in the Book of Exodus:

> If you do not believe that I AM, you will die in your sins. (John 8:24*)

> When you have lifted up the Son of Man, then you will know that I AM, and that I do nothing on my own authority but speak thus as the Father taught me. (John 8:28*)

These words make quite a claim. We have just seen that in early Judaism the divine Name gradually ceased to be used publicly, although it continued to be so used in the temple liturgy. In the Mishna we are informed that the Name was employed in connection with the high-priestly blessing in the temple: "In the Temple they pronounced the Name as it was written, but in the provinces by a substituted word" (*m. Tamid* 7:2 and *m. Sota* 7:6). Furthermore, an especially sacral moment occurred in the context of the great Day of Atonement when the priest pronounced the Name and all those assembled in the forecourt fell to their knees (cf. *m. Yoma* 6:2). In so doing, the priest will presumably have "swallowed" the Name (*b. Qidd.* 71a), that is, pronounced it unclearly, so that its mystery might not be broached and profaned.

When Jesus proclaims his "I AM," he is unambiguously playing on a formula that recalls the Old Testament text about the revelation of the divine Name. In other words, when a reader of the Bible puts himself in the vantage point of the New Testament "I AM" expressions and looks backwards at the Old Testament, he sees a line of tradition that goes back to Exod 3:14. But, there is another kind of flashback to Isaiah 40—55.

In the Old Testament we frequently encounter a formula with which God introduces himself: "I am the Lord" (Hebrew, *ʾănî YHWH*). In Isaiah 40—55, however, we repeatedly encounter a variant of this formula, "I (am) he" (Hebrew, *ʾănî hûʾ*). In the LXX this formula is several times translated with an unconditional *egō eimi*, "I AM" (cf., e.g., Isa 41:4; 43:10; 43:25; 46:4).[53] Here is one example:

"You are my witnesses," says the Lord,
"and my servant whom I have chosen,
that you may know and believe me
and understand that I am He [*ʾănî hûʾ*]." (Isa 43:10)

Several scholars have called attention to the connection between the *ʾănî hûʾ* passages and Jesus' "I AM" statements in the Gospel of John.[54] It has been observed that this particular Hebrew formula plays an important part in the Jewish festal liturgies of Passover and the Feast of Booths. Here we encounter the Hebrew formula as a divine name. And we are concerned here with passages that really help to shed some light on the New Testament.

During the celebration of the Passover, a particular liturgical narrative of the exodus from Egypt was read aloud in the homes; this was the so-called Passover Haggadah. The narrative quotes, among other things, Exod 12:12: "For I will pass through the land of Egypt that night, and I will smite all the first-born . . . ; and on all the gods of Egypt I will execute judgments: I am the Lord." The short commentary on this passage, which contains the proclamation of the Name, twice uses the formula *ʾănî hûʾ*.[55] However, the oldest textual witnesses to the Haggadah lack this section, and it is most probably a later addition to the account; this does not rule out the possibility that it may be an ancient tradition.

The other Jewish festival of importance in this connection is the Festival of Booths. By necessity we have to reconstruct the way this festival was celebrated on the basis of the Mishna. Every day during the course of the festival there was a procession around the altar, on which occasion the following words from the Psalter were recited: "Save us, we beseech thee, O Lord! O Lord, we beseech thee, give us success!" (Ps 118:25). In order to avoid pronouncing the Name, the worshipers cited the passage in the form,

" *'ănî wĕhû'!* save us we pray! *'ănî wĕhû!* save us we pray!" (*m.Sukka* 4:5). In other words, we find the formula *'ănî hû'* here in the slightly altered form *'ănî wĕhû'*. We know from Jewish sources that it was usual to "swallow" the name YHWH (cf. *b. Qidd.* 71a). That is, out of respect for the sacredness of the Name the priest avoided pronouncing it in the correct manner. It is presumably for the same reason that the Old Testament revelatory formula was changed from *'ănî hû'* to *'ănî wĕhû'*. The latter form of the expression may be translated "I and he," although the quotation shows that in reality the formula functioned as a divine name; it has replaced the name YHWH in the quotation.

In brief, the absolute "I AM" expressions of Jesus have a double background (see Fig. 6). On the one hand, they point to the divine Name of Exod 3:14. On the other hand, they reflect certain expressions in Isaiah 40—55, where we find the formula *'ănî hû'*. The latter "I am" formula (*'ănî hû'*) apparently played a role in Jewish cultic celebrations in the time of Jesus, above all in the celebration of the Festival of Booths. The Jewish materials show that Jesus may well have employed the Hebrew revelatory formula; they also show what reaction was to be expected if he had done so. For those who did not accept Jesus' claims, he would in so doing have infringed upon the sacredness of the divine Name. He would have committed blasphemy.

FIGURE 6
"I AM" IN THE OLD AND
NEW TESTAMENTS

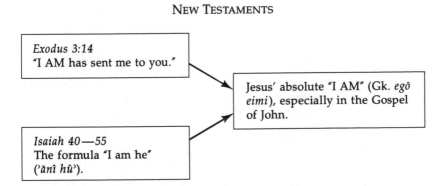

Jesus' absolute "I AM," that is, "I am" with no subsequent complement, has a twofold Old Testament background.

45

In Search of God

We now need to take a closer look at the relevant passages in the New Testament. It will become clear that certain of these texts, especially in the Gospel of John, may be associated with the Jewish festivals.

John 6:16–21 relates the story of how Jesus walked on the waters. The disciples take his appearance for an apparition, but Jesus calms them, saying, "It is I (*egō eimi*); do not be afraid" (v 20). The translation "It is I" is completely legitimate (cf. John 9:9); however, I am inclined to agree with those exegetes who have held the words to be more significant than this. The injunction "Fear not!" is a standard assurance in the context of Old Testament theophanies (cf. Gen 15:1, et al.). Thus the description of Jesus' walking on the waters can easily be understood as a scene of self-revelation, in the context of which Jesus says, "I AM (*egō eimi*), do not be afraid." Both the episode and Jesus' words are well attested in the earliest Gospel tradition (cf. Mark 6:50). Note also that Matthew's version of the scene containing Jesus' "I AM" (Matt 14:27) concludes with the disciples' confession of Jesus as the son of God (v 33). What we see in John is a revelation in which Jesus in his majesty is viewed for a moment by his astonished disciples. The medium of this is Jesus' deed—his miracle—and his word: the majestic "I AM." If such expressions enjoyed a particular role in the contemporary Jewish festivals, then it is important to see when this event is said to have taken place. The evangelist relates, "Now the Passover, the feast of the Jews, was at hand" (John 6:4).

The "I AM" expressions that we have just cited come from John 8. We shall now examine John 8 in its wider context of chapters 7—9. These chapters are to be read against the background of the Jewish Feast of Booths (cf. John 7:2, 10). (See Fig. 7.) For our purposes three elements of this cultic celebration are particularly important:[56] (1) Every morning of this week-long festival the ritual of a water libation took place. The water was fetched from the Pool of Siloam and poured out at the altar; the rite itself seems to have anticipated the advent of the harvest rains. (2) The festival was also characterized by a grand Festival of Lights (Hanukkah) in the forecourt of the women, in the course of which the golden candlesticks were lit and the participants danced joyfully with torches in their hands. (3) Furthermore, there was a procession around the altar, in the course of which there was the divine proclamation—'*ănî wĕhû*'. On the last day of the festival this feature was repeated seven times.

FIGURE 7

JOHN 7—9 AND THE JEWISH FESTIVAL OF BOOTHS

The Jewish Festival of Booths	*John 7—9*
1. The water-libation ceremony	Jesus' characterization of the Spirit as living water (7:37–39).
2. The Festival of Lights	Jesus heals the blind man and says, "I am the light of the world" (9:5; cf. 8:12).
3. The proclamation of the Name	Jesus' absolute "I AM" (8:24, 28, 58).

On point after point, John 7—9 are to be read against the background provided by the Jewish Festival of Booths.

Even a cursory reading of John 7—9 reveals a number of details that appear in special relief when beheld against the background of the Jewish festival. First, Jesus presents an alternative to the Jewish water libation with the words, "If any one thirst, let him come to me and drink. He who believes in me, as the scripture has said, 'Out of his heart shall flow rivers of living water'" (John 7:37–38). Jesus speaks these words of the Spirit. Second, Jesus palpably recalls the Jewish Festival of Lights when he heals the man born blind (9:1–12) and proclaims, "I am the light of the world" (8:12; 9:5). These correspondences naturally lead us to wonder what Jesus has made of the rite in which the formula *'ănî wĕhû'* is employed? The answer is quite simple: the formula repeatedly finds its counterpart in Jesus' several "I AM" expressions (cf. John 8:24 and 28 above).

One detail needs special attention. As we have seen, in Isaiah the formula is *'ănî hû'*, "I (am) he," a phrase which was varied in the context of the Jewish Festival of Booths to *'ănî wĕhû'*,[57] with the meaning "I and he." In John 8, we find yet another expression that provides a factual counterpart to the Jewish formula in all its multiplicity. The Greek text of 8:16 may be translated as follows: "Yet even if I do judge, my judgment is true, for it is not I alone that judge, but I and he who sent me." Here the words "I and he who sent me" look like yet another reference to the divine proclamation that took place in the Jewish Festival of Booths (cf. also John 10:30).

Yet another passage in John 8 reads: "Truly, truly, I say to you, before Abraham was, *I am*" (John 8:58*). Here, too, one suspects that it is the *'ănî hû'* formula of the Prophet of Consolation and the divine "I

47

Am" of Exod 3:14 that form the background. Once this is acknowl-
edged, the Jews' reaction becomes intelligible: "So they took up stones
to throw at him" (8:59). Note what the law of Moses commands: "He
who blasphemes the name of the Lord shall be put to death; all the
congregation shall stone him" (Lev 24:16). Thus, when Jesus uttered
the Semitic revelatory formula that underlies the Greek *egō eimi* ("I
AM") his Jewish listeners felt that he had gone too far; he had profaned the Name and deserved to die.

Thus we now must deal with the arrest of Jesus in John 18. When
the emissaries announce that they are seeking Jesus of Nazareth, Jesus
proclaims his *egō eimi* (v 5), which could well mean, "I am he" (cf. John
9:9). The continuation, however, shows that here the formula also
serves as a formula of self-revelation: "When he said to them, *'egō
eimi,'* they drew back and fell to the ground" (v 6). The event takes
place during the last Passover that occurred during Jesus' earthly life.
We are reminded of what the Jewish texts say about the Day of Atonement: when the priests and the people hear the high priest call out the
divine Name, they fall to their knees with their faces turned towards
the earth (*m.Yoma* 6:2).

Finally, we note a few more attestations of this "I AM" (John 4:25;
13:19; Mark 13:6; cf. 14:62). It is of course appropriate that our formula is so frequently attested in the Gospel of John, for it is in John
that we find an understanding of Jesus that displays both his glory
and his pre-existence. The self-revelatory formula "I AM" is at home
in this theological context. The deeper perspective of these matters is
reflected in Jesus' high priestly intercessory prayer in John 17. Here
Jesus speaks to his Father of "the glory which I had with thee before
the world was made" (v 5); he also speaks of "thy name, which thou
hast given me" (vv 11–12). And finally, he also tells how his life had
been a proclamation of this divine Name—and thereby of the nature
of God (vv 6 and 26):

> I have manifested thy name to the men whom thou gavest me out of the
> world. (John 17:6; cf. v 26)

SUMMARY

We now draw the following conclusions concerning the mysterious
Hebrew divine name YHWH:

- The name YHWH began to play a role among the Hebrew tribes in
  the time of Moses—the historical point of departure (*terminus a*

quo). We have no certain attestation from the pre-Mosaic age, although there is some likelihood that the Name had a prehistory among certain tribes in what is now eastern Sinai. The Ebla materials do not include the name YHWH, but they do contain a parallel of considerable interest.

- In philological terms the Name probably means "He is." At the earliest phase of the tradition (the period of Moses and subsequently) it was understood as an assurance that God was present helping those who worshiped him. In the period of the Josianic reform the Name was probably also understood as an existential statement: "He is the one who exists [and no other god does]."
- It has also been possible to recognize some lines of development traceable into the New Testament.

  1. The sacredness of the Name became more and more pronounced, so that it was gradually replaced by *Adonay*, "Lord." For this reason most translations use the word "Lord" or some equivalent whenever the Hebrew text reads *YHWH*. This fact also enables us to understand the designation of Jesus as "Lord" (*Kyrios*).

  2. The "I AM" expressions of Jesus have a double background: that of the divine "I AM" of Exod 3:14 and of another "I am" formula (*ănî hûʾ*), which is attested in the Old Testament and in Jewish festal liturgies.

3
The God of the Fathers:
Divine Designations in
the Patriarchal Narratives

In the previous chapter we directed our attention to the texts in Exodus dealing with Moses and the name YHWH. We shall now step backwards in the Bible and investigate the materials in the Book of Genesis that refer to "the God of Abraham, Isaac and Jacob." Which features of the countenance of God do these texts permit us to glimpse?[1]

Yet his bow remained unmoved,
his arms were made agile
by the hands of the Mighty One of Jacob
by the name of the Shepherd, the Rock of Israel,
by the God of your father who will help you,
by God Almighty [El Shaddai] who will bless you
with blessings of heaven above,
blessings of the deep that couches beneath,
blessings of the breasts and of the womb. (Gen 49:24–25)

The quotation is part of Jacob's blessing upon Joseph. Among the divine names that occur here, three have attracted special attention:
1. "the God of your father"
2. "the Mighty One of Jacob"; in Hebrew, "Jacob's *'ābîr*"
3. El Shaddai, which was earlier thought to mean "God the Almighty"
These three divine names will be the basis of the investigation in this chapter.

First, we ask, Did the patriarchs, too, worship God under the name of YHWH, or should we search for another divine name? We have already seen that the texts in Exodus regard the revelation of the name of YHWH as a major milestone in the history of salvation:

> I am YHWH. I appeared to Abraham, to Isaac, and to Jacob, as God
> Almighty, but by my name YHWH I did not make myself known to
> them. (Exod 6:2–3)

It is nevertheless the case that the name YHWH occurs around ninety
times in the narratives about Abraham, Isaac, and Jacob (e.g., Gen
12:1, 4, 7; 15:1, 7; 17:1; 18:1). This poses a problem: Exodus 6 seems
not to agree with the facts as related in Genesis.

In such a situation, we can do one of two things: either question the
usual interpretation of Exodus 6, or else strive to arrive at a more sophisticated understanding of the state of affairs in Genesis. For centuries, scholars have attempted the first sort of approach; both the
ancient rabbis and modern biblical scholars have squeezed and con-
torted the words in Exod 6:2–3. None of these attempts, however, has
ever produced a generally accepted new interpretation of the passage.
The passage must then be taken in its most literal sense, as was ac-
knowledged already by the earliest translators of the Bible (cf. the
LXX, the Vulgate, and the earliest of the Targums). This literal interpretation is no less incumbent on contemporary biblical scholars.[2]

The text, then, maintains that God did not reveal himself to the
patriarchs under the name of YHWH. But how are we to understand
the situation in Genesis? Why is the name YHWH employed in the
texts dealing with the patriarchs? The most reasonable answer is that
the patriarchal traditions were transmitted orally during the very
centuries when the most commonly employed divine name was in
fact YHWH. The Old Testament testifies to the certainty of a fundamental continuity throughout the history of salvation; it is always
one and the same God who acts. The God who spoke to Moses was
the same one who had earlier spoken to "the fathers" (Exod 3:6, 15;
6:2–3). Thus the use of the name YHWH in Genesis is yet another
example of this certainty.

This means that when we encounter the name YHWH in the patriarchal narratives, it is not to be regarded as a survival of the patriarchal
period.[3] It derives, instead, from the later editors of these materials.
There is some supporting evidence to this effect in our Bible. An example is provided by the narrative of Jacob in Bethel. When Jacob awakens from his dream he says, "Surely *YHWH* is in this place, and I did
not know it." And then he names the site in question *Beth-El* (Gen
28:16, 19). An equally clear example is to be found in Genesis 16,
which deals with Hagar and Ishmael. Here the angel of the Lord says
to Hagar, "Behold, you are with child, and shall bear a son; you shall

call his name *Ishma-El*, because *YHWH* has given heed to your afflic-
tion" (Gen 16:11). The names Beth-El and Ishma-El contain the ancient
semitic divine name "El." It is routinely assumed by scholars that in
both of the quoted passages the name "YHWH" has replaced an earlier
"El"; however, the passages also demonstrate that the narrator felt free
to use "YHWH" instead of "El," not only in his own narrative but also
in the quoted dialogue between a mortal and a divine being.

Thus patriarchal narratives have come down to us through the
hands of those people in later Israel who transmitted the various
traditions in such a way that they were gradually written down and
ultimately came to constitute our long patriarchal epic (Genesis 12—
50). We may conceive of this epic as a gigantic oil painting which was
gradually embellished with new brushstrokes by later artists. Unlike
art historians, however, biblical scholars have no definitive scientific
method to distinguish between the different accretions to the original tradition. This is why scholars must devote so much attention to
the present form of the Genesis texts, even when addressing the historical problems raised by these texts.

From the point of view of the historian, it is a daring undertaking
to attempt to penetrate behind the Mosaic period in order to draw
some conclusions about conditions in the patriarchal era. Indeed, the
very genres of the narratives in question urge one to be cautious.
Nevertheless, some observations deserve our attention:

- In the patriarchal narratives a number of names of persons and
  places are mentioned that have long attracted scholarly interest:
  Abram, Sarai, Jacob, Laban, Serug, Nahor, and Terah; all of them
  have been studied in the light of extrabiblical comparative material. Recent studies have shown that one must be careful about
  drawing historical conclusions on the basis of these names.[4] On
  the other hand, it is clear that the biblical names are not products
  of some scribe's imagination. The name "Jacob" is of particular
  interest; comparative materials from the ancient Near East have
  shown that it means either "El protects" or "El is near."[5] Its use as
  a proper name is based on these contents. In later biblical tradition, however, this meaning has waned, and we find the name
  secondarily associated with other meanings, such as "to seize by
  the heel" (cf. Hosea 12:3).
- Next there is the matter of the ethnic origins of the patriarchs.
  There is a well-established tradition that associates the patriarchs with the Arameans and that also manifests itself in the

texts about Jacob, since he is said to be related to the Arameans
through his mother, Rebecca. Rebecca was the daughter of the
Aramean Bethuel and the sister of Laban, likewise referred to
as Aramean (cf. Gen 25:20; 28:5; 31:20, 24). A text from the D-
literature records that "a wandering Aramean was my father;
and he went down into Egypt" (Deut 26:5). Such information
may be combined with extant extrabiblical information concerning an Aramaic population migration in the ancient Near East.[6]

- Certain negative observations are also worthy of note. We know
that Jerusalem and Zion played a major role in the cult of the
monarchy. Thus, when earlier scholarship maintained that the
patriarchal narratives were products of the monarchical period
and as such had no source value about the pre-monarchical period, it was palpably difficult for adherents of this approach to
explain why Jerusalem plays no role of importance in the patriarchal stories.

- Another empty space on the "map" applies to Baal. We happen to
know that the conflict with the worship of Canaanite Baal was a
significant problem subsequent to the patriarchal period. It is thus
astonishing to note to what degree the patriarchal stories keep silent about Baal. If these texts were really explicable as literary
products of the period of the monarchy, this would hardly be
the case.

"MY FATHER'S GOD"

Our point of departure is Albrecht Alt's classical study. In 1929
Albrecht Alt issued what was for quite some time the definitive
scholarly answer to the question of the faith of the patriarchs. Up
until then the situation had been largely influenced by the skepticism of Julius Wellhausen, the great nineteenth-century German Old
Testament scholar, for whom the patriarchal texts were reflections of
Israel's faith during the period of the monarchy. Then Alt issued
"Der Gott der Väter" ("The God of the Fathers").[7] The contribution
was a scientific breakthrough to a new way of understanding matters, and Alt had achieved it by directing his attention to the divine
names in the patriarchal narratives.

Alt had become aware of a certain way of referring to God in
Genesis, which at first sight does not seem at all strange. He pointed
to a number of passages in the patriarchal texts which refer to "the

God of my father," "the God of your father," "the God of Abraham," and so forth. Let us examine these materials.

Genesis 26 informs us about a nocturnal revelation to Isaac in Beer-Sheba, in which God speaks to him and says, "I am the God of Abraham your father; fear not, for I am with you and will bless you" (v 24). The address to Jacob during his nocturnal revelation is similar: "I am the Lord, the God of Abraham your father and the God of Isaac" (28:13). Jacob also receives a similar message in Beer-Sheba as he is on his way to his sons in Egypt: "I am God, the God of your father; do not be afraid to go down to Egypt; for I will there make of you a great nation" (46:3).

It is also interesting to note that this way of speaking about God does not occur in theophany texts alone; it occurs in other literary forms. For example, in conjunction with his conflict with Laban, Jacob experiences God's special protection and says, "If the God of my father, the God of Abraham and the Fear of Isaac, had not been on my side . . ." (Gen 31:42; cf. vv 5 and 29).

EXCURSUS 4
WHERE DO WE FIND REFERENCES TO
THE "GOD OF THE FATHERS"
IN GENESIS AND EXODUS?

"The God of my father": Gen 31:5, 42; Exod 15:2; 18:4
"The God of your father" (2d m.sg.): Gen 46:3; 49:25; 50:17; Exod 3:6
"The God of your father" (2d m.pl.): Gen 31:29; 43:23
"The God of their father": Gen 31:53
"The God of your fathers": Exod 3:13, 15, 16
"The God of their fathers": Exod 4:5

"The God of Abraham": Gen 24:12, 27, 42, 48; 26:24; 28:13; 31:53
"The God of Isaac": Gen 46:1
"The God of Abraham, your father, and the God of Isaac": Gen 28:13
"The God of my father Abraham and the God of my father Isaac": Gen 32:9 [10]
"The God of your father(s), the God of Abraham, Isaac, and Jacob": Exod 3:6, 15, 16; 4:5

The conflict between Jacob and Laban is eventually resolved when both parties enter into a pact: it is described in the latter part of Genesis 31. The covenant is guaranteed by the gods of the contracting parties who are, respectively, "the God of Abraham" and "the God of Nahor" (v 53). The accompanying verb is in the plural: "may they judge between us," which suggests that the God of Abraham and the God of Nahor are two separate deities.

In his study of "the God of the Fathers," Alt emphasized two matters in particular. First, he noted that the type of divine designation itself is strange. It seems as if we have a "nameless" god, a god who had no proper name as such. This god is instead referred to in terms that speak of a connection to a given individual: "my father's God," "Abraham's God," and so forth. The type of name in question may be described as "the God of X," where X stands for some worshiper of this god. The emphasis of the name is on the connection between this deity and some individual mortal, whom Alt assumed was the head of the family or tribal group. The personal character of this relationship to the divine is striking. We are not dealing with religion on the level of the tribe or the people but on the level of the individual and his or her personal encounter with God. Abraham, Isaac, and Jacob were the first who received revelations from this "God of the fathers," and it is for this reason that they have been commemorated century after century. It is not because of any deeds of heroism that we recall the Hebrew patriarchs, but because of their faith.

Second, unlike so many deities, the God of the fathers is not bound to the locality where his temple is situated. The God of the fathers is not only "nameless"; he is also, in a manner of speaking, "siteless"— not bound to any given locality.

Alt also attempted to find comparative material among related Semitic peoples. He found what he was seeking in some inscriptions of the Nabateans, a nomadic people who frequented the region to the south and southeast of Palestine in the centuries around the beginning of our era. The Nabateans also spoke of their gods as "the god of so and so," that is, they used names of the type "the god of X." This fact led Alt to suppose that the worship of the God of the fathers was a special type of religion rooted in the nomadic way of life.

If this presumption is correct, then we would have in "the God of the fathers" an example of interplay between way of life and understanding of God, evidence to the effect that the understanding of God evolves in conjunction with the challenges presented by life itself. The patriarchal way of life was characterized by the nomadic lifestyle; for the nomads it was a feature of their existence that God was not confined to any particular geographical location. Their god was a god who went with his own. The notion that the God of the fathers has certain aspects that correspond to the vital necessities of the patriarchs has been especially emphasized by Victor Maag.[8]

Now we shall attempt to complete and partly correct the portrayal of the god of the fathers—the "nameless" and "siteless" god of the ancestral fathers—which Alt proposed.

EXCURSUS 5

THE SEARCH FOR A CRITICALLY
ASSURED MINIMUM

The historical-critical scholar attempts to arrive at a critically assured minimum. Such a "critical minimum" is that territory which rational historical analysis demonstrates to be more or less historically reliable "facts." This can happen, for example, when scholars combine the use of biblical with extrabiblical materials (e.g., archaeological discoveries from Palestine or its environment).

One should note that in this context the word "critical" does not express a negative attitude towards the texts. It means instead simply a study in the sense of an intensive investigation. To search for such a "critical minimum"—the demands of intellectual integrity being what they are—one must be willing to distinguish among those features which can be asserted *as facts*, those which represent *probable conclusions*, and those which are merely *possibilities* among other, equally valid ones.

This does not mean that only the critically assured minimum can be of interest for whatever faith the scholar himself professes. In the church or synagogue, one and the same scholar may experience God's address through a biblical text which may not belong to what the same scholar regards as belonging to the critically assured minimum.

THE GOD OF THE FATHERS:

THE PERSONAL GOD

The gods of the ancient Near East were, to a large extent, associated with particular places and temples. Marduk was worshiped in Babylon; and Sin, in Haran. As for YHWH, there are suggestions that he was originally thought to be connected with Sinai (see Chapter 2, under "In Historical Perspective: Some Indications of the Origin of the Name"). The idea of such a connection perhaps underlies certain texts in which there appears to be some question as to whether YHWH is able to follow his wandering tribes after the departure from Sinai (Exod 17:7; 33:14–15). Also another and rather peculiar text may be explained on the basis of the conception of the association of the gods to particular sites or territories (territoriality). A passage in the Books of Kings relates that a Syrian general was healed by the prophet Elisha and

56

converted to the worship of YHWH on the same occasion. When the Syrian is about to return home, he makes a remarkable request of the prophet—that he be allowed to take with him as much earth as two mules can carry (2 Kings 5:17). This "newly converted" Syrian heathen still believed that gods were attached to their territories. Thus, believing that the God of Israel could be worshiped only in Israel, he wanted to take back some of Israel's earth with him to his own country.

The God of the fathers whom we encounter in Genesis lacks all such territorial ties. This can hardly be accounted for by the assumption that the texts are the result of later ages' attempts to present the materials. This characteristic can hardly have been added during the development of the tradition. Here we note the correspondence between the life situation of the semi-nomadic patriarchs and their understanding of God. The God of the fathers accompanied his faithful during their wanderings!

Furthermore, the God of the fathers is not attached to places, but to persons! This comes into relief when we examine a group of personal names that were typical before the divided monarchy, but became rare subsequently. These are composite names in which a *kinship term* is the first element: '*āb*, "father"; '*āḥ*, "brother"; and *ʿam*, "uncle" (father's brother).[9] We immediately recognize such elements in names like Abram, Ahi-ezer, or Ammi-nadab. We happen to know that the kinship terms in such names do not refer to any earthly relative, but to God. This is so because we also possess a parallel group of names in which the first element is a clear divine designation, such as "YHWH" or "El." Note the following:

Ab-ram	Jeho-ram
Abi-melech	Eli-melech
Abi-ezer	Eli-ezer

The kinship term in the names in the left-hand column refers to God as father. The names signify, respectively, "my (divine) father is high," "my (divine) father is king," and "my (divine) father is an aide."

In other words, personal names of this type bear witness to the fact that it was possible to speak of one's god as a close relative—a father, a brother, or an uncle. In names like Ab-ram we even possess the Old Testament roots of the address to God in the Lord's Prayer.

Personal names like these (i.e., with kinship terms as the "theophoric elements") suggest that the God of the fathers was a personal god. In this connection it is possible to point to yet another group of names;

this time, however, they are not personal names, but special designations of the God of the fathers. In Jacob's blessing of Joseph we found the name "the Mighty One of Jacob," in Hebrew "Jacob's *ʾābîr*" (Gen 49:24; the name is also found in Isa 49:26; 60:16; Ps 132:2, 5; and in the form "the *ʾābîr* of Israel" in Isa 1:24). In another similar name, the God of the fathers is related to Isaac in the name "Isaac's *paḥad*" (Gen 31:42, 53). The name means approximately "the Fear of Isaac," although this is hardly a fear experienced by Isaac, but rather a panic sent out by the God of the fathers to strike Isaac's enemies.[10] The God of the fathers protects Isaac and his group.

These names, "Jacob's *ʾābîr*" and "Isaac's *paḥad*," have one major feature in common: they speak of God in terms of a personal association with the chief of the tribal group; he is a god who protects the group of his faithful.

Alt held that the God of the fathers represented a special type of religion that was rooted in the life of nomadic groups. Scholars who have examined the oldest Semitic comparative material have criticized Alt on this issue. The attempt to classify the worship of the God of the fathers as a special type of religion has resulted in a preference for "the God of the fathers" as relating to an observable trend in the ancient Near East, and not merely among nomads—the worship of the personal god who is often referred to as "my god," "NN's god," "my protector," "my shepherd," and so forth. In particular, Herbert Vorländer has studied the God of the fathers against this background.[11] Continuing studies of the problem—above all the work of Rainer Albertz—have led scholars to locate this sort of personal piety in the sociological context of the family, in contradistinction to varieties of worship practiced in the context of the temples.[12]

THE GOD OF THE FATHERS:
THE GUARANTOR OF THE PROMISE

The divine promises are an important element in the patriarchal narratives. There are three distinct promises: the promise of progeny, the promise of land, and the promise of presence and protection ("I am with you").

In the research of recent decades, the discussion of the promises has been intense. Certain scholars, such as Erhard Blum, have preferred to regard the promise texts as literary compositions the intention of which is to link disparate tradition complexes together.[13] It has of course been observed that the promise of a great and numerous people arches all the way from Gen 12:1–2 to 46:3–4, connecting all that falls within its compass. Other scholars have reasoned along the following lines: it cannot be proved that the promise texts are an original element in the oldest tradition, but the promises deal with matters that would have been both appropriate and fitting for nomads of the patriarchal type. This line has been argued by Albrecht Alt and Claus Westermann, among others.[14] In other words, they have emphasized the interplay between situation and religion. The promise of a son deals with the birth of the heir, whose appearance would ensure continuity in the clan. The promise of land deals with new pasturage sufficient to meet the future needs of the group.

The Promise of Progeny

Westermann[15] especially has emphasized the authentic character of the promise of a son, in which connection he offers several thought-provoking observations. He notes that in texts like Genesis 18 the promise of a son is part of the contents of the narrative itself, and it would be unthinkable to attempt to excise it from the context: "At the appointed time I will return to you, in the spring, and Sarah shall have a son" (Gen 18:14). Without the promise, the text would no longer be a meaningful narrative. Similar considerations apply to the function of the promise of the son in Genesis 16, which speaks of Ishmael. Westermann also observes that in certain texts we find the promise that Abraham's descendants will grow into a mighty people (Gen 15:1–6; 17:2–6; 22:16–18). Here the horizon of the texts is wide ranging, whereas the patriarchal promise of a son is limited in relevance to the life of the patriarch in question alone. In short, the promise is immediately relevant, and its fulfillment does not lie in the distant future. This supports the conclusion of the historical nature of the promise of a son.

In this connection, it is appropriate to call attention to the sacrifice of Isaac (Gen 22). When Abraham abandoned his land and his kinship group (Gen 12), he simultaneously sacrificed his past to the one who had called him. When he set off on his journey to Mount Moriah to sacrifice his son, the son of the promise, he was by the same token equally prepared to sacrifice his future to the same God.

The Promise of Land

The promise of a son expands to become a promise of an entire people. Other scholars see a similar "expansion" in the promise of the land, which we encounter in a number of texts (Gen 12:7; 13:14–18; 15:7–21; 17:8). They seem to detect underlying it an earlier promise of immediate interest to nomads: the promise of new pasturage.[16]

The promise of the land is accorded especial theological weight in Gen 15:7–21, a notoriously difficult dating problem. In the introduction of the text God presents himself as the one who had led Abraham out of Ur of the Chaldees in order to give him "this land to possess." Abraham then asks, "O Lord God, how am I to know that I shall possess it?" Abraham is ordered to slaughter a number of animals, cut them in two, and position the various halves opposite one another.

What is expressed in this rite? Other biblical texts as well as extra-biblical materials provide some significant clues. It appears that in the process of making contractual agreements in the ancient Near East, rites were sometimes employed that expressed the threat of a curse upon any party who failed to live up to their obligations. In the course of such rites a person cut up one or more animals with either the implicit or the explicit understanding that a similar fate would befall whomever failed to uphold the contract.[17]

Jeremiah 34 offers a good example of such a covenantal rite. It deals with a covenant made during the reign of the last Judaean king; according to its terms, the inhabitants of Jerusalem had pledged themselves to free their slaves. The obligation was expressed by means of a covenantal rite: a calf was slaughtered and halved, and those who entered into the covenant signified their acceptance of its terms by marching in procession between the halves of the slaughtered animal. But the people of Jerusalem did not live up to their covenant and instead re-enslaved their once-manumitted servants. This calls for the actualization of the covenantal penalties, the central formulation of which is as follows:

> And the men who transgressed my covenant and did not keep the terms of the covenant which they made before me, I will make like the calf which they cut in two and passed between its parts. (Jer 34:18; cf. v 19)

The rite in Genesis 15 has a similar content. The text describes how the sun goes down and Abraham falls asleep. We then read,

> When the sun had gone down and it was dark, behold, a smoking fire pot and a flaming torch passed between these pieces. (Gen 15:17)

But who is it who passes between the animal sections and thereby takes upon himself the obligation in question? Abraham is completely passive in this scene. What the text implies is that God comes forth in a fiery form between the halves of the slaughtered animals and that in this solemn fashion God assumes the obligation. We are also told the nature of the obligation: "On that day the Lord made a covenant with Abram, saying, 'To your descendants I give this land'" (v 18). In this passage Abraham is depicted solely as the recipient of the pact; God solemnly pronounces his promise concerning the land, and the promise is accorded special emphasis via the ancient rite. Moreover, this rite states that God is willing to jeopardize his own existence in the event he should fail to keep his promise. With paradoxical sharpness the narrative describes God as the guarantor of his promise. The essential content of Gen 15:7–21 is the same as that expressed in Deuteronomy, where the promise of the land is repeatedly expressed as a divine oath (e.g., Deut 1:8; 6:10, 18; 7:8, 12–13).

The Promise of God's Presence

There is a third kind of divine promise in the patriarchal narratives, one in which God delivers to the fathers an assurance of his presence and continual protection: "I am with you." These are formulas that use one of the Hebrew prepositions, notably either ʾet or ʿim. [18] These notices are especially evident in the accounts dealing with Jacob; some of them appear in sentences in which God himself expresses his promise, while in others Jacob or other people refer to it.

Jacob's life is set off by two nocturnal revelations. The first takes place at Beth-el, when the young Jacob is fleeing from the brother whom he has cheated of his birthright. En route from Beer-sheba to Haran, Jacob stays overnight in Beth-el. In a dream God reveals himself to him and says, among other things,

> Behold, I am *with you* and will keep you wherever you go, and will bring you back to this land; for I will not leave you until I have done that of which I have spoken to you. (Gen 28:15)

Later in Genesis we meet the aged patriarch, en route to Egypt to join his sons. He spends his last night in the land of promise at the sacred site of Beer-Sheba. In another nighttime vision God reveals himself to Jacob and renews the promise of his presence:

> I am God, the God of your father; do not be afraid to go down to Egypt; for I will there make of you a great nation. I will go down *with you* to Egypt, and I will also bring you up again; and Joseph's hand shall close your eyes. (Gen 46:3–4)

61

This divine promise stretches between the two poles of the narrative—the dream in Bethel and the revelation in Beer-sheba.

The same promise recurs as a divine address in Gen 31:3: "Return to the land of your fathers and to your kindred, and I will be with you." The description of the revelation in Beth-el concludes when Jacob makes a vow: "If God will be with me, and will keep me in this way that I go" (Gen 28:20). His words point forward to Genesis 35, where Jacob returns to Beth-el to build an altar "to the God who answered me in the day of my distress and has been with me wherever I have gone" (Gen 35:3). The promise may also be glimpsed in 31:5 (cf. v 42).

In brief, the promise of the divine presence plays an important role in the Jacob narratives; notice, however, that it also occurs in the Abraham stories (Gen 21:22) and in the Isaac narrative (Gen 26:3, 24, 28).

The Hidden God and the Promise
of God's Presence

The Abraham narrative is introduced by the following majestic command from God: "Go from your country and your kindred and your father's house to the land that I will show you" (Gen 12:1). The divine command for Abraham to break with his previous life is his fundamental experience. There is another context later in Genesis in which Abraham recollects the time "when God caused me to wander from my father's house" (Gen 20:13). Where the usual translation reads "caused me to wander," the Hebrew original is far stronger, for there Abraham says literally "when God led me astray" (the verb *tāʿâ* being in the Hiphil). The Hebrew shows to what extent the patriarch had been sent out to face the unknown. Abraham had encountered the *Deus absconditus*, the impenetrable and hidden God.

It is correct to affirm that the promise of the divine presence offers a theological counterweight to this theme. God is not merely the one who sends his chosen out into the darkness of existential uncertainty; he is also the one who pronounces the assurance of his presence: "I am with you." This aspect is already understood in God's command to break away "to the land that I will show you" (Gen 12:1). The words imply that God will accompany Abraham and show him the way. We find the same thought more explicitly formulated in the words of the Philistine king Abimelech to Abraham: "God is with you in all that you do" (Gen 21:22); and in the narrative of how Abraham's servant obtains a wife for Isaac (Gen 24:48).

When we review the patriarchal narratives and compare them with literature that arose during the period of the monarchy, we reach these two conclusions concerning the promise:

- In the patriarchal narratives, God's promise has no antithesis: *the word of judgment is notably absent.* This is to be compared with the alternation between judgment and promise that we find in the prophetic writings, for example.
- God's promise to the fathers is freely given: *any condition for the promise is strikingly absent.* Elsewhere in the Old Testament we find a radically different situation, for we see that the divine promise is usually supplied with a "conditional clause," which is introduced by the conditional conjunction "if" (cf., e.g., 1 Kings 2:4; 6:12–13; 9:1–9; 11:38).

EXCURSUS 6

THE PROMISE OF THE PRESENCE
OUTSIDE OF THE PATRIARCHAL NARRATIVES

Horst Dietrich Preuss (1968) has done us the service of assembling all of the occurrences in the Old Testament of the promise of "the Presence." On the basis of his collection we shall call attention to certain connections in which either this promise or the observation of its effects is important:

- The Joseph Story: Gen 39:2, 3, 21, 23.
- The History of David's Rise to Power: 1 Sam 16:18; 18:12; 2 Sam 5:10; 7:3, 9.
- Call narratives: certain call narratives are characterized by the following structure: commission from God; protest of the call recipient; God's promise; God's sign (see Chapter 2, "The Two Key Texts in Exodus"). Here God's promise normally consists of the assurance of his presence and assistance. See Exod 3:12 (the call of Moses), Judges 6:12, 17 (Gideon's call), and Jer 1:8 (the call of Jeremiah).
- The name "Immanuel": Psalm 46:7, 11 [8, 12] contains the expression "YHWH Sabaoth is with us." In Hebrew this expression consists of (a) a divine name and (b) the preposition *'immānû,* "with us." In Isa 7:14 the name "Immanuel" has the same contents, although the sequence differs: (a) *'immānû,* "with us," plus (b) a divine name, which in this case is "El."
- The Gospel of Matthew: When we turn to the New Testament, we find that the Gospel of Matthew is framed by the promise of the presence. Matthew 1:22–23 quotes the "Immanuel sign" promise from Isa 7:14. This is one of Matthew's "formula" or "fulfillment quotations." Then at the end Jesus utters the command for missionary activity, which ends with the words "and lo, I am with you always, to the close of the age" (Matt 28:20). In literary terms this is the Gospel's inclusio.

THE GOD OF THE FATHERS:
THE SOURCE OF BLESSING

The divine blessing also plays a major role in our texts. It is closely related to the motif of the promise.[19] Of course the semantic field of the notion of "blessing" is comprehended in Hebrew by a number of words, all of which are derived from the Hebrew root *b-r-k*. In the patriarchal narrative these words occur no less than eighty-two times. Many scholars have taken this fact as an indication that the blessing motif was intensified during the process of tradition. Nevertheless, one should note that the motif of blessing emerged as an important element in the earliest material.

In the Jacob narrative the blessing serves as a leitmotiv. Jacob strives so fiercely to obtain the divine blessing that he does not even draw the line at cheating his brother Esau. And once the aged Isaac has pronounced his blessing, it cannot be withdrawn (Gen 27). The blessing manifests itself during Jacob's years as a shepherd working for his father-in-law (Gen 31); and, working through Jacob, it benefits the latter as well. Laban says to Jacob, "I have learned by divination that the Lord has blessed me because of you" (30:27; cf. v 30). Later the theme of blessing receives its classical formulation in the account of Jacob's wrestling at the Jabbok, when the patriarch says to his opponent, "I will not let you go unless you bless me" (32:26). At the end of his life, Jacob passes on the blessing to Joseph's two sons (Gen 48).

But the Abraham texts, too, know of the motif of blessing. In this connection Gen 12:1–3 is particularly important. As P.D. Miller has contended, the passage should be translated as follows:[20]

And the Lord said to Abram:
"Go from your land, from your kindred, and from your father's house to the land that I will show you,
that I may make you a great nation, and bless you, and make your name great that you may effect blessing,
and that I may bless the ones blessing you—and should there be one who regards you with contempt I will curse him.
So, then, all the families of the earth can gain a blessing in you."

In the final literary complex comprised of the primeval history (Gen 1—11) *and* the patriarchal narratives (Gen 12—50), the divine word of promise points far beyond the immediate context; it points *forward* to Israel as a leading nation. The expression "a great nation" uses the Hebrew political term for "people, nation" (*gôy*), rather than the ethnic term (*ʿam*). But the word of promise also points *backward* into the primeval history. It does so in the implied contrast between the human attempt to "make oneself a name" (cf. Gen 11:4) and God's promise to make Abraham's name great (12:2). Above all, the promise to make Abraham himself into a blessing points back to the primeval blessing of the creation in the first chapter of the Bible. There God pronounces a double blessing, one upon the animals (1:22) and one upon humankind (1:28). A third blessing applies to sacred time—the seventh day (2:3). With the Fall, however, the curse comes into the world; thus we have the curse of the serpent (3:14), the curse of the field (3:17; cf. 5:29), and the curse of Cain (4:11). If we place ourselves in Genesis 12 and look backward, Abraham's blessing points back behind the context of the Fall and to God's original blessing upon creation. Thus the divine blessings comprise a bow, which implies that the curse of the Fall is not God's last word in the matter.

THE GOD OF THE FATHERS
AND EL

DIVINE NAMES WITH AN EL COMPONENT

Alt once claimed that the God of the fathers was a "nameless" deity. Close examination of the relevant texts, however, leads us to question this description.[21]

In Exod 6:2–3 we read how God revealed himself to the patriarchs under the name El Shaddai (RSV: "God Almighty"). Here the God of the patriarchs has a special proper name, and, moreover, one which repeatedly appears in Genesis (17:1; 28:3; etc.).

In the patriarchal narratives, the name El also functions as part of a number of divine names. These names can usually be associated with a particular site.

EXCURSUS 7
THE EL NAMES IN THE
PATRIARCHAL NARRATIVES

Divine Name	Place	Passage
El Elyon, "El Most High"	Salem	Gen 14:18–22
El Roi, "El of Seeing"	Beer-Lahai Roi	Gen 16:13
El Olam, "El the Everlasting"	Beer-Sheba	Gen 21:33
El Elohe Yisrael, "El, the God of Israel"	Shechem	Gen 33:18–20
El Bethel, "El of Bethel"	Bethel	Gen 31:13; 35:7
El Shaddai, see the analysis below	—	Gen 17:1; 28:3; 35:11; 43:14; 48:3; 49:25

The table shows the local attachments of the "El" names. At the same time, however, it shows that the name El Shaddai is not associated with any particular place. How is this difference to be explained? We shall approach the problem below in our analysis of "El Shaddai."

Furthermore, the divine name El is also an element in several important names of persons and places in the patriarchal narratives. We recognize it easily in such names as Beth-El (Gen 28:19), Peni-El (32:30), Ishma-El (16:11), Isra-El (32:28), and Bethu-El (24:15). We also know that this El element is sometimes left out of such names (cf. Jephtah-El: Josh 19:14, 27; and Jephtah, Judges 11:1). There are good reasons to believe that the patriarchal names Isaac and Jacob are abbreviated El names of this sort (originally: Isaac-El and Jacob-El). One such El name, Jaqub-El, is attested in Babylonia about one hundred years before the time of Hammurabi,[22] whose dates are ca. 1729–1686 B.C.E. It is, then, clear that the divine name El plays an important part in the patriarchal narratives. What do we really know about the background of this divine name El in connection with the patriarchs?

The Comparative Materials:
El in the Canaanite Texts

The discovery of new extrabiblical texts in this century has led to a series of surprises. The discoveries from Israel's neighbors provide us with indispensable comparative materials. When Alt published his study of the "God of the fathers" in 1929, the most important comparative material available to him came from inscriptions deriving from the Nabateans in the centuries around the dawn of our era. Various finds have now made it possible to place the patriarchs in a wider cultural and religious framework. The Hebrew patriarchs came from an ancient culture to a new but related one. Also in 1929, one of the most important discoveries of modern biblical research was made: the discovery of the city of Ugarit on the Mediterranean coast of Syria. The city had been destroyed around 1200 B.C.E.; its last centuries left us with a library of texts that give us a detailed new picture of the religious world of ancient Canaan.[23]

Among the gods whom we encounter in the Canaanite texts from Ugarit are El and Baal. Baal was a young fertility deity who was closely associated with the cycle of vegetation. It is striking that Baal is never referred to in the biblical patriarchal narratives.

The god called El was of a different character from Baal. El was old and wise, a mild and merciful god. El was called both "father of humankind" and "creator of all created beings." El is the one who gives a child to the childless king Keret. El is sometimes referred to as "king," but if we wish to describe his peculiarities accurately, we can justifiably characterize him as the patriarch among the gods of Canaan. El emerges from the texts as an aged father figure with an air of mild and generous wisdom.[24]

In short, we have actual Canaanite texts that tell us how the Canaanites understood the highest god—El. On the other hand, we also have the biblical texts that speak of a God of the fathers who had a variety of El names. These El names are easily situated against the background provided by the extrabiblical materials from the eastern Mediterranean. It develops that the names El Elyon,[25] El Olam, and El Bethel seem to be rooted in the Canaanite conceptual world. This fact may also be detected in the biblical texts. El Elyon is the name of the deity whose priest was Melchizedek, the king of Salem (Jerusalem). As the name of a deity, the name Bethel is cited in some passages, where it is a parallel to the gods of other peoples and seen in contradistinction to YHWH (cf. Jer 48:13 and Amos 5:4–5).

A Reasonable Conclusion

What conclusions may be drawn on the basis of the closeness of the biblical El names to the Canaanite conceptual world? Admittedly it is true that the word $\check{}el$ is not only used as the proper name of a deity, that is, El with a capital *E*. The word is also the common Semitic word for "deity." In the biblical tradition the word $\check{}el$ in the El names has gradually acquired this reduced content; to Israelites in later times names such as "El Elyon" and "El Olam" meant "God the Most High" and "God the Eternal."

When we work back through history in order, whenever possible, to get behind the biblical texts, we are tempted to see some connection between the phenomena we meet in the patriarchal narratives and the worship of a supreme god called El in Canaan far before the emergence of Israel. There are certain biblical passages that at one and the same time speak of $\check{}el$ and the God of the fathers or the God of Israel. These passages are difficult to interpret, but in precisely this connection they ought not to be overlooked:

Genesis 33:20. The altar at Shechem was to be called "El [is] the God of Israel" (*'ēl 'ĕlōhê yiśrā'ēl*).

Genesis 46:3. In the nocturnal revelation to Jacob in Beer-Sheba we are told, "I am El, the God of your father." Here the word *'ēl* bears the definite article.

Genesis 49:25. In Jacob's blessing to Joseph we find the words, "by the El of your father."

It is indeed difficult to conceive of reliable criteria to determine the precise relationship between the God of the fathers and El. Modern research, however, has presented us with two main alternatives:

1. Scholars like Alt and Werner H. Schmidt[26] see two different stages in a historical course of development. From their original milieu in Mesopotamia and Transjordan, the patriarchs brought the worship of the God of the fathers with them. After their settlement in Palestine, they came into contact with numerous local sanctuaries and settled around such sacred sites as Mamre (near Hebron), Beer-Sheba, and Shechem. At these sites the sacral traditions about El were perpetuated. It was here perhaps that these traditions were gradually attached to the God of the fathers. This two-stage argument suggests that the God of the fathers appropriated traditions that had originally to do with El. It has been held that such ancient El traditions are especially evident in texts that speak of such sacred sites as Bethel (Gen 28) and Penuel (Gen 32).

2. Other scholars, the most prominent among them being Frank Moore Cross,[27] maintain that we do not have to do with two different phases in a developmental scheme. They feel instead that the God of the fathers represents a special type of El worship. In this event, we have to do with an original identity between the God of the fathers and El. Some scholars who argue along these lines have emphasized that the worship of El could have been practiced among the patriarchs even before they became sedentary. The divine name El is, after all, common Semitic and so emerges as part of a common Semitic inheritance.[28]

The extant materials scarcely permit us to decide between the two above-noted solutions, although I personally regard the latter suggestion to be the more probable one.[29] At any rate, it is difficult to distinguish any decisive contrasts between the picture we presently possess of the worship of El in pre-Israelite Canaan and the picture the biblical texts provide us of the piety associated with the God of the fathers.

EL SHADDAI: THE OLDEST DIVINE NAME IN THE BIBLE?

Among the various names used to designate the God of the fathers, one in particular appears to be quite special: El Shaddai.[30] There are a number of questions about this name; here we are concerned with two:

- What does it really mean? Biblical translations usually render it "God Almighty" (RSV). Does this correctly reflect the contents of the name El Shaddai?
- In earlier biblical research it was customary to make much of the fact that El Shaddai is mainly employed in the Priestly strand of the Pentateuch. Here belongs not only Exod 6:3 but also Gen 17:1; 28:3; 35:11; 43:14; and 48:3. According to the usual view, the Priestly tradition was fixed in written form at a late stage—around the time of the exile. Earlier scholarship has accordingly maintained that the use of the name El Shaddai is not historically motivated in the patriarchal texts; it has no roots in the patriarchal era. Thus our second question: How old is this divine name actually?

We tackle the latter question first. Of the forty-eight occurrences of the name, quite a number appear in late literature, such as Ezekiel (twice) and Job (thirty-one times). Nevertheless, there is practically no contemporary scholar who claims that the name El Shaddai was a late invention of the exilic period. This is because there is broad agreement about the antiquity of some of the other biblical passages in which the name occurs; for example, Jacob's patriarchal blessing (Gen 49:25), the Baalam texts (Num 24:4, 16), and an ancient list of names (Num 1:5–16) in which Shaddai is the theophoric element in several personal names: Shede-ur, Zuri-shaddai, and Ammi-shaddai (vv 5, 6, 12). There is also a single extra-biblical attestation. An Egyptian figurine bears the legend "Shaddai-ammi." Thus it contains the same elements as the previously mentioned biblical "Ammi-shaddai." The figurine in question is datable to ca. 1300 B.C.E.[31]

EXCURSUS 8
WHERE DOES THE OLD TESTAMENT REFER TO EL SHADDAI?

The divine name (El) Shaddai occurs 48 times in the Old Testament:
- The Pentateuch: 9 times
  Three of these occurrences are in ancient tribal blessings, like the blessing of Jacob (Gen 49:25) and Balaam's blessing (Num 24:4, 16); the other

six occurrences are usually assigned to the so-called "Priestly tradition" in the Pentateuch: Gen 17:1; 28:3; 35:11; 43:14ff; 48:3; Exod 6:3.

- The Book of Ruth: 2 times (Ruth 1:20–21)
- The Prophets: 4 times (Isa 13:6; Joel 1:15; Ezek 1:24; 10:5)
- The Psalter: 2 times (Ps 68:14 [15]; 91:1)
- Job: 31 times

In addition to these attestations, the name Shaddai is a component in the personal names Shede-ur, Zuri-shaddai, and Ammi-shaddai (Num 1:5, 6, 12). This "map" of the distribution of the name in the texts raises the question of its age.

These facts point to El Shaddai being an ancient divine designation. This conclusion is reinforced by the next step in our investigation when we examine the derivation and significance of the name. Over the years, the name El Shaddai has been interpreted and rendered in a wide variety of ways.[32]

- A common Greek rendering of "El Shaddai" is *pantokratōr*, "the ruler of all" (16 times in LXX Job). It is clear, however, that this does not represent an actual attempt to translate the divine name. Rather, it is a conventional rendering and not an effort at a linguistic interpretation of "El Shaddai."[33] What we usually find in modern biblical translations of the name "El Shaddai" are reflections of this convention. As a result, the expression "the Almighty" in the biblical translations provides no key to the understanding of "El Shaddai."

- Early Judaism understood the contents of the name as "he who is sufficient" (derived from Heb. *še* + *day*). This interpretation underlies the translation *hikanos* ("he who is sufficient"), which we find in certain Greek translations. Today, however, this is not held to be a convincing alternative.

- An early interpretation associated "El Shaddai" with a Hebrew root signifying violence and destruction—*š-d-d*. This view is expressed already in the Old Testament in the expression "as destruction from the Almighty" (thus RSV). The texts in question speak of a *šōd*, "violence, destruction," which comes from Shaddai (cf. Isa 13:6; Joel 1:15). But this is probably a pun, not a linguistic-historical derivation.

- The derivation that has won broadest acceptance does not associate the name with any Hebrew word, but with an Akkadian one found in Babylonian texts—*šadû*—the usual Akkadian word for "mountain." On this theory the name "El Shaddai" would then signify something like "El, the One of the mountain."[34]

What sorts of associations were originally attached to the name El Shaddai? A number of scholars have felt that it was a notion of God as protector and refuge. Similar thoughts are presumably expressed when the God of Israel is characterized as the "rock" of his people (cf., e.g., Deut 32:4, 15, 18, 30, 31; 2 Sam 23:3; Ps 18:46). Another possibility is the notion that the name El Shaddai designates God as the One of the mount of the divine council (cf. Isa 14:13). In this event El Shaddai would be a name that characterized the God of the fathers as the chief of the heavenly council. The use of the name (El) Shaddai in close association with (El) Elyon, "God the Most High" (Num 24:16 and Ps 91:1), provides a degree of support for this conjecture, as does the occurrence of the name in the Deir Alla inscriptions.[35] At this point, however, the question remains open.

Now, I shall briefly depict a new perspective on "El Shaddai" made possible by recent research. The Amorites dwelt in northern Mesopotamia, at the upper course of the Euphrates; they were a nomadic people whom scholars have designated "proto-Arameans," and they have been held to have been related to the tribal groups that eventually made up the people of Israel. These Amorites worshiped a god called "Amurru." In some texts, it develops that this deity was characterized as *bēl šadê*, "the lord of the mountain."[36]

It is naturally impossible to prove, but it is tempting to suppose that the name "El Shaddai" had something to do with this deity concept. If this is correct, then we may further assume that this divine name was already used by patriarchal groups prior to the settlement in Canaan. This may help to explain the disparity between "El Shaddai" and the other El names in Genesis: all of them, with the exception of "El Shaddai," are associated with a given geographical site in Palestine. Of course, if the name "El Shaddai" was part of the baggage of the immigrating nomadic groups, then this would explain why such a geographical localization is lacking in this particular case. Moreover, if this was the case, then "El Shaddai" would be one of the oldest divine names in the Bible!

In other words, there is much to suggest that "El Shaddai" is an ancient divine name. It even may have been used by the patriarchal groups before they settled in Palestine. But how do our observations concerning El Shaddai agree with our conclusions about the God of the fathers?

If we turn to the biblical materials,[37] we quickly discover that El Shaddai frequently appears in contexts which deal with a divine blessing; one has only to think of the blessings of Jacob and Baalam (Gen 49:25; Num 24:4, 16, respectively). Most of the occurrences in the patriarchal narratives appear in similar contexts. Thus El Shaddai reveals himself to Abraham and promises him innumerable offspring (Gen 17:1); in the name of El Shaddai, Isaac blesses Jacob and communicates to him the assurance of numerous progeny and the blessing of Abraham (Gen 28:3–4). The same motif recurs in Gen 35:11 in the words, "I am El Shaddai. Be fruitful and multiply."

The fact that El Shaddai is so often attested in the Book of Job is in some way related to the characterization of Job as a patriarch. While the occurrences in Job can hardly be reduced to a simple scheme, the motif of blessing does occur in some of them. Eliphaz the Temanite tells how Shaddai fills a man's house with good things (Job 22:17–18), just as Job, speaking of the past days of his prosperity, relates how Shaddai was with him and his children stood about him (Job 29:5). A few passages in the Book of Ruth indirectly confirm this picture (Ruth 1:20–21).

These observations permit the following conclusions: El Shaddai's radius of action is in the family and the lineage; the blessing he confers expresses itself in numerous progeny, and he guarantees the continued survival of the lineage. In other words, this view of God expressed by "El Shaddai" agrees with our observations about the God of the fathers.

Summary. Accordingly, our main impressions of El Shaddai are as follows: first, the divine name itself is probably related to a Babylonian word that means "mountain"; second, the expressions most often associated with El Shaddai have to do with divine blessing; third, El Shaddai's radius of action is above all the family and the lineage; and finally, there is hardly room for doubt that it is an ancient divine designation, perhaps one of the oldest divine names in the Bible.

THE GOD OF THE FATHERS
AND YHWH:
CONTRAST AND CONTINUITY

In the introduction to this work, we posited that people in new situations become aware of new features in the face of the hidden God.

We now want to clarify the ways in which the worship of YHWH entailed something new in relation to the worship of the God of the fathers.

We have observed that the God of the fathers mainly appears as the source of blessing and the guarantor of the promise and that his sphere of action was the realm of the family and its extensions. The God of the fathers was a generous giver; his blessing continued on from generation to generation. The birth of new children and the increase of the flocks bore witness to blessings of his presence.

From the time of Moses, the Hebrew tribes began to worship a God called YHWH. This new divine name marks a milestone in that "wandering with God" to which the Old Testament bears witness. At this time God came forth in a new way; new aspects of God's countenance became visible.[38]

Just as Moses himself was not a patriarch, the name YHWH is not associated with a piety of the sort that we encounter in connection with the God of the fathers. The latter was by no means bound to any given locale, whereas the God who revealed himself to Moses at the sacred mountain in the desert was a God who linked himself to a sacred site. It is not for nothing that he is characterized as *zeh sînay*, "he [who comes from] Sinai" (Judges 5:5*, Ps 68:8[9]). We are subsequently able to follow YHWH on his journey from Sinai to Zion (cf. Exod 15:17; Ezek 20:32–44; Ps 68:17[18]).

The patriarchs were able to use words about their God that were otherwise used to address close kinfolk, like a father or a brother. The forms through which the people at Mount Sinai related with YHWH may be described as somewhat more distant. We read about this in Exodus 19: the preparations for the divine revelation require a special purification rite for the people (v 10). Moses is told to set boundaries around the sacred area (vv 12 and 23). The sacred area was not to be profaned through human contact; do not touch, do not see—that is the basic attitude (vv 12 and 21). The mount of God itself serves as the specially demarcated sacred area (the *temenos*). And when YHWH later appears, his presence is manifested in lightning and thunder, smoke and the clashing of horns, which cannot but awaken the people's fear in relation to the sacred.

To begin with, then, YHWH is closely associated with the mountain, and he manifests his presence through the heavy cloud. These are characteristics rather different from those of the God of the fathers.[39]

In order to describe the God of Sinai, a German scholar has used the compound term "Eiferheiligkeit" (approximately: "jealousy-holiness"). YHWH is at one and the same time characterized by his jealousy and his holiness; he is "the jealous God," Hebrew *ʾēl qannāʾ* (Exod 20:5; 34:14; Deut 4:24; 5:9; 6:15; cf. Josh 24:19 and Nahum 1:2). This particular divine designation expresses God's unconditional reluctance to allow his people any parallel relationship to any other, competing, deity. Elsewhere in the Bible, when the root in question, *q-n-ʾ*, is used of human relations, it signifies, among other things, jealousy between two partners or two lovers (e.g., Prov 6:34; 27:4).

The designation *ʾēl qannāʾ* sounds like the El names we otherwise encounter in Genesis and whose background was mainly Canaanite. In this case, however, we have a name which distinguishes itself from its Near Eastern environment. YHWH's violent "jealousy," which tolerates no rival, is without parallel in the religious literature of the ancient Near East.[40]

The contrast between "the God of the fathers" and "YHWH" testifies to the fact that Israel's understanding of God is not static. The journey together with God entails new surprises. At the same time, however, the texts emphasize that it was one and the same God who spoke to both Abraham and Moses (Exod 3:6 and 6:2–3).

4
Some Background: Gods and Myths in Canaan

The Old Testament contains a remarkable piece of history, a people's wandering together with their God. In ever new historical situations this people was continually awakened to new insights as to new features in the countenance of the hidden God.

We now proceed to study a few divine designations that the evidence suggests were employed during the period of the judges, the period separating the exodus from Egypt (most likely in the thirteenth century B.C.E.) from the emergence of the Israelite monarchy under Saul and David (around 1000 B.C.E.). Specifically, we shall be concerned with the divine designations "the living God," "YHWH Sabaoth," and the use of the term "king" with respect to God.

Certain lines of thought and patterns of symbols present in the biblical texts become clearer when we examine them against the background provided by the cultural world of which Israel was only a part. Therefore, we shall first glimpse at the conceptual world which was dominant in that Canaan which the God of Israel assumed as his inheritance (cf. Deut 32:8–9).

Thanks to the finds from Ugarit, or Ras Shamra, we now know much about the gods and myths of the Canaanites.[1] A sizable text cycle consisting of six multicolumned clay tablets inscribed on both sides in cuneiform and dating from the decades around 1370 B.C.E. relates how Baal defeats his opponents and seizes royal power. This Baal cycle has two main parts.

In the first main part we are told about Baal's battle with "Prince Yam" (the Sea), who is also called "Judge Nahar" (the River). Yam requests that El and the council of gods on Mount Lel deliver Baal up to him, a request to which El accedes. But the smith-god intervenes and urges Baal to resist, conquer Yam, and seize power as king. To this end he gives Baal two clubs, the names of which imply that they will expel

Yam from his kingdom. Baal defeats Yam, after which we are told, "Yam is indeed dead! Baal shall be king!" Later on, the first main part of the myth tells us how El, after some deliberation, decides that Baal is to have a palace. When Baal takes possession of his house, he opens a window, thereby rending the cloud cover. Through this opening, Baal sends forth his thunder-voice, so that the earth shakes and the mountains tremble. Baal's enemies flee to the woods and the mountain reaches, and Baal explains, "I alone am he who is king over the gods."

The second main part of the Baal myth describes another divine battle, this time taking place between Baal and Mot (Death). A summer drought shows that Mot is in power and that Baal must surrender and enter into the kingdom of death. He is to take with him the clouds, winds, rain, the dew, and his seven servants. But before he descends into the underworld, Baal mounts a cow and begets offspring with her. It is then announced to El that Baal is dead: "Mightiest Baal is dead, the prince, lord of earth has perished." After this, El installs the god Athtar on Baal's throne, although this proves to be a mistake, as Athtar is unequal to the task: his feet do not reach down to the footstool, and his head fails to reach the top of the backrest of the throne.

After this, we read how the goddess Anath seeks the deceased Baal. In the text, her search is associated with a drought. In order to force Mot to deliver Baal up to her, she subjects the death-god to harsh treatment: she splits, winnows, burns, and grinds him. The conclusion of the text tells us about a battle between Baal and Mot; here Mot falls in the field with Baal, triumphant, over him. Some words from the sun-goddess make clear that power is transferred from Mot to Baal.

This is the basic story-line of the Canaanite myth. We shall return to it shortly. For the moment, these general observations will suffice:

- Scholars have debated what is the main theme of the Baal myth. Clearly, one should take care not to attempt to reduce the lot to a single formula. But there is much to be said for the view that the main theme is the *gods' battle for the kingship.*[2] Baal wins his royal title via his victory over the sea-monster, Yam, just as he preserves it through his victory over the king of the underworld, Mot. Now, Israel, too, speaks of her god as King. To what extent is it legitimate to speak of connections and contrasts between the Israelites and the Canaanites when each group speaks of its god as king?

- Baal is *the dying and rising god.* In the myth, this motif is associated with the changing of the seasons. The motif plays a particular role in the description of the combat between Baal and Mot. The continually recurring death and renewal of the vegetation finds its projection in the fate of the deity.[3] We know of course that Israel spoke of her god as "the living God." What conclusions may we draw when we study this designation against its Canaanite background?

Questions of this sort will be central to the next three chapters of this work. Here we shall examine three important Old Testament divine designations: first, "the living God"; then, the Lord as "King"; and finally, "YHWH Sabaoth."

First, however, it will be appropriate to say a few words about the relationship between Israelite faith and Canaanite religion during the era of the judges. The basic question is, How are we to conceive of the emergence of the people who in the course of time created the Hebrew portion of the Bible? Recently this question has become the object of considerable scientific controversy. There are, of course, two extreme alternatives:

1. *The invasion hypothesis.* The traditional, historical reconstruction of Israel's history rests above all on the biblical sources. According to these, a group of Hebrews who had escaped from Egypt acquired Palestine by conquest (Albright, Wright). Thus it is meaningful to speak of a meeting, perhaps even a confrontation, between the Yahwistic faith of the exodus group and the Canaanite religion.

2. *The revolution hypothesis.* Recently another group of scholars offered a reconstruction that is mainly based on extrabiblical materials from the Late Bronze Age, as well as on ethnographic and sociological comparisons (Mendenhall, Gottwald; cf. Ahlström, Lemche).[4] These scholars play down the role of the exodus group or eliminate it wholly. A "revolution" alternative is proposed instead; it maintains that Israel emerged as the result of a peasant revolt against the feudal upper classes of the Canaanite city-states in the plains. Those who abandoned the Canaanite habitations in the plains sought refuge up in the mountains. From this perspective, certain scholars have been able to claim that there was continuity in both cultural and religious terms: the faith of Israel evolved out of the welter of Canaanite religious conceptions.[5]

For my own part I am inclined to see the problems from the perspective of a theory recently presented by Volkmar Fritz (1987) that builds on previous work by Alt and Noth. We could call this theory *the infiltration-symbiosis hypothesis:* "Nomadic" Hebrews in search of new pasture infiltrated Canaan, gradually becoming sedentary people. These tribal groups to some extent lived in symbiosis with the Canaanite population.[6] Over against the revolution hypothesis (above, no. 2) I would like to stress that the exodus tradition plays such a fundamental part in the faith of Israel at a later date that it is a reasonable historical hypothesis that an important part of the ancestors of the Israelites in fact did emigrate from Egypt to Palestine. Here the exodus group encountered other (related?) tribal groups. One such already extant tribal group presumably bore the name "Isra-el," a name which implies a faith centered around the god El (note the name of the altar that Jacob built: El-Elohe-Israel, "El, the God of Israel," Gen 33:20). For the exodus group, by way of contrast, the important divine name was, of course, "YHWH." If we pose the question as to the relationship between the faith that was to characterize the later Israel with the religion that characterized Canaan in the period prior to the exodus (the thirteenth century B.C.E.), we must assume degrees of contrast and of continuity. Simple generalizations are unacceptable. In the search for features that were peculiar to the faith of Israel vis-à-vis Canaanite religion, the following considerations need to be taken into account:

- YHWH is the god who was worshiped by the exodus group. This deity was a newcomer to Palestine; his name is utterly lacking from the array of gods known from extant Canaanite pantheon lists.[7]

- The exodus tradition, grounded in a concrete historical experience, was undeniably a major difference between Israel and the other peoples of the ancient Near East.

- The blood rites that are so typical of Israelite religion have no counterparts in Canaanite practice; they are presumably of nomadic origin.

- The Israelite cult is thought from its inception to have lacked divine images. On this issue, Israel differs radically from the surrounding peoples; the aniconic injunction was unique in the ancient Near East.[8]

- The God of Israel was above and removed from the sexual polarities. This was apparently not the case with such Canaanite deities as El and Baal, whose sexual activities play a significant part in the myths. In Canaan, the sexual union of the god with the goddess (the *hieros gamos* motif) was expressed in myth, and perhaps also in the ritual of worship services.[9] The God of Israel, however, was radically different.[10] Therefore Israel was able to describe how God created humanity in his image and at the same time created male and female (Gen 1:27).[11] From this perspective we discern that Hebrew has no specific word for "goddess." See further Excursus 24, "God-Language and Gender."

EXCURSUS 9
EL AND BAAL:
TWO CANAANITE DEITIES

FIGURE 8
THE GOD EL ON HIS THRONE

FIGURE 9
THE GOD BAAL READY FOR BATTLE

This relief in serpentine stone (47 cm high) was excavated at Ugarit in 1936. According to many scholars it represents the god El. (See Mettinger [1982 A: 131, note 96].)

This limestone relief (140 cm high) was also excavated at Ugarit. It was found in the great west temple and very probably represents the god Baal. (See Börker-Klähn [1982] no. 284.)

Any study of these two representations should concentrate on the situations, clothing, and attributes of the two deities.

	Situation
El is sitting.	Baal is either standing or in the act of walking.

	Clothing
El wears a long robe. His crown is equipped with horns.	Baal wears a short cloth wrap. His helmet is also horned.

	Attributes
The throne, footstool, and crown symbolize El's kingship.	Baal wears a sword on his hip. In his right hand is a club; in his left, a lance. Note the special shape of the lance, which indicates that it symbolizes lightning and rain and the fertility they bring. Note, too, the wavy lines under his feet; they probably represent Baal's defeated opponent Yam, that is, the Sea.

These two images provide us with a clear summary of the main characteristics of both gods. El, the old wise monarch, is the eternal ruler among the gods. El is the reigning god whose authority in the last instance is final and who awards other deities royal honors. Baal, by way of contrast, is the young warrior. Through his victory over the powers of chaos he wins his kingship and receives in return a palace, a temple. The lightning in his hand reminds us that Baal is responsible for lightning and rain. He is the god of weather and fertility.

Literature: Detailed information and extensive bibliographies on these two graphic representations are to be found in Börker-Klähn ([1982] no. 288 El; and no. 284 Baal). On the iconography of El, see also Wyatt [1983].

EXCURSUS 10
WHEN NATURE TREMBLES:
BAAL'S THUNDER THEOPHANY

In the process of completing his palace on the "heavenly mountain" Zaphon, Baal also constructs a window in it and raises his voice. The reference here is to a "thunder theophany" ("theophany" meaning the self-revelation of the god). The voice of the thunder-god strikes the earth with terror; the earth shakes, and the enemies of the god seek refuge in deep caves. Thus the Ugaritic text reads,

> Baal opened a window in the mansion,
> a lattice in the midst of the palace,
> he opened a rift in the clouds.
> Baal uttered his holy voice,

Baal repeated the issue of his lips;
he uttered his holy voice and the earth did quake,
he repeated the issue of his lips and the rocks did quake. . . .
the high places of the earth shook.
The foes of Baal clung to the forests,
the enemies of Hadad [i.e., Baal] to the hollows of the rock.
(KTU 1.4.VII.25–37; Gibson [1978]:65.)

It is clear that the "thunder theophany" played a part in Canaanite religion, or so we learn from other pre-Israelite Canaanite texts (KTU 1.101 and EA no. 147). In their attempts to describe the majesty of God, the Israelites, too, seized on the experience of the roar of thunder and nature's terror (Ps 29; cf., e.g., Job 37 and Ps 18:13–15). This is not surprising; nor is it astonishing that in so doing the Israelites made use of already existing literary patterns.

5
"The Living God"

YHWH went from Sinai to Canaan; this step introduced a new, highly dramatic section in God's "biography." It is a chapter that deals with a fascinating trial of strength between YHWH and the gods of Canaan; and the God of Israel emerged from this trial with three new names written on his banner: "the living God," "the King," and "YHWH Sabaoth."

The designation "the living God" occurs only fifteen times in the Old Testament (see Excursus 12). The Old Testament also knows an oath formula, "as the Lord lives." The divine designation and the oath formula, taken together, make up eighty-five passages in which the living God may be found. The modern accounts of Old Testament theology and the religion of Israel do not have much to say on this account.[1] This is regrettable, since a study of these texts reveals a fundamental difference between YHWH and the Canaanite gods. This first becomes apparent when the biblical texts are viewed against the background of a particular concept that was widespread in Syria and Palestine: the Canaanite myth of the fertility god.

THE MYTH OF THE DYING AND
RISING GOD

The climate in the eastern Mediterranean is characterized by rainy winters and rainless summers. The rainy season is introduced by the "early rains" in October; it ends with the "late rains" of April to May.[2] Winter is thus the green season of the year. When summer comes with its scorching winds, the vegetation withers (cf. Isa 40:6ff). The Canaanite myth of the dying and rising god reflects this cycle of nature.

In its classical form, the myth about Baal and Mot is part of the great Baal cycle mentioned above (see Chapter 4). In the myth, the death-god, Mot, corresponds to the withering summer drought. When Baal, the god of rain and lightning, becomes Mot's prisoner in

82

the kingdom of death, he takes with him the clouds, winds, and the rain. Then El, the chief of the divine assembly, receives the report of Baal's death:

> Mightiest Baal is dead,
> the prince lord of earth has perished![3]

Baal's wife, the goddess Anath, then sets out to look for Baal. She encounters the death-god, Mot. In order to force him to surrender Baal to her, Anath subjects Mot to a treatment that has several interesting features:

> She seized divine Mot,
> with a sword she split him,
> with a sieve she winnowed him,
> with fire she burnt him,
> with mill-stones she ground him,
> in a field she scattered him,
> his flesh indeed the birds ate,
> his limbs indeed the sparrows consumed.[4]

What we have so far seen reflects the transition from winter rain to summer drought. Baal has disappeared with his clouds and his rain; nature dies. Anath's treatment of Mot is thought to have something to do with the harvest and thrashing, which ordinarily took place in the summer months.

Then the scene changes. The god El has a dream in which the clouds drip with oil. The dream anticipates the harvest rains and symbolizes Baal's return. Thus El feels relieved,

> for mightiest Baal is alive,
> for the prince lord of the earth exists.[5]

Baal's return is related in a section that depicts the combat between him and Mot. Some damaged lines of the text seem to contain an address by Mot to the other gods, asking them to reinstate Baal on his royal throne.

This is a myth that closely follows the seasons of the year; in it Baal is the dying and rising fertility god. In the ancient Near East there were a variety of myths about the dying and rising god. *De dea Syria* ("Of the Syrian Goddess") from the second century C.E. speaks of the celebration of the dying and rising Adonis in Byblos. The name "Adonis" may be traced back to one of the epithets applied to Baal.[6] During the first day of the Adonis celebration, the worshipers participated in the funeral of the god. On the second day, they celebrated his resurrection. The dying vegetation god was the lover of the goddess, and his rites were mainly celebrated by women.

A number of passages in the Bible show that Israel was familiar with the concept of the dying and rising fertility god, whose passing was bemoaned by the women and who was hailed with miniature gardens on clay platters, symbolic of the fate of the god (Isa 1:29, 17:10; Ezek 8:14; Zech 12:11; Dan 11:37; cf. also Ps 126:5 and Hos 6:1–3).

EXCURSUS 11

THE DYING GOD: FROM BAAL TO
ADONIS AND MELQART

In the biblical account of the struggle between Elijah and the prophets of Baal on Mount Carmel, Elijah is sarcastic towards his opponents. He urges the Baal prophets to "cry aloud" to awaken Baal, if possible: "Perhaps he is asleep and must be awakened" (1 Kings 18:27). The fourteenth-century Baal texts from Ugarit provide the background for this. Other text finds have shown that the concept of the dying and rising vegetation god was very much alive through the centuries. This deity was known by many names: Adonis, Melqart, and so forth; in reality, these are merely local variations on Baal.

- The author of *De dea Syria* ("On the Syrian Goddess") describes the Adonis rites performed in Byblos, some 25 km to the north of modern-day Beirut:

> Furthermore, I saw in Byblos a great temple of Aphrodite Byblia, in which they also perform the rites in honour of Adonis. I was also informed about the rites. They assert that the event involving Adonis and the boar took place in their country. In commemoration of the occurrence they mourn and lament every year and perform the rites, and great mourning solemnities are arranged all over the country.
>
> When their mourning and weeping is over, they first sacrifice to Adonis as if he were dead; then, on the next day, they declare that he is alive and take him in a procession out of the temple. They shave their heads, as the Egyptians do when Apis is dead.
>
> Those women who refuse to shave are subject to the following punishment. For one day they are exhibited with their beauty for sale. Only strangers are admitted to the market, and the payment becomes a sacrifice for Aphrodite. (*De dea Syria* § 6. Text: Attridge and Oden [1976]: 12–14. Quoted translation: Jerker Blomqvist).

- A Phoenician inscription deriving from Pyrgi, about 40 km northwest of Rome, probably dating from 500–300 B.C.E., speaks of "the day of the burial of the deity" (NERT 243–44; Gibson [1982]: 151–59).
- Phoenician inscriptions from the Mediterranean region mention a priestly office (?) called "the resuscitator of the god" (*mqm ʾlm*) (cf. de Vaux [1967]: 493–94; Gibson [1982]: 144–47; KAI III, p. 15).

84

- The Jewish historian Flavius Josephus mentions an "awakening" of Heracles-Melqart (Antiquities VIII.5.3 §146). A Greek inscription from Amman seems to refer to a "rouser" of Heracles (de Vaux [1967]: 399, 494).

In particular, the Swedish historian of religion Geo Widengren has claimed that YHWH was a similar dying and rising god.[7] Widengren bases this claim on two observations. First, he feels that the statement in the Baal myth "mightiest Baal lives" underlies the phrase "the Lord lives!" (Ps 18:46 [47]). Second, he maintains that passages that speak of the "sleep" of God bear witness to the same understanding of God (e.g., Ps 78:65–66). Is Widengren correct?

"THE LIVING GOD" IN THE
OLD TESTAMENT

The Canaanite myth of the vegetation god is dominated by the oppositional pair death-life. The biblical texts that speak of the living God of Israel offer a different picture. The passages insist in a variety of ways that the Lord lives; on the other hand, they nowhere claim that he is supposed to have died. The only time in the entire Old Testament the verb "to die" is associated with the Lord occurs in a negative statement in Habakkuk:

Art thou not from of old, O Lord?
my God, the holy, the immortal. (Hab 1:12, NEB)[8]

The God of Israel was not enclosed within the cycle of seasons of vegetation; he was a living God who never died.

Of particular interest in this connection is the prophet Hosea. There are suggestions in the Book of Hosea that some of his people adhered to the myth of the vegetation god and that Hosea seriously combated this heresy. In the beginning of Hosea, we encounter "the living God" (1:10) in a context which consists of 1:10—2:23 [2:1–25]).[9]

Hosea 2 informs us that the Israelites assumed that the produce of the fields came from Baal (2:5). The people had not understood that it was YHWH who sent "the grain, the wine, and the oil" (2:8). Therefore, the Lord will now take these gifts back; he will reduce the land to a wasteland (2:12).

This occasions an important conclusion: the God of Israel differed from Canaanite Baal in one fundamental way. Their God was not the projection of the changing of seasonal vegetation. Their God stood above all this mutability and ruled the entire process from its very beginnings. Thus, if he wanted to, he could also employ the forces of drought and destruction. In the figure of YHWH were combined activities that the Canaanites assigned to two different actors: Baal and Mot.

This means that in Hosea's proclamation the reference to the living God occurs in a context that is polemical towards the Baal cult. One formulation in particular has a special undertone: "And in that day, says the Lord, you will call me, 'My husband,' and no longer will you call me, 'My Baal'" (2:16). The statement seems to presuppose that the popular piety in the northern kingdom of Israel had taken the form of a worship of YHWH as Baal. They had become identified with one another. Hosea turned against this syncretism with extreme sharpness. In so doing, he spoke of YHWH as "the living God."

It would probably not be an exaggeration to say that the basic character of Canaanite religion was expressed in the vegetation myth—in the myth of the dying and rising fertility god, the god whose fate mirrored the course of nature. When we examine the Old Testament's expressions about "the living God" of Israel against this background, our attention is drawn to an important feature of Israel's faith: *history* comprised the radius of action of "the living God." In several passages it is the special quality of "the living God" that he intervenes in history; he manifests himself on the arena of salvation history. To these passages we now turn.

First, there is the account of Israel's crossing the Jordan:

> Hereby you shall know that the living God is among you, and that he will without fail drive out from before you the Canaanites, the Hittites, the Hivites, the Perizzites, the Girgashites, the Amorites, and the Jebusites. Behold, the ark of the covenant of the Lord of all the earth is to pass over before you into the Jordan. (Josh 3:10–11)

Here the living God is preparing the final act of the drama of the exodus. The passage of the waters of the exodus (Exod 14) is mentioned when the waters of the Jordan rise up and stand "in one heap" (v 13; cf. Ps 114). Notice also that God's lordship is emphasized here. "The living God" is also "the Lord of all the earth" (vv 11, 13). Is this a Hebrew formulation (*ʾădôn kol hāʾāreṣ*) that was consciously created as an alternative to the Baal epithet, "lord of the earth" (*bᶜl arṣ*)?

Two passages describe the consequences of insulting "the living God." One of these occurs in the account of David's battle with Goliath (1 Sam 17).

Through his challenge, Goliath has insulted "the armies of the living God" (vv 26, 36). The few glimpses that our sources allow us of the religion of the Philistines suggest that they followed the cult of the god of vegetation. If this is correct, it is interesting to note what David says in v 46:

> [A]nd I will give the dead bodies of the host of the Philistines this day to the birds of the air and to the wild beasts of the earth; that all the earth may know that there is a God in Israel. (1 Sam 17:46)

I suspect that David's words here reflect that section of the Baal myth in which Anath threshes the death-god, Mot. We are there told (*a*) that Mot's body will be food for the birds of the air, and, subsequently, (*b*) that El receives a sign that Baal "lives" and "exists."[10] Thus the narrative of the combat between David and Goliath may be a polemical allusion to these features: David's victory will leave the foe slain on the battlefield as food for the birds, and thus "all the earth may know that God exists [*yēš*] for Israel," which is how the final words in the quotation may also be translated.

In other words, this passage tells about the intervention of the living God to save his people—his action in history. This is also the case in Isaiah 37, which deals with the crisis that arose in conjunction with the siege of Jerusalem in 701 B.C.E. The Assyrian general has been sent by his king "to mock the living God" (v 4; cf. v 17). We then read that the divine images of other peoples' gods have been burned up in the course of the Assyrians' ravages (v 19). Thus it will now be made clear that the Lord alone is God (v 20). In this way the text paints the contrast between the gods of the rest of the world and the God of Israel, "the only," "the living God."

The same contrast between the living God and the idols occurs in Jer 10:1–16. The idols are unable to speak or walk; nor can they act (v 5); they are as dead. There is not even a spark of life in the idols (v 14). And against the idols the text marshals "the living God" (v 10). While the idols are lifeless products of human creativity, the living God is the God who acts; he acts by creating (vv 12–16).

Now we are ready to turn to one of the most important passages for Widengren's argument that the God of Israel was a dying and rising God: the expression in the Psalter, "YHWH lives!" (Ps 18:46 [47]). In one respect, though, we must agree with Widengren: what we find here is a close linguistic parallel to the phrase in the Baal myth: "mightiest Baal lives." The context in which the hymnic phrase belongs (vv 32–49), however, does not contain anything that even remotely recalls the myth of the Canaanite vegetation god. Israel's "living God" is neither twin nor son of the Canaanite fertility god. On the contrary, in the psalm this divine name figures in a context that deals with how God rescues David and Israel from their enemies. Once again it is the field of history in which "the living God" is manifest.

REFERENCES TO GOD'S "SLEEP"

Widengren's second main argument for including the God of Israel among the dying and rising deities of the ancient Near East is based on certain passages in the Old Testament that speak of God's "sleep." But there is some question as to what conclusions one may legitimately draw on the basis of this observation.

A passage that may provide some useful information is the narrative of Elijah's struggle with the priests of Baal on Mount Carmel (1 Kings 18) in conjunction with a lengthy period of drought (17:1; 18:1). To the Canaanites, Baal was the god of lightning and rain. Therefore the Baal prophets had no choice but to accept the proposition which Elijah laid before them: "the God who answers by fire, he is God" (18:24). The sacrifices were prepared, each on its respective altar. The Baal prophets cut themselves with swords and lances "after their custom" (v 28). This phrase suggests that we here have the ordinary rites of the Baal cult in conjunction with the summer drought. The priests of Baal called on their god in vain for the sign, for the fire that would ignite the sacrifice. But when Elijah called, YHWH answered: "Then the fire of the Lord fell, and consumed the burnt offering" (v 38). The God of Israel had wrenched the lightning-shaped lance out of Baal's hand! (Cf. Excursus 9, Chapter 4). But not only that; he sent the rains as well (vv 43–45).

In this account we subsequently find a new section in which Elijah scorns the prophets of Baal: they call upon Baal, but he does not seem to hear them:

> Cry aloud, for he is a god; either he is musing, or he has gone aside, or he is on a journey, or perhaps *he is asleep* and must be awakened. (1 Kings 18:27)

This is presumably a polemic that uses the mythical language of the worshipers of Baal themselves. The biography of the god of vegetation could well be compressed into the twin terms "sleep" and "awakening."

Israel, then, knew of this usage. The indications are that the Israelites transferred it to their own god but gave it a wholly new content, as we shall see.

Psalm 78 is a historical exposé intended to demonstrate the contrast between God's fidelity and Israel's continual faithlessness. The people provoke their God again and again. Finally they go too far, and the Lord abandons Israel to her enemies; even the ark falls into enemy hands, and the youth of Israel become political prisoners (vv 55–64). Verse 65 introduces an entirely new description:

> Then the Lord awoke as a sleeper awakes,
> like a warrior heated with wine. (Ps 78:65, NEB)

The psalm proceeds to describe the consequences of God's "awakening." Here it is not a matter of the renewal of the vegetation, as in the Baal myth. Instead, we find that once again history is God's preeminent territory: the enemies are beaten back and defeated, Judah is elected and the kingdom of David is established.

There is a similar theme in Psalm 44, where the psalmist prays for his God to awaken:

> Rouse thyself! Why sleepest thou, O Lord?
> Awake! Do not cast us off for ever!
> Why dost thou hide thy face?
> Why dost thou forget our affliction and oppression?
> (Ps 44:23–24 [24–25])

Here, too, the context must be determinative for our exegesis. This prayer is directed to God in a situation in which Israel thinks herself forgotten by him. The military disaster bears witness to this (vv 10, 13). The prayer to God to awaken is a prayer for divine intervention, for salvation from oppressors. It may be that the exile was the historical situation of this psalm; such expressions were appropriate then (cf. Isa 51:9–11).

The Old Testament phrases about the sleep and awakening of God seem ultimately to derive from the mythic language of the Baal cult, but they have now been put into a new context and given a new function. When the singers and prophets of Israel speak of God's "sleep" and "awakening," they do so as a rule in the psalms of lamentation. In such texts the sufferer can in prayer and desperation describe God's concealment as sleep. These texts nowhere speak of God's death; what they offer us are expressive metaphors for God as the *Deus absconditus,* the hidden God, the God who "hides himself" (Isa 45:15).[11] Here we also find texts that speak of God's "awakening" (Pss 7:6; 35:23; 44:23; Isa 51:9) and that contain prayers to God asking him to "get up" and come to aid the supplicant (Pss 3:7; 7:6; 9:19; 10:12; 44:26).

SUMMARY AND PERSPECTIVE

The Old Testament uses the expression "the living God" as a sharply focused name for the God of Israel. Among the divine names used by Israel's neighbors it is difficult to find anything comparable.[12]

The Old Testament textual material bearing on this divine designation does not permit us to say with certainty just when it came into use, although certain features suggest that this occurred already in the period of the judges[13] (or perhaps later).

We happen to know that the idea of the dying and rising god was pervasive throughout the history of the eastern Mediterranean basin. Throughout her religious history, Israel was confronted with such deities: the Canaanite Baal, Assyrian and Babylonian Tammuz, the Adonis, Melqart, and Eshmun of the Syrian city-states. An array of deities like these offers an effective background and contrast against which Israel's confession to "the living God" can be seen to be a conscious protest.

Against the background provided by Israel's Canaanite neighbors, it is now possible for us to make the following observations about Israel's faith, which indicate the differences between that faith and the beliefs extant in Israel's environment:

- The polarity of the sexes belongs to the area of creation; YHWH, by way of contrast, was *one*. It is irrelevant that in the Old Testament masculine pronouns and verbs are employed of YHWH in a language that possesses two genders. Ultimately, YHWH is both above and removed from the distinction between male and female. The sexual polarity as such is significant in the Old Testament in symbolic passages where God is described as a bridegroom and where the people of God are his bride.
- The God of Israel was "the living God." This confession demarcated Israelite thought from the conception of a dying and rising god whose cyclical biography reflected the vegetational seasons, and which was ubiquitous in Israel's surroundings.
- The characterization of YHWH as "the living God" does not signify that fertility and agricultural abundance were his preeminent manifestations. Rather, the field of expression of "the living

God" was history. YHWH intervened in the fates of both individuals and nations.

EXCURSUS 12
WHERE DOES THE OLD TESTAMENT REFER
TO "THE LIVING GOD"?

- The expression "the living God" is not among the most common divine designations in the Old Testament. It occurs 13 times in the Hebrew Old Testament and 2 times in the Aramaic section of Daniel: Deut 5:26; Josh 3:10; 1 Sam 17:26, 36; 2 Kings 19:4, 16; Isa 37:4, 17; Jer 10:10; 23:36; Hos 1:10 [2:1]; Pss 42:2 [3]; 84:2 [3]; Dan 6:20, 26 [Aram vv 21, 27]. In all passages we find either *'ēl* or *'ĕlōhîm* (or Aram. *'ĕlāhā'*) used for God.
- In addition to this 2 occurrences of the expression "the Lord lives": 2 Sam 22:47; Ps 18:46 [47]. One should also note Job 19:25 ("that my Redeemer lives").
- The Old Testament contains some oath formulas in which God's "life" is an element, that is, oaths of the type "as the Lord lives." Such oaths occur 67 times in the Old Testament. *'ēl* and *'ĕlōhîm* occur only twice (in Job 27:2 and 2 Sam 2:27, respectively), while we meet the formula "he who lives for ever" once (Dan 12:7). YHWH dominates with 41 occurrences in such oaths (e.g., Judges 8:19; 1 Sam 14:39, 45; 19:6). There are also 23 occasions in which God swears by himself, that is, "as I live."

These statistics are based on the investigation by Kreuzer ([1983]: 21–29, 259).

6
The Lord As "King":
The Battling Deity

What is the center of the Old Testament understanding of God? Although this question is not easy to answer, nevertheless the idea of the Lord as "King" can stake a claim to a position of importance.

When the prophet Isaiah experiences his prophetic call, he finds himself in the presence of one whom he must acknowledge as king: "for my eyes have seen the King, the Lord of hosts" (Isa 6:5). When the biblical psalmists sing hymns, it is the royal majesty of God they single out for praise. When they address themselves to God in prayer, they often do so presupposing that God is King. The Psalter and Isaiah are profoundly influenced by this understanding of God. Nor would it be an exaggeration to claim that this understanding of God links the two Testaments together. "Thy Kingdom come!" is, of course, a prayer which presupposes someone who bears the royal title.

In speaking of God as "King," the Bible is making use of a metaphor. Naturally, there are metaphors of varying degrees of power. When God is called "the Rock," "the Shepherd," or "the Healer," we encounter metaphors which enliven the texts, but these terms scarcely influence the overall portrait of God. Matters are different, however, with the metaphor of the Lord as "King"; here we have a "root metaphor." When I employ this terminology I mean a metaphor that serves as a basic analogy or model; it is used to describe the nature of the world. It is a way of seeing "all that is" through a specific key concept. A root metaphor feeds a whole family of extended metaphors; it comprises the genetic code for a broad complex of ideas.[1]

In other words, the Lord as "King" is a metaphor that generates other, related metaphors; it supports an entire tree and its attendant ramifications. Among these ramifications is the notion of the temple as God's royal dwelling—God's "palace." Here, too, we find the concept of God as the enthroned Ruler, surrounded by a heavenly court and divine armies. Moreover, this aspect of the Israelite understanding of God sheds light on a wide range of pronouncements concerning a final divine demonstration of power in history—the "Day of the Lord."

The kingship of the Lord, then, provides an organizational matrix for a whole cosmos of ideas. This understanding of God lies beneath the surface of numerous texts, even of some that do not use "king," "to rule," "throne," and so forth.

Our lead question therefore will require a concentrated effort as we search for an answer. We do well to pay attention to conceptual connections that unify the otherwise varied materials and to keep our root metaphor in mind—the Lord as King.

Note that there are two central divine designations, which, taken together, endow the "royal aspect" with terminological precision: "the King," and "YHWH Sabaoth." As we shall see below, these two designations are associated with two different sides of the monarchical metaphor: YHWH as *the warring deity* and YHWH as *the enthroned and reigning deity.*

Here we turn to those passages in which the Lord is called "King," in Hebrew, *melek* (see Excursus 13). In terms of language, there are no particular problems with this usage; the usual Hebrew word for "king" is simply applied to God. But the far more important question is, which ideas and associations were activated when the ancient Israelites spoke of God as "the King?"[2]

First, however, we must discard a stubborn misunderstanding propagated even by some modern biblical scholars: the claim that the idea of God as "the King" first arose after Israel became a territorial state around 1000 B.C.E.[3] The divine kingship has been held to have been a reflex of the earthly Israelite monarchy as represented by Saul, David, and Solomon. In extension of this view, we find the vulgar notion that the Old Testament understanding of God was in reality a heavenly projection of oriental despotism.

There are, however, a number of indications that Israel began to call her God "King" long before the introduction of the monarchy—already in the period of the judges. In the first place, there are both personal names and some terminology associated with Shiloh in the era of the judges which suggest that the Lord was worshiped there as King.[4] In the second place, we happen to know that other Semitic peoples called their deities "king" long before the kingdom of David arose. Thus, for example, the idea of the deity as king played an important role already among the Canaanites.

YHWH IS KING—NOT BAAL!

A drama unfolded during the period of the judges, one which many scholars have described as the encounter between the Yahwistic faith of the Hebrew tribes and the Baal worship of the Canaanite populace. Such religious encounters have often proven to be complex historical processes. Victor Maag has characterized some of the more usual patterns of reactions in the following terms:[5]

1. Identification: the god of one religion becomes identified with the god of another.
2. Elimination: one of the religions in question actively repudiates motifs and conceptions present in the other.
3. Integration: in the course of the encounter, one of the religions receives from the other stimuli that lead to new formulations of the original faith.

It is natural to expect that two or more of these patterns of reaction can take place simultaneously when two religions meet one another. The reactions may thus be positive on one point and negative on another.

Sometimes we have to reckon with the possibility of *identification* having taken place. Within certain strata of the population—one thinks here of the popular piety among the Hebrew landowners—we must assume that there was a tendency to efface the distinctions between YHWH and Baal (the god of vegetation and fertility). Various prophetic criticisms are directed against such an identification (e.g., Hos 2:16). In later, normative Yahwistic belief, the boundaries were sharply drawn indeed.

It is also clear that a degree of conscious distancing took place. That is, *elimination* also characterized Israel's reaction to the sexual athleticism and the dying and rising features of the Canaanite deities.

Third, there is *integration*. Perhaps a modern example would be useful to illustrate the phenomenon. In one of his novels, the Swedish author P.C. Jersild recounts how a small Pentecostal congregation in the town where he grew up once bought the town movie theater and made it into a chapel. Jersild offers an entertaining description of how, shortly before the chapel was to be consecrated, the pastor of the congregation happened to notice the friezes, which were adorned with naked nymphs, high up on the walls of the former cinema. A scandal was averted by the use of a paintbrush and some paint: the ladies in question were supplied with demure garments, which transformed them into chaste examples of biblical womanhood! It requires little imagination to conceive of the atmosphere of victory and triumph when the church was ultimately taken in use: the devil had been conquered in the here and now! One should note that the theater building had been taken over, but in the process it received *an entirely new function*; in its new context it also had a new content, having been dedicated to the Lord.

In the confrontation between the powers, we may assume that similar things happened time and time again. In our study of the Lord as "King," we proceed on the hypothesis that the use of the designation "king" in Israel was inherited from the Canaanites. It is an interesting but undemonstrable speculation that this process was a conscious confiscation, that is, that the confession of the Lord as King was at one and the same time a protest against Baal's claim to this title: YHWH is King, not Baal! Here the historical development is important. To be sure, such a note of religious polemics was hardly present when the Hebrew tribes first began to designate their God as "king" during the period of the judges. In the "Enthronement Psalms" (Pss 93; 96—99) which were composed later there is, however, a decided tendency to repudiate the royal prerogatives of other gods. Here we find the formula *YHWH malak*, "the Lord has become king" (see below, Excursus 16). The word order of this Hebrew formulation gives emphasis to the word *YHWH*, and the sentence assumes the character of a triumphant protestation: YHWH, and no other god whatsoever.

On the assumption that Israel adopted the royal epithet from the Canaanites, we begin by noting some views of the Canaanite use of the word "king" in connection with their deities.

In the Baal myth (see Chapter 4), both El and Baal are described as king. El is the eternally enthroned god who distributes kingship among the other gods. Baal is the young warrior who wins and defends his kingship through battles against hostile powers. One could, with W.H. Schmidt, characterize El's reign as static, while that of Baal is dynamic.[6]

Baal is declared king after having conquered a chaos monster, who in the texts is called Yam, that is, "the Sea," and Nahar, meaning "the River." He subsequently receives a palace. In the myth, Baal's palace on Mount Zaphon apparently corresponds to the earthly Baal temple in Ugarit. We are thereafter informed of Baal's battle with Mot, "Death," a battle in which Baal defends his kingship.

The original text of the Baal cycle consists of six large cuneiform tablets. In the modern critical editions[7] the text in transliteration takes up about twenty-five pages. Thus I have given only a compressed summary of an extensive plot with numerous complications (see Chapter 4).

Israel inherited the epithet "king" and applied it to YHWH; but in the process the term acquired a new context. In the Old Testament there is nothing that precisely corresponds to the extensive Baal myth of Canaan; we find instead only scattered fragments which, whether taken together or singly, do not form a narrative comparable to the Baal myth. On the other hand, the Israelites did use pieces of the mosaic of the myth, which they introduced into hymns, prayers, and similar contexts. The myth lost entirely its independent function.[8]

Here are the apparent implications: *Israel did not use the Baal myth as a unit. It is nevertheless possible to point to three structural elements from this context which may have played a role in Israel.* These structures may be described in the following manner:

1. The god's victory over the forces of chaos
2. His acclamation as king
3. Construction of his palace/temple

These basic elements are also present in the Babylonian creation epic, *Enuma Elish.*[9]

At this point one might object: Is it, then, so obvious that the use of the title "king" in connection with the God of Israel is to be traced back to the influence of Canaanite religion? Could this usage not have arisen spontaneously? I would not rule out this alternative as a theoretical possibility, but what speaks in favor of the supposition offered above are the tangible similarities between certain Old Testament passages and the formulations in the Canaanite texts. Here are a few examples:

Psalm 74 is a collective psalm of lament, probably dating from the time of the exile. The country has been ravaged by the enemy, for which reason the populace prays together for divine intervention. The psalmist has interpolated vv 12–17 into this prayer; these verses comprise a retrospect of God's gracious actions in the past. We now read:

Yet God my King is from of old,
working salvation in the midst of the earth.
Thou didst divide the sea [*yām*, without the article] by thy might;
thou didst break the heads of the dragons on the waters.
Thou didst crush the heads of Leviathan. (Ps 74:12–14)

In another passage the motif of the chaos battle is used to describe God's eschatological demonstration of power on the Day of the Lord:

In that day the Lord with his hard and great and strong sword
will punish Leviathan the fleeing serpent,
Leviathan the twisting serpent,
and he will slay the dragon that is in the sea. (Isa 27:1)

In the first example, we find a combination of the kingship of God and the chaos battle in one and the same text. In the latter text only the chaos battle is mentioned, but the kingship of God plays a prominent role in the wider context (cf., e.g., Isa 24:23). In particular, the latter passage contains Hebrew expressions that have close parallels in a certain Ugaritic text. The phrases "Leviathan the fleeing serpent" and "Leviathan the twisting serpent" have their immediate Ugaritic counterparts.[10] Moreover, that the "sea" in the former text refers to more than just a body of water is demonstrated by the parallel reference to the many-headed dragon.

What does this mean for our study of God as King in the Old Testament? Well, by studying the Old Testament in the light of the archaeological materials bearing on Israel's neighbors—in this case the Baal cycle—we are on the trail of a conceptual, deep structure that endows certain Old Testament texts and ideas with a surprising sort of internal coherence. This basic structure consists of three main elements, in which God as King is the very center: (a) God's battle with the forces of chaos; (b) God's kingship, understood as having been asserted and established through battle with evil; and (c) God's temple, understood as the earthly sign of his worthiness to rule. This is how I describe the Old Testament root metaphor.

Our main task now is to answer the following question: Are there texts in the Old Testament in which *the kingship of God* is seen in relation to (a) *a divine battle against the powers of chaos* and (b) *the temple, understood as God's royal palace on earth*? We shall now observe how the kingship of God manifests itself in four different "situations":

1. The creation battle: descriptions of a divine conflict in the primeval time (*Urzeit*).
2. The Zion battle: descriptions of how God defends his temple-mountain against hostile assaults.
3. The exodus battle: passages in which the exodus and the miracle at the Sea of Reeds are described in terms of symbols deriving from the chaos battle.

4. The battle on the Day of the Lord: descriptions of the great eschatological drama in which it is seen as a rehearsal and conclusion of God's continually varying struggle with the forces of chaos.

It should be borne in mind, however, that we are primarily concerned with the motif of the Lord as King. We are in search of a better understanding of precisely this motif.

THE LORD AS KING:
THE CREATION BATTLE

The Old Testament expressions about God as King reveal a basic common feature: God manifests royal power through battle with an opponent. In Psalm 74, the statement that "God my King is from of old" (v 12) is immediately succeeded by the description of such a battle. In question is God's primeval victory over the anti-divine forces: "the sea," "the dragons," and the many-headed "Leviathan" (vv 13–14). Note that the immediate context also includes other formulations that are of importance for our purposes. The chaos battle is followed by a creation account:

> Thou didst cleave open springs and brooks;
> thou didst dry up ever-flowing streams.
> Thine is the day, thine also the night;
> thou hast established the luminaries and the sun.
> Thou hast fixed all the bounds of the earth;
> thou hast made summer and winter. (Ps 74:15–17)

In other words, the text presents God as a king in battle with the forces of chaos. Through its very existence and by virtue of its beauty and purposeful design, the creation proclaims God's victory over chaos.

The same combination of motifs recurs in Psalm 89, in which verses 5–18 deal with God as King. In v 18 [19] the final expression should be rendered "The Holy One of Israel, he is our king" (thus NEB). The chaos battle may be glimpsed in vv 9–10, where it is immediately followed by a creation account:

> Thou dost rule the raging of the sea;
> when its waves rise, thou stillest them.
> Thou didst crush Rahab like a carcass,
> thou didst scatter thy enemies with thy mighty arm.
> The heavens are thine, the earth also is thine;
> the world and all that is in it, thou hast founded them.

The north and the south, thou hast created them;
Tabor and Hermon joyously praise thy name. (Ps 89:9–12 [10–13])

Furthermore, observe that both passages in Ps 74:12–17 and Ps 89:9–12 display an identical structure: in each the chaos battle and the description of creation are linked together by means of a phrase that characterizes God's ownership of the created world. Thus Ps 74:16 informs us that "thine is the day; thine also the night," while Ps 89:11 states that "the heavens are thine, the earth also is thine" (cf. also Pss 24:1–2 and 95:5).[11]

An important term in the battle descriptions of the Old Testament is the verb *gāʿar*, and the noun form *gĕʿārâ*, (usually translated by "chastise", "rebuke," or by the corresponding nouns, respectively). Psalm 104 offers an example; here we are told how the *tĕhôm*-waters envelop the earth so that the waters are high above the mountains:

At thy rebuke [*gĕʿārâ*] they fled;
at the sound of thy thunder they took to flight. (Ps 104:7)

We note from this and previous examples that this topos seems to refer to God's thundering against the waters of chaos (cf. Job 26:11; Ps 18:15; Nah 1:4). We will soon observe how the same terminology reappears in other Old Testament battle descriptions and even has left its imprint on some New Testament texts.[12]

The concept of the Lord as King has many dimensions; central, however, is the idea of God's battle with the hostile powers. To ancient Israel, the existence of evil was a real and uncontested fact whose dimensions were unfathomable. God, however, was held to manifest royal sovereignty through battle with these same forces of evil, so that the creation emerges in the texts as a witness to the God who is stronger than the powers of chaos.

There is thus great emphasis on the fact that God is superior to the forces of chaos. A few texts go even further and subject the chaos powers to conscious demythologizing. Psalm 104:26[13] seems to be a text in which this takes place. Here we meet the chaos power called "Leviathan." In the RSV the verse has been translated, "There [i.e., in the sea] go the ships, and Leviathan which thou didst form to sport *in it.*" It can, however, also be rendered, "Leviathan whom thou created to play *with*" (cf. the NEB). The likelihood of this translation is supported by consideration of Job 41:5 [40:29]. In brief, Leviathan has been reduced to the more modest dimensions of a household pet; this is no doubt an example of the Israelite demythologization of a Canaanite motif, which has been realized with rare humoristic appropriateness!

Summary. The concept of the Lord as King is associated with the idea of the chaos battle. We have just seen how the chaos battle also serves as a motif of creation.[14] In this context, the creation bears witness to God's victory over chaos. This establishes a connection between the Lord as King and his creation of the world, and this connection is attested in other biblical texts (e.g., Jer 10:7, 12–16) and in other Jewish literature. (See Chapter 9 for a discussion of the creation battle and the divine order of creation.)

THE LORD AS KING:
THE TEMPLE AND THE
ZION BATTLE

The kingship of the Lord is the center of a biblical thought pattern consisting of (a) God's battle with the forces of chaos, (b) his kingship, and (c) his palace/temple. In the texts we have examined up to this point, the temple has not played any significant role; now, however, we shall examine some materials in which this is not the case. We shall encounter the Old Testament ideas of the temple and of Zion, a name for the temple mountain that originally referred to the hill south of the temple mountain that was conquered by David (2 Sam 5).[15]

We begin with Psalm 24. Close examination of this psalm shows it to be a fine example of the combination of all three elements in our conceptual structure: chaos battle, kingship, and temple. The psalm tells us how the "King of glory" enters into his temple—his palace (vv 7–10). God's royal progress into his temple is indeed the main motif of the psalm. In the very beginning of the psalm we read:

> The earth is the Lord's and the fullness thereof,
> the earth and those who dwell therein;
> for he has founded it upon the seas,
> and established it upon the rivers. (Ps 24:1–2)

We glimpse behind all this the Creator's battle with the powers of chaos; God created the world and thereby subdued the waters of chaos. Thus the psalm provides its own answer to the question as to why the "King of glory" is characterized as both "strong" and "mighty in battle" (v 8). The struggle from which the Lord has just emerged when he enters his temple is the Creator's battle with the powers of chaos; through his victory over those powers, God manifests himself as King. Of course, this entails that he is entitled to a royal palace, and the temple on Zion serves in this capacity:

Lift up your heads, O gates!
and be lifted up, O ancient doors! (Ps 24:7, 9)

God's creation of the world and his entrance into his temple are here placed alongside one another. This understanding may have been celebrated during the annual Festival of Booths in the autumn. At all events, the temple itself was consecrated and the ark of the covenant was placed in its holy of holies on the occasion of one such autumn festival (cf. 1 Kings 8:1–2, 65). Psalm 24 is thought to have been composed for the regular celebration of this event.

The temple, then, is God's royal palace. This is the site where God is present in a special way as King. The role of the temple as the royal dwelling of God is expressed in several ways in the Old Testament. When the temple is dedicated, Solomon makes an announcement:

I have built a royal house [*bêt zĕbūl*] for thee,
an established place for thy throne forever. (1 Kings 8:13*)

In this connection, recall that the temple in Jerusalem is often referred to as *hêkāl* (RSV, "temple"; cf., e.g., Ps 27:4; Isa 6:1). The same word is also used with reference to the palaces of earthly kings (1 Kings 21:1; 2 Kings 20:18), where we automatically translate it as "palace." The term has an ancient prehistory; from the West Semitic languages, it is possible to follow it back to Akkadian and Sumerian. Already in Mesopotamia its equivalent was used with reference to both the divine temples and the palaces of earthly monarchs.

In other words, the theology cultivated in the temple centered around the concept of God as King. Scholars have frequently used the term "Zion theology" for this sort of theology; some have also spoken of a "Zion tradition" or of a "Jerusalemite cult tradition." The various designations all refer to different aspects of the same phenomenon; they all have to do with the theology which was cultivated in the milieu of the temple and which received its clearest expression in the so-called Zion psalms of the Psalter (cf., e.g., Pss 46, 48, and 76). Attempts to describe the main thrust of this "Zion theology" have concentrated on the motifs of the temple mountain (Ps 48:2), the temple streams (Ps 46:4; Ezek 47; Joel 3:18 [4:18]; Zech 14:8), and God's defense of Zion from her enemies (e.g., Ps 48:4–8).[16] I claim that neither the various terminologies nor the different determinations have been adequate.

I maintain that we gain a clearer view of the matter when we acknowledge that the center of this theology is the concept of the Lord as King. This insight was arrived at by Sigmund Mowinckel in 1922 in *Psalmenstudien II*; it has recently been re-emphasized by Josef Schreiner and J.J.M. Roberts.[17] This is the central motif of these psalms, in relation to which everything else is peripheral. In agreement with Roberts, I would describe this theology in the following manner:

1. The Lord is the great King (Ps 48:2).
2. God has chosen Jerusalem (Pss 78:68–69; 132:13); the temple on Zion is his royal palace, and God is always present in it.
3. The royal presence of the god on Zion has a series of consequences:
   a. God's blessing emanates from Zion (Pss 128:5; 134:3); the temple river is a manifestation of this (Ps 46:4; Ezek 47:1–12).
   b. In a virtual repetition of the chaos battle, the Lord intervenes against the enemies who are threatening Zion. God's presence makes Zion inviolable; God is the guarantor of Zion's security (Ps 46:5).
   c. God's presence entails special demands on the inhabitants of Zion, as sinners cannot endure the presence of God (Pss 15; 24:3–6; Isa 33:13–16).

We now turn to those Zion texts in which the notion of the Lord as King is the theological center. In particular, notice the role played by the battle motif in these passages.

Our first text is, admittedly, not one of the "Zion psalms"; however, it does show how the motif of the chaos battle is transformed so as to apply to God's battle with the enemies who attack Zion:

Ah, the thunder of many peoples, they thunder like the thundering of
   the sea!
Ah, the roar of nations, they roar like the roaring of mighty waters!
The nations roar like the roaring of many waters,
but he will rebuke [*gā'ar*] them, and they will flee far away,
chased like chaff on the mountains before the wind
and whirling dust before the storm.
At evening time, behold, terror!
Before morning, they are no more!
This is the portion of those who despoil us,
and the lot of those who plunder us. (Isa 17:12–14)

Here the sea's furious rebellion against God (cf. Ps 93:3–4) is used as a metaphor for the attack of the hostile peoples on Zion. But just as God rebuked the chaos waters, so, too, he roars at the hostile peoples, who flee from his wrath (cf. Ps 65:7). This scenario may be labeled the "Zion battle."

Proceeding to the Zion psalms, we begin with Psalm 48. Here we find explicitly formulated the notion of God as King, as v 2 refers to Jerusalem as "the city of the great King." The same verse also contains a curious reference to "Mount Zion in the far north" (RSV), which, however, is probably better rendered "Mount Zion, the heights of Zaphon." The historical Mount Zaphon, up in Syria, was regarded as the throne of Baal;[18] in Psalm 48, however, the name has been transferred to the temple mountain in Jerusalem. After all, it was not Baal but YHWH who was King. The motif of the battle with the peoples is introduced in verses 4–8: when the enemies attack Jerusalem, God rises up for battle, and the attackers are destroyed just as ships of Tarshish are swept away by the east wind (v 7). In this fashion, God keeps Zion inviolate (v 8).

The symbolism of the chaos battle is even clearer in Psalm 46. When the enemies attack the city in which God dwells, he responds with his mighty rebuke. Admittedly, the specialized terminology *gāʿar/ gĕʿārâ* is not attested here, but the reference to God's "voice" presumably describes the same phenomenon:[19]

> God is in the midst of her, she shall not be moved;
> God will help her right early.
> The nations rage, the kingdoms totter;
> he utters his voice, the earth melts. (Ps 46:5–6 [6–7])

The continuation of Psalm 46 describes the peace that God brings about. By dint of the fact that he is the battling King—by intervening against every new manifestation of the forces of chaos—God is here also the peacemaker: "he breaks the bow, and shatters the spear, he burns the chariots with fire!" (v 9).[20]

One more expression in this psalm is noteworthy: "Be still, and know that I am God" (v 10). The various translations available fail to grasp the essence of the Hebrew text. The verb that is translated "be still," *rāpâ* (Hiphil), sometimes has "the hands" as its object, in which case it signifies "to let one's hands fall." Thus we venture the following translation: "let [your hands] fall and know that I am God." This would then be an admonition to acknowledge the senselessness in attempting to resist the God who possesses ultimate power, as he is the battling King.

The third of the Zion psalms to be considered here is Psalm 76. The introductory verses speak of God's presence on Zion: "His abode has been established in Salem, his dwelling place in Zion" (v 2). A description of God's intervention against the enemy attack follows; the means in question are not human weapons, but a royal word of power (as in Ps 46):

> The stouthearted were stripped of their spoil;
> they sank into sleep;
> all the men of war
> were unable to use their hands.
> At thy rebuke [*gĕʿārâ*], O God of Jacob,
> both rider and horse lay stunned. (Ps 76:5–6 [6–7])

Of course, this statement is to be seen in the light of the words in verse 8, which tell us how God utters his word of judgment. Furthermore, the hands that fall impotently when confronted with God's majesty is a topos that we encountered in Ps 46:10.

As in Psalm 46, God makes peace by destroying the weapons of war: "There [i.e., on Zion] he broke the flashing arrows, the shield, the sword, and the weapons of war" (Ps 76:3).

Thus the Zion psalms tell us how God's royal presence on Zion serves to guarantee the safety of the city. If we read Psalm 137 against this background, we grasp a sense of its bitter irony. During their Babylonian captivity, the Jewish prisoners are urged by their captors, "Sing us one of the songs of Zion!" (v 3; cf. also Lam 2:15, which quotes the Zion psalm 48:2).

Summary. So far we have witnessed the importance of the temple to the metaphor of the Lord as King. Its architecture and cult symbols (e.g., the cherubim throne, concerning which see Chapter 7) imply that the structure in question is the palace of the great King. In the biblical ideological complex in which the Lord as King is the very center, there are three components: chaos battle, kingship, and temple. It is logical to assume that this root metaphor was especially cultivated in the milieu of the temple, which would help to explain its occurrence in the Psalter and related literature. The question as to whether these notions about the Lord as King were ingredients in the ritual of the great autumn festival, as Mowinckel had maintained (see Excursus 16), is another matter. Whether one accepts the theory of an Enthronement Festival of YHWH or not, the concept of God as King does play a central role in the texts in question. In other words, we have put off dealing with the problem of the Enthronement Festival in favor of a study of the objectively demonstrable presence of the king motif in the relevant materials. Many scholars have neglected this motif in their eagerness to do battle with Mowinckel's grandiose theoretical construction. In the milieu of the temple, the motif of the chaos battle probably always played an important part in attempts to describe God as Creator. However, the motif was also transferred to the historical plane, and in this connection we should note that the use of the term *gā'ar* is ever present in the various occurrences of the motif: God "rebukes" the waters of chaos (Pss 18:15; 104:7; Nahum 1:4), just as he "rebukes" the peoples who are attacking Zion (Isa 17:13; Pss 9:5; 68:30). The motif of the battle with the peoples implies the "historicization" of the chaos battle. This process no doubt had pre-Israelite roots, but in the form in which we find it in the Old Testament it is genuinely Israelite and a typical development.[21] The same "historicization" is also discernible in the adaptation of the motif of the exodus, to which we shall now turn.

THE LORD AS KING:
THE EXODUS BATTLE

The fact is that the exodus from Egypt is mentioned in prose texts (Exod 14). In addition, there are a number of short poetic texts, most of which are in the Psalter. They all display contact with the traditions of the temple in various ways. The poetic exodus accounts describe the miracle itself as an act of God's royal sovereignty by adapting in various ways the root metaphor (consisting of battle-kingship-temple) to the exodus.[22]

First, we have passages describing the miracle of the exodus as a re-enactment of God's battle with the powers of chaos. Thus the waters retreat just as the sea of chaos once receded in the face of God's rebuke.

Psalm 114 speaks of Israel's exodus from Egypt (v 1); here God demonstrates his royal power (v 2), after which we are told that,

The sea looked and fled, Jordan turned back.
What ails you, O sea, that you flee?
O Jordan, that you turn back? (Ps 114:3, 5)

Just as the Canaanite version of the chaos battle deals with "the Sea" and "the River," here we have the waters of the exodus and the Jordan. Note, however, that in the biblical texts there is no mention of mythical primeval time, but of God's actions in the history of his people.

105

Psalm 77 contains a similar exodus account (vv 13–20). The reality of the exodus reference emerges from the framework: vv 15 and 20. The symbolic language of the chaos battle is plain:

When the waters saw thee, O God,
when the waters saw thee, they were afraid,
yea, the deep trembled.
The clouds poured out water;
the skies gave forth thunder;
thy arrows flashed on every side.
The crash of thy thunder was in the whirlwind;
thy lightnings lighted up the world;
the earth trembled and shook.
Thy way was through the sea,
thy path through the great waters;
yet thy footprints were unseen. (Ps 77:16–19 [17–20])

The chaos waters, more precisely the exodus waters, retreat in the face of the battling King. The references to the thunder and lightning (vv 17–18) obviously complement the other battle accounts that speak of God's "voice." But, one might ask, does the term *gāʿar* not occur in this sort of exodus account? As a matter of fact, we do find an example of it in Ps 106:9, which speaks of how God "rebuked the Sea of Reeds." The miracle of the exodus, then, is a re-enactment of God's struggle with the chaos waters. In accordance with this, the waters of the exodus are in fact termed "the deep," *tĕhôm*, in Ps 106:9 (cf. Exod 15:5, 8; Isa 51:10; 63:13; Ps 77:17).

Second, other passages speak of the exodus and of the temple as God's royal palace at one and the same time. That is, not only the chaos battle, but also the kingship of God and his palace (temple) may be glimpsed simultaneously in such texts.

Ezekiel 20:32–44 is an interesting but often overlooked case in point. The text concerns the calling of Israel from among the peoples, a process expressed as a new exodus, desert wandering, and covenant making (vv 34–37). The wandering leads to the temple mountain, Zion, where all Israel will serve the Lord (v 40) and where God will reign over the people as King, as the Hebrew text explicitly states (v 33). In abbreviated form, one might characterize the basic structure here as "from Sinai to Zion," or more exactly, "from Egypt to Zion"— where Zion is the site of God's royal rule.

The same route also figures in another important exodus passage—Exod 15:1–18. Here the desert wandering leads to Zion, which is identified with the words "the mount of your possession," "the dais of your throne which you made," and "the sanctuary, O Lord, which your own hands prepared" (v 17*). The text ends immediately thereafter with the words "The Lord will reign for ever and ever."

Exodus 15:1–18 also contains a battle account! In v 3 God is described as "a man of war." Here, however, God does not do battle with the waters. Rather, God uses the waters as a weapon with which to destroy the enemy army (vv 4–8).

The same conjunction of the exodus with the chaos battle is also present in Isaiah 51:

> Awake, awake, put on strength, O arm of the Lord;
> awake, as in days of old, the generations of long ago.
> Was it not thou that didst cut Rahab in pieces,
> that didst pierce the dragon?
> Was it not thou that didst dry up the sea,
> the waters of the great deep;
> that didst make the depths of the sea a way
> for the redeemed to pass over? (Isa 51:9–10)

The adaptation of the battle motif to the exodus leads to an interesting double exposure of creation (battle motif) and salvation (exodus).[23] This in turn sheds a special light on the biblical miracle: when God acts miraculously, it is as Creator. It is against this background that we are to understand Exod 34:10: "Before all your people I will do marvels, such as have not been wrought in all the earth or in any nation." In actual fact, the Hebrew of this text does not speak of "doing" marvels, but of "creating" them, as it employs the theologically significant verb *bārā'* (cf. Gen 1:1).

We have now seen how the motif of the chaos battle is used in the Old Testament in a variety of ways: to show how God created this world in an act of royal sovereignty and how God acts in new ways on the historical plane. In this connection we find the "historicization" of the motif in order to describe God's saving action in the exodus. Here, too, we find God's defense of Zion against the attacking enemy peoples.

The original mythological motif was "historicized" in Israel. The texts to which we now turn reveal another interesting feature, a specifically Israelite development: the same motif was employed to describe certain central aspects of the events at the end of days. God as the warring King became "eschatologized."

THE LORD AS KING:
THE BATTLE ON THE DAY OF
THE LORD

What does the future hold in store? To the major prophets it was obvious that God's sphere of action included, not just the past and present, but the future as well; the future, too, belonged to the Lord. The prophets' visions include images of dramatic overturnings, of catastrophes of judgment upon the earth which at the same time make for the beginning of something completely new. For this reason the coming disaster is not only, or not merely, the final chapter of world history; the event also has the character of birth pangs—the beginning of a completely new life (cf., e.g., Isa 26:17; Mark 13:8).

It is easy to see that certain of the "Day of the Lord" texts have only a short chronological horizon (e.g., Isa 22:5 and Jer 46:10). The day of God's intervention is always a "Day of the Lord"; furthermore, various circumstances and events anticipate his great and final intervention. If we choose to use the term "eschatology" in dealing with such passages, we do so conscious of the fact that the term has a different content from its usual meaning for other theological disciplines.

Scholars who have studied the "Day of the Lord" have attempted to analyze the main ideas and motifs present in the texts and to see these in relation to other, related materials in the Old Testament. As a result, two major understandings have competed with each other in modern scholarship.

On the one hand, Gerhard von Rad maintains in his theology of the Old Testament[24] that the "Day of the Lord" implied a renewal of that intervention which the Lord once undertook in connection with the "holy war" which took place after the exodus from Egypt and in conjunction with the conquest of Canaan. Of course, we know that the prophets sometimes looked to the past when they spoke of that which was to come. Thus, for example, it is possible to interpret Isa 9:4 in the light of Judges 7, or Isa 28:21 on the basis of 2 Sam 5:20. Moreover, it is clear that the descriptions of the "holy wars" of the past contain a number of miraculous details (e.g., Exod 14:20; Josh 10:11; 1 Sam 7:10).

On the other hand, in 1922, Sigmund Mowinckel[25] claimed that the "Day of the Lord" entailed a re-enactment of the events of the time of the Festival of Booths, when the Israelites celebrated the Lord as King. According to Mowinckel, in the autumn New Year celebration the

Israelites celebrated the Lord's accession to the throne (see Excursus 16), and the "Day of the Lord" was an eschatological re-enactment of this. On this theory, the "Day of the Lord" was the day of the enthronement. This means that, for Mowinckel, the center of Israelite eschatology was the Lord as King.

In particular, continental Old Testament research has rejected Mowinckel's theory that there was an enthronement festival, thereby discarding some wisdom. Those who resolutely opposed Mowinckel's theory about the connection of eschatology with the autumn festival have also tended to be fairly deaf to what the texts actually say about the Lord as King. Here we have chosen to concentrate on the incontestable facts: the texts' undeniable attestation of the motif of the Lord as King. Here we have an objective Archimedean point on which scholars of widely different views should be able to agree and to progress.

It is a simple fact that certain of the texts that speak of the "Day of the Lord" or of "the Day" also expressly speak of the Lord as King. Here I content myself with a brief reference to Obad 15–21; Micah 4:6–8; Zeph 3:11–15; and Zech 14:9, 16.

Since the Lord as King is specially associated with the conceptual structure of chaos battle-kingship-temple (Zion), this prompts an important question: Do the Old Testament eschatological texts contain traces of this central conceptual structure?

Recall here the ancient rule that a meaningful question yields a meaningful answer. Using our question to establish the route, we shall quickly see the connective lines that lead from our texts about the Day of the Lord back to those that deal with the creation battle and the Zion battle. At the end of days, the battling king's struggle will finally culminate. It is a battle against the forces of chaos, and it has gone on since the creation of the world. The judgment and consummation of all things correspond to the beginning.

Now we proceed to see to what extent the kingship of the Lord has to do with the chaos battle or with the temple (or Zion) as the site of God's royal presence.

The Isaiah Apocalypse. Chapters 24—27 in the Book of Isaiah are conventionally termed the "Isaiah apocalypse."[26] The name implies that there is some degree of kinship between these chapters and Revelation and similar literature; the contents are difficult to interpret. Isaiah 24 describes the divine destruction of the earth, an earth that "lies polluted under its inhabitants" (v 5; cf. Jer 5:24–25). Of particular interest for our purposes is Isa 24:21–23. Here a cosmic battle is first depicted in which the Lord punishes "the host of heaven, in heaven, and the kings of the earth, on earth." This battle description subsequently leads to a confession of the Lord as King: "Then the moon will be confounded, and the sun ashamed; for the Lord of hosts will reign on Mount Zion and in Jerusalem" (v 23). Note that here the kingship of the Lord is associated with Mount Zion, the temple mountain. The three verses contain, in miniature, the entire complex of battle-kingship-temple.

In Isaiah 25, vv 6–8 offer a description of the eschatological feast: "On this mountain the Lord of hosts will make for all peoples a feast" (v 6). The reference to "this mountain" must point back to the words in 24:23, which describe the Lord's kingly rule on Mount Zion. Thus the characterization of the eschatological meal is to be read in the light of the words about the Lord as King. The festivity on Mount Zion is God's coronation banquet!

All this does not mean that the Bible speaks of a time when God was not King; on the contrary, God has been King ever since he battled, as Creator, with the forces of chaos. The drama of the last days, however, signifies that he will then manifest his kingship for all to see. This may be compared with Revelation. We are told that in the final act God "has begun to reign" (Rev 11:17; 19:6, with the twin aorists *ebasileusas* and *ebasileusen*), although already at the beginning of the book we find a vision of the Lord on his throne (Rev 4). Thus the final drama leads to the definitive revelation of that sovereignty which God has all along possessed.

Then in the final chapter of the Isaiah apocalypse we read,

In that day the Lord with his hard and great and strong sword
will punish Leviathan, the fleeing serpent,
Leviathan the twisting serpent. (Isa 27:1)

Thus the final drama repeats the primeval event. Basically the powers hostile to God which we encounter in the final conflict are merely new incarnations of those beings which, in the texts dealing with the creation battle, represent the most monstrous evil. Thus the Isaiah apocalypse displays a center composed of statements about the Lord's coronation and battle against the powers of chaos. When certain extrabiblical texts claim that the main dish to be served at the coronation banquet will consist of Leviathan and Behemoth (the monster of Job 40:15–24),[27] this is presumably an expression of confidence in the finality of the divine victory: "Death is swallowed up in victory."

In Isaiah 24—27 one encounters the hope of resurrection. Isaiah 26:7-21, v 19 in particular, deals with this subject: the dead receive new life, those who dwell in the dust will arise, and the earth will give birth to those who have fallen asleep. As in the other chapters of this apocalypse, the Lord acts as King. Moreover, the promise of resurrection is not an isolated fragment. This is evident when we remember the similar expressions in the case of the eschatological coronation banquet on Zion (Isa 25:6-8). There we find a description of how God will destroy "the covering that is cast over all peoples, the veil that is spread over all nations" (25:7). In the Old Testament a covering for the face is an expression of sorrow (Esth 6:12; cf. 2 Sam 15:30; Jer 14:3-4). That this custom is presupposed here is made clear by the following: "He will swallow up death for ever, and the Lord God will wipe away tears from all faces" (Isa 25:8). Sorrow, death, and tears—one day God's creation will be liberated from all such things. Having observed what are the binding elements in Isaiah 24—27, one begins to recognize the power supply of the Old Testament faith in resurrection: the confession of the Lord as King and the certainty of this King's unlimited sovereignty.[28]

Thus Isaiah 24—27 speaks of the final manifestation of God's royal sovereignty, of how he will confront the anti-divine powers (those powers in the creation battle) once and for all. And the seal on God's ultimate victory consists of the triumphant words describing how death will be permanently eliminated from God's creation.

In the Isaiah apocalypse the final eschatological crisis has the character of a repetition of God's primeval battle with the powers of chaos. We found above a historicization of the chaos battle, so that it became the motif of the battle with the peoples, or Zion battle, the battle that takes place when God deals with the peoples who attempt to destroy Zion (p. 102). We now turn to some eschatological texts in which the Zion battle and the security of Zion play an important part, in which texts the kingship of God is also expressly mentioned.

Zechariah 14. This description of the "Day of the Lord" (v 1) paints a picture of an enormous combat.[29] The peoples rise up against Jerusalem (vv 1-3), but the Lord intervenes before the city is completely in their grasp (vv 3, 12-15). This is a re-enactment of the drama in the Zion psalms: the warring God defends his city against the assaults of the enemies. The tone is the same as in the Zion psalms: "The nations rage, the kingdoms totter; he utters his voice" (Ps 46:6). In other words, we find here the motif of the chaos battle transformed into that of the battle with the peoples. The same motif also recurs in the latter chapters of the Book of Zechariah (Zech 12:3, 9; 13:7–9). It is within this context that the expressions in the texts about the Lord as King are to be understood:

> And the Lord will become king over all the earth; on that day the Lord will be one and his name one. (Zech 14:9)

> Then every one that survives of all the nations that have come against Jerusalem shall go up year after year to worship the King, the Lord of Hosts, and to keep the feast of booths. (Zech 14:16)

The Book of Zephaniah. Chapter 1 contains the classical description of the Day of the Lord as a "day of wrath" (v 15). Notice that the wrathful God in this context is not an arbitrary despot; the day of God's wrath is the day of his judgment upon sin (vv 4, 9, 17). The connection between the Day of the Lord in Zephaniah 1 and the Zion concepts is evidenced by chapter 3, which contains a long eschatological scene in which the idea of the security of Zion is significant (vv 9–20):

> Sing aloud, O daughter of Zion;
> shout, O Israel! . . .
> The Lord has taken away the judgments against you,
> he has cast out your enemies.
> The King of Israel, the Lord, is in your midst;
> you shall fear evil no more. (Zeph 3:14–15)

A few verses later we find some expressions that are directly reminiscent of Psalm 24 and Psalm 46:

> The Lord, your God, is in your midst,
> a warrior who gives victory. (Zeph 3:17)

SOME LINES OF THOUGHT IN THE NEW TESTAMENT

The fact that God is understood as the warring King is a central aspect of the Old Testament understanding of God. Now we want to examine briefly its trajectory in the New Testament.

JESUS STILLS THE STORM AND "REBUKES" THE DEMONS

We have seen that the Hebrew verb *gāʿar*, "to rebuke, chastise," plays an important part in the Old Testament chaos battle texts. H.C. Kee has shown that this word has its New Testament counterpart in the Greek *epitimaō*, which is usually translated "rebuke," "correct," and so on.[30]

The narrative in which Jesus stills the storm (Mark 4:35–41) contains an expressive example. The disciples awakened Jesus, following which he "rebuked the wind and said to the sea, 'Peace! Be still!'" (v 39). Just as God in the Old Testament "rebukes" the chaos waters, so here Jesus "rebukes" both wind and sea. This makes the disciples' reaction intelligible: "Who then is this, that even wind and sea obey him?" (v 41). Jesus' sovereign command to the elements leads his disciples to be suspect. Here we are seeing the same power that we have read about in the Scriptures. Furthermore, they know from Psalm 89 (esp. vv 9–13 and 25–27) that the Son, the messianic King, will receive delegated power over the elements.

A point of special interest is of course that the Greek verb *epitimaō* is often used when Jesus "rebukes" the demons. In Mark 1:23–28 we are told how Jesus meets a man who is possessed by an evil spirit in the synagogue: "But Jesus *rebuked* him, saying 'Be silent, and come out of him!'" (v 25). Once again it is Jesus' majestic word of power that conquers the demon, who represents that kingdom which opposes God and his plans. Of course, this makes the demon's remark to Jesus quite understandable: "Have you come to destroy us?" (v 24). This passage gives us a clear indication as to what Jesus' exorcisms are all about: they bear witness yet again to the struggle between the divine power and the powers that are hostile to it. The *epitimaō* of the New Testament (cf. Old Testament *gā'ar*) shows that Satan's power is about to be broken, that the kingdom of God has drawn near. Other cases in which the same verb is used in this way are to be found in Matt 17:18; Luke 4:38–39; Mark 9:25 and 8:33 (cf. Zech 3:2). Other passages that lack the explicit terminology, but that obviously deal with the same issue, are Luke 11:21–22; Eph 4:9–10, and 1 Peter 3:18–22.

THE PAROUSIA OF CHRIST: THE ROYAL ARRIVAL OF JESUS

It is an established fact that the New Testament ideas about the last things are deeply rooted in the eschatology of the Old Testament. The important difference is that what is said about God in the Old Testament is transferred to Christ in the New Testament. In the Old Testament the Day of the Lord is the time of God's final demonstration of his royal power. In the New Testament such expressions as the "Day of the Lord" or the "Day of Jesus Christ" designate the day of Jesus' return, the day when he will make the ultimate manifestation of his sovereign power.

113

In the New Testament, precisely the royal character of Christ's return has been expressed in a new way by means of terminology borrowed from Hellenistic court language.[31] In particular, one should note the key Greek term applied to Jesus' return—*parousia*. With the exception of 1 John 2:28, this word is invariably rendered by "coming" in the RSV (Matt 24:3, 27, 37, 39; 1 Cor 15:23; 1 Thess 2:19; 3:13; 4:15; 5:23; 2 Thess 2:1, 8; James 5:7–8; 2 Peter 1:16). The word itself means both "presence" and "arrival"; in Hellenistic court language it was applied to the arrival of the king or emperor. The Latin counterpart of this term is *adventus;* it was customary when the emperor paid a state visit to a city for that city to mint a special "advent coin" to commemorate the event. This occurred, for example, when the emperor Nero visited Corinth.

A number of important terms are to be found in 1 Thess 4:15–18. In v 15, which speaks of those "who are alive, who are left until the coming of the Lord," we find the term *parousia* used to designate the arrival of Christ. In v 17, in reference to those being led away "to meet the Lord in the air," Paul uses a different term, *apantēsis*, which normally signified the official reception of a ruler during a state visit. This term, too, has a Hellenistic background. In these two expressions we find a reference to Christ's "cry of command," the word of power which awakens the dead at the resurrection. The Greek term is *keleusma* (v 16), meaning a military order; it was also well known in the Hellenistic world, although in Paul's usage the term has deep Old Testament roots. This divine command is the last link in the long chain of divine interventions against the forces of chaos—of God's "rebukes" of his opponents. It is the final command to Death to surrender those who slumber.

THE BOOK OF REVELATION:
GOD'S ROYAL TRIUMPH

When we read the description of the various phases of the end-time in the last book in the Bible, we cannot avoid this question: Are we not here faced with the problem of God's impotence and the consequent triumph of evil? For an answer, we turn to the beginning and the end of the Book of Revelation.

Revelation 1:19 contains a clue as to the structure of the composition: "what is" (usually taken to refer to chaps. 1—3), and "what is to take place hereafter" (chaps. 4—22). The vision of the future is introduced in chapters 4—5 by a vision of God seated on his throne. The throne is clearly a symbol of power, and it is by no means "empty," since God himself occupies it (4:2–3). Chapter 5 deals with the famous scroll with the seven seals, which contains the secrets of the future; the text is explicit as to the situation of this work: "in the right hand of him who was seated on the throne" (5:1). It could not be more clearly stated that the world has not been abandoned to the forces of evil. Here is the theme: someone is sitting on the throne!

The same theme re-emerges in full in what might be called the "hallelujah chorus" at the end of the work (19:1–10). In particular, one should note v 6: "Hallelujah! For the Lord our God the Almighty reigns." The Lord has been King since the very beginning; and now he manifests his lordship. Thus we see how the biblical reference to the reign of God points back to the morning of creation and forward to judgment and completion.

SUMMARY

Whereas the Canaanite population of Palestine spoke of Baal as king, Israel confessed that her Lord was King. This "monarchical" understanding of God was formulated with a root metaphor consisting of God's chaos battle, his kingship, and his palace (temple). God asserts sovereignty through battle with the forces of chaos, which continually threaten his creation. This divine activity stretches from creation, across the pages of history, and ahead to the eschatological completion. Protology, history, and eschatology are unified in God and ruled by God the warring King.

A postscript on the history of the chaos battle motif is in order. My presentation has focused on "the Creation battle," "the Zion battle," "the Exodus battle," and "the battle on the Day of the Lord" in this order. This presentation does not purport to delineate the history of the motif. What seems clear to me is that the battle motif had a Sitz im Leben in the worship of the Solomonic temple and that the adaptation of the motif to the exodus and to eschatology represents genuinely Israelite developments. It is more difficult to be definite about the earliest contents of the originally Canaanite motif as used in pre-monarchic Israel. I think it is wise to leave open the question whether the motif, as used in Israel, was from the outset connected with the idea of creation. It appears, however, that such a connection is later displayed in texts such as Psalms 74 and 89.

In Search of God

EXCURSUS 13
WHERE DOES THE OLD TESTAMENT SPEAK
OF THE LORD AS KING?

The Old Testament speaks of the Lord as King a total of 85 times (ignoring personal names in which this concept is also expressed). These are contexts in which such words as "king," "reign," "throne," and the like are used of God. Here is a tabulation of them:

- The epithet "king," *melek*, is used 43 times of God.
  Pentateuch, 2 times: Num 23:21; Deut 33:5
  Samuel, 1 time: 1 Samuel 12:12
  Prophets, 18 times: Isa 6:5; 33:17, 22; 41:21; 43:15; 44:6; Jer 8:19; 10:7, 10; 46:18; 48:15; 51:57; Micah 2:13; Zeph 3:15; Zech 14:9, 16, 17; Mal 1:14.
  Psalter, 21 times: Pss 5:2 [3]; 10:16; 24:7, 8, 9, 10; 29:10; 44:4 [5]; 47:2, 6, 7 [3, 7, 8]; 48:2 [3]; 68:24 [25]; 74:12; 84:3 [4]; 89:18 [19] (translate: "the Holy One of Israel, he is our King"); 95:3; 98:6; 99:4; 145:1; 149:2
  Daniel, 1 time: Dan 4:37 [Aram v 34]
- The verb "to be king," *mālak*, is used 13 times of God.
  Pentateuch, 1 time: Exod 15:18
  Samuel, 1 time: 1 Sam 8:7
  Prophets, 4 times: Isa 24:23; 52:7; Ezek 20:33; Micah 4:7
  Psalter, 6 times: Pss 47:8 [9]; 93:1; 96:10; 97:1; 99:1; 146:10
  Chronicles, 1 time: 1 Chron 16:31 (= Ps 96:10)
- Terms signifying "kingdom" occur 10 times in connection with God.
  malkût: Pss 103:19; 145:11, 12, 13 (2 occurrences in v 13); Dan 4:3 [Aram 3:33]; 4:34 [Aram 4:31]
  mălûkâ: Obad v 21; Ps 22:28 [29]
  mamlākâ: 1 Chron 29:11
- The Lord's sitting on his throne is mentioned 11 times. (This does not include the passages containing the expression "he who thrones upon the cherubim," [on this see p. 127]: 1 Kings 22:19; Isa 6:1; 66:1; Jer 3:17; 17:12; Ezek 1:26; Pss 9:4, 7 [5, 8]; 47:8 [9]; 89:14 [15]; 93:2; 103:19
- The verb *māšal*, "to rule, govern," occurs 8 times with God as subject: Judges 8:23; Isa 63:19; Pss 22:28 [29]; 59:13 [14]; 66:7; 89:9 [10]; 1 Chron 29:12; 2 Chron 20:6

These statistics are based on the study by Eissfeldt (KS 1 [1962]: 179–81), plus my corrections.
A brief glance at this tabulation shows that the terminology in question mainly occurs in poetic usage, as the terms tend to cluster in the prophets and the Psalter. The Pentateuch and the D-literature are conspicuously underrepresented, and the few occurrences in the Pentateuch are without exception in poetic passages:
Exod 15:18—The Song of Moses
Num 23:21—The Oracles of Balaam
Deut 33:5—The Blessing of Moses

116

The Lord As "King": The Battling Deity

In the Psalter, special attention should be paid to Psalms 47, 93, and 96—99, all of which express the idea of the Lord as King with especial poignancy. They have been designated "enthronement psalms," as they deal with the enthronement of YHWH. These psalms are hymns. Another genre in which this terminology occurs is that of the collective lament. Is it possible that these occurrences in hymns and collective laments imply that the concept of the Lord as King was particularly at home in the collective piety of the temple?

EXCURSUS 14

THE MORE IMPORTANT OLD TESTAMENT
"DAY OF THE LORD" TEXTS

In the New Testament, the expression "the Day of the Lord" refers to the day Jesus arose from the dead—Sunday. Alternatively, it sometimes refers to the day of the return of Christ. In the Old Testament, the phrase often has eschatological connotations. There it has to do with the day of God's final intervention in world history, the day when he will judge the peoples. "The Day of the Lord" and related expressions occur virtually only in the prophetic literature. Here is a brief survey of the evidence:

- The expression "the Day of the Lord" occurs 18 times: Hebrew *yôm (lě)YHWH:* Isa 2:12; 13:6, 9; Ezek 13:5; 30:3; Joel 1:15; 2:1, 11; 2:31 [3:4]; 3:14 [4:14]; Amos 5:18 (twice), 20; Obad 15; Zeph 1:7, 14 (twice); Mal 4:5 [3:23]; cf. Zech 14:1.
- The expression is subsequently specified in some way 8 times: "the day of the wrath of the Lord" (Ezek 7:19; Zeph 1:18; 2:2, 3; Lam 2:22) "a day of vengeance" (Isa 34:8) "the day of the Lord's sacrifice" (Zeph 1:8) "a day of tumult and trampling and confusion" (Isa 22:5).
- There are also a number of related expressions of the type "in that day," "at that time," "in days to come," and so forth.

On the basis of this terminological inventory, we may conclude that the more important of the "Day of the Lord" texts include Isa 2:6–22; 13:1–22; 22:1–14; 34:1–8; Jer 46:1–12; Ezek 7:1–27; Joel 1:1–20; 2:1–17; 2:28–32 [3:1–4]; 3:1–21 [4:1–21]; Amos 5:18–20; Obad 15–21; Zeph 1:2–18; 3:9–20; Zech 14:1–21. In addition to these texts, the following should be considered. They do not contain the technical terms of the "Day of the Lord" texts, but are nevertheless related: Isa 24—27; Jer 4:23–31; 50–51; Ezek 38—39.

EXCURSUS 15

THEOPHANY AND NATURAL CATASTROPHE IN
THE "DAY OF THE LORD" TEXTS

We have already noted that the expression for the Lord's rebuke (*gā'ar* and *gě'ārâ*) of the anti-divine forces occurs in texts that deal with the creation

117

battle, the Zion battle, and the exodus struggle. If our interpretation of the eschatological texts is correct, then we should also expect this terminology to be present in the eschatological "Day of the Lord" texts. And in fact the "rebuke" does occur, although only once:

For behold, the Lord will come in fire,
and his chariots like the stormwind,
to render his anger in fury,
and his rebuke [*gĕ'ārâ*] with flames of fire.
For by fire will the Lord execute judgment,
and by his sword, upon all flesh;
and those slain by the Lord shall be many. (Isa 66:15–16)

God comes in his cloud chariot, accompanied by his storm wind. Here his "rebuke" has the character of a divine act of judgment (cf. Ps 76:6, 8); on the day of judgment, then, the final word of power of the warring King will resound (cf. v 6).

Now we know that the terminology of God's "rebuke" is at home in descriptions of theophanies, that is, in accounts of how the battling God departs from his dwelling, with the attendant results on the natural realm. This is evident from Ps 18:9–15 and Nahum 1:3–6, two sections with a similar structure. Here we are told (a) how YHWH comes with his cloud chariot, (b) how he raises his thunderous voice and rebukes the chaos waters, and (c) how nature reacts to his arrival: the foundations of the earth are laid bare and the mountains tremble. The same theophanic scene recurs repeatedly, also in texts that lack the terminology for God's "rebuke" (e.g., Hab 3:6–10).

Such theophanies show us an important part of the prehistory behind the various descriptions of eschatological catastrophes in the texts dealing with the Day of the Lord. The most prominent features are the Lord's raising his voice and the subsequent earthquake (parts *b* and *c* above).

In the Book of Joel, the Day of the Lord plays a major part (2:1, 11; 2:31 [3:4]; 3:14 [4:14]). In the final chapter we are told that "the Lord roars from Zion . . . and the heavens and the earth shake" (3:16). Here the earthquake of the eschatological texts is directly connected with the theophanic motif.

Ezekiel's two famous chapters about Gog (38—39) are correctly perceived when they are viewed against the background of the Zion psalms and the depictions of the chaos battle. Ezekiel 38 contains a description of an earthquake. The connection between the earthquake motif and the theophany is shown by vv 18–20; these are the same effects of God's royal arrival which we read about in other theophanies.

In this connection one should recall Zechariah 14. Here the mountains begin to tremble when the battling God approaches, and more, too: the mountains themselves change so as to fit God's purposes better. The Mount of Olives breaks apart from east to west (Zech 14:4–5); one half moves to the north and the other to the south, thus creating a gateway for God's triumphal march from the southeast (cf. Judges 5:4; Deut 33:2; Hab 3:3).

The Lord As "King": The Battling Deity

Isaiah 2:6–22 presents the Day of the Lord as the day when human arrogance will be terminally confronted with God's majesty, the result of which meeting is inevitably destructive:

And men shall enter the caves of the rocks
and the holes of the ground,
from before the terror of the Lord,
and from the glory of his majesty,
when he rises to terrify the earth. (Isa 2:19)

What all of these texts attempt to do is to describe the overwhelming majesty of God's arrival (cf. also Isa 13:13; 34:4; Jer 4:24; 51:29). In the face of the warring King, all opponents are afflicted with powerlessness; their hands drop in despair (Isa 13:7; Ezek 7:17), a partial motif that we again recognize from the Zion psalms (see above, "The Lord As King: The Temple and the Zion battle," and cf. Pss 46:10 and 76:5). God's presence becomes unendurable for sinners (Isa 33:14; cf. Ps 24:3–6). Now one realizes that God is God.

Literature: Jörg Jeremias (IDBSup [1976]: 896–98) and Hanson ([1983]: esp. 369–401).

EXCURSUS 16

THE FESTIVAL OF THE LORD

AS KING

As we have hinted, in 1922 a major scientific breakthrough occurred with the publication of Sigmund Mowinckel's *Psalmenstudien II*, which bore the title *Das Thronbesteigungsfest Jahwäs und der Ursprung der Eschatologie* ("The Enthronement Festival of Yahweh and the Origin of Eschatology").

The most important festival in pre-exilic Israel was not the Passover, but the great autumn temple festival, the Festival of Booths, which took place in the month of Tishri (i.e., September–October). According to Mowinckel, the three festivals in this month, New Year's Day (on the first of the month), the Great Day of Atonement (the tenth), and the Festival of Booths (the fifteenth to the twenty-first), had made up a single festival in preexilic times.

Mowinckel used the "enthronement psalms" (Pss 47; 93; 96—99) along with other biblical texts to describe the contents of this festival. He compared these biblical materials with two different sorts of textual materials. On the one hand, he referred to the Babylonian New Year festival, which diverse archaeological finds had made accessible. Here the battle of the god with the powers of chaos and his acclamation as king were celebrated (see now NERT 80–84 and ANET 331–34 and 60–72). On the other hand, Mowinckel referred to the later Jewish celebration of New Year's Day (Rosh Hashanah). Here the Lord as King was the center of the festival, and its most important partial motifs were the creation of the world and the final judgment.

119

On the basis of these comparisons Mowinckel proposed the theory that the great autumn festival celebrated the Lord as King. He found the most important aspects of the ritual drama to have been *(a)* the chaos battle and creation of the world, *(b)* the battle with the enemies of Zion, and *(c)* the Lord's accession to the throne.

Subsequent discussions of this thesis reflected skepticism about Mowinckel's theory. Among other things, the dominant theological current of the dialectical theology of Karl Barth and Barth's own concept of revelation led those Old Testament scholars who were influenced by him to be only marginally interested in comparisons with other ancient religions. They concentrated instead on what they took to be specifically Israelite features, like the exodus and the idea of the covenant. Indeed, the victory of Barthian theology back in the 1930s was so complete that it virtually spelled the end, in some quarters, to exegesis concerned with religio-historical comparisons. This explains to some extent why Mowinckel's theories won so little attention on the Continent and in the United States. Elsewhere, however, the climate was somewhat different. Thus, for example, in England the "myth and ritual" school achieved a brief vogue, and in Scandinavia there was the "Uppsala school." Both schools proposed developments of Mowinckel's theories which, however, did not make their original architect completely happy. One of these was Geo Widengren's suggestion that the idea of YHWH as a dying and rising god was a central part of the festival of YHWH's enthronement.

The critical attitude towards Mowinckel was exemplified by H.-J. Kraus, one of the great students of the Psalter in this century. In a number of works, particularly in his massive commentary on the Psalter, Kraus explicitly criticized Mowinckel's conception of the enthronement festival of the Lord. He found the notion to be foreign to the Old Testament understanding of God, in that it subjected YHWH to the cyclical course of the dying and rising god. Instead of this, Kraus found the central features of the autumn festival to be the celebration of the election of Zion and of the Davidic line (cf., e.g., Kraus [1961]: 201–5; [1966]; and [1979]: 105–13; 139–50). Other scholars such as von Rad and Weiser held the centerpiece of the autumn festival to have been a covenant celebration (see Helmer Ringgren's survey [1969]: 192–95). In short, numerous alternatives to Mowinckel were proposed.

An important new contribution to the discussion was made in 1982 by Peter Welten. Welten made two important observations, both of which favor Mowinckel's position. First, the idea that the enthronement festival of YHWH automatically made him into a dying and rising god was the result of the fallacious combination by scholars of two Mesopotamian texts in their attempts to describe the Babylonian New Year festival. According to Welten the texts in question did not belong to the ritual texts of the New Year festival, nor did they necessarily characterize Marduk as a dying and rising god.

Second, Mowinckel had placed great emphasis on the suggestion that the Hebrew expression *YHWH mālak* actually meant "the Lord has become

King." The expression in question occurs in Psalms 93:1; 96:10; 97:1; and 99:1. By contrast, Kraus maintained that the expression signified that "the Lord is King [now and forever]." Both translations are philologically possible (cf. Ulrichsen [1977]). However, the Old Testament also contains some expressions with the reversed sequence, *mālak YHWH* (or *'ĕlōhîm*); and there is general agreement that these are to be taken to mean "the Lord has become King" (cf. 2 Sam 15:10; 1 Kings 1:11). This sort of expression occurs in Ps 47:8 [9] and in Isa 52:7. Mowinckel's critics, however, have tended to regard these variants as curiosities, which they have subjected to various forced interpretations. But in this connection Welten has noted that the same sequence also occurs in two other texts: Isa 24:23 and Micah 4:7. Since there are four such occurrences, it is inviting to suppose that these were not mere "curiosities," but rather normal expressions that show that YHWH was annually proclaimed King. The ambiguous expression *YHWH mālak* should be understood against this background. It expresses the same meaning but with added emphasis on YHWH. Thus: "The Lord—and no one else—has become King!"

I myself am inclined to understand the situation in the following manner. We have noted that YHWH's accession to royal power plays a central role in some important texts, both superficially and in their deep structure as well. The motif in question was specially associated with the temple and with Zion. If we should attempt to point to the central motif of the most important festival of the year, then it would be reasonable to assume that this was the celebration of the Lord as King. This main motif of the festival was probably realized in the form of a sacred drama, as we may perhaps sometimes glimpse in expressions of the type "come and behold the works of the Lord" (Pss 46:8 [9]; 48:8 [9]; 66:5). Concerning these, Ringgren once remarked, "However these passages are to be understood in detail, one thing can be stated with assurance: on the great festivals something took place in the Temple that could be described as seeing the deeds of Yahweh" (Ringgren [1969]: 183). So what were the most important motifs associated with this celebration of the Lord as King?

- The chaos battle and creation (while neither the exodus nor the covenant played any important part in the festival in pre-exilic Jerusalem)
- The battle against the enemies of Zion and the judgment of the peoples (the point of departure for OT eschatology)
- The enthronement of the Lord, which was probably realized as a procession in which the ark was led up to the temple (cf. Pss 24 and 47).

It should also be stressed that the ancient Israelites cannot be held to have associated the enthronement of the Lord with any sort of temporary divine abdication of royal power. Notice the way Revelation states that God has become king, which is expressed with the Greek aorist (Rev 11:17; 19:6), while the narrative itself begins with a vision of God on his throne (Rev 4). Taken together, these features emphasize God's constant sovereignty. In a corresponding way, in the Israelite autumn festival the Lord's enthronement

In Search of God

took place as a re-enactment of the primeval events of the creation battle and the reception of royal honors, but this re-enactment does not suggest that God was thought to have lost power at any time.

Literature: An impressive survey of the discussion is that of Cazelles (1960). See also the balanced review by Ringgren ([1969]: 185–200). On the transfer of the emphasis from autumn festival and creation battle to Passover and exodus in the late pre-exilic or exilic period, see Mettinger ([1982 B]: 67–77).

EXCURSUS 17
THE DIVINE NAME ELYON,
"THE HIGHEST"

The divine name *'elyôn* is rightly translated "the Highest." The word comes from the same root as the Hebrew verb meaning "to ascend" (*'ālâ*). The adjective is not only used to characterize God but also to refer to something that is spatially higher in relation to something else (cf., e.g., 2 Kings 15:35; Isa 7:3; 36:2). The word is used of God 31 times in the Old Testament, while its Aramaic counterpart occurs 14 times.

This divine designation is a facet of "monarchical" theology; it is similarly expressed when God is characterized as "the King," "the Lord Sabaoth," and so forth. That the term was specially associated with the temple services is attested by the fact that about 20 of the occurrences of its use are in the Psalter. Moreover, all of the attestations outside of the 4 in Gen 14:18, 19, 20, and 22 appear in the poetic materials of the Old Testament.

As *'elyôn* the Lord is "exalted far above all gods" (Ps 97:9), so indeed the other gods are the "sons of the Most High" (Ps 82:6), who are accordingly urged to sing praises to their ruler (Ps 47:2, 6–7; cf. Roberts [1976]). "The Most High" is a typical power epithet for God: the texts in question speak of his power "over all the earth" (Pss 47:2 [3]; 83:18 [19]; 97:9). The Most High establishes the boundaries of the peoples (Deut 32:8); and as the ruler of the world, "the Most High" deserves songs of praise (Pss 7:17 [18]; 9:2 [3]; 50:14; 92:1 [2]). To deny the Highest One just praise and to rebel instead is a vicious sin (Pss 78:17, 56; 107:11). The superficial powerlessness of "the Most High" is a source of despair for the righteous (Ps 77:10 [11]; cf. 73:11), although in reality the one "who dwells in the shelter of the Most High" is secure (Ps 91:1).

It is probable that this divine name was used in Jerusalem already before the time of David, as suggested by the narrative of Abraham and Melchizedek (Gen 14:18–22). Ugaritic knows a comparable designation (KTU 1.16.III.5–8), and it is also attested in the later Aramaic Sefire inscriptions (KAI 222 A 11).

Literature: Wehmeier (THAT 2: 285–87) and Kraus ([1979]: 27–28).

7

"The Lord of Hosts":
The Regnant God

In Hebrew the divine name "The Lord of hosts" reads as *YHWH ṣĕbāʾôt*. The first part of the name is immediately recognizable; the second element, *ṣĕbāʾôt*, would seem to be an ordinary plural of the fairly frequently attested noun *ṣābāʾ*, the Hebrew word for "army," "host," "horde." However, this apparently simple word constellation, "YHWH of hosts," poses so many problems that scholars have not agreed on how to understand it. The RSV unfailingly renders it "the Lord of hosts."

The disagreement is naturally regrettable, since the Sabaoth name appears frequently in the Old Testament (284 times), above all in the prophetic writings; and it occurs in some of the most sublime passages in the entire Old Testament. When, on the occasion of the call of the prophet Isaiah, the seraphs sing out their praise of God in the heavenly sanctuary, this very name is employed:

> Holy, holy, holy is *YHWH ṣĕbāʾôt*
> the whole earth is full of his glory. (Isa 6:3)

And the prophet reacts to this overpowering experience with the words,

> Woe is me! . . . for my eyes have seen the King,
> *YHWH ṣĕbāʾôt*. (Isa 6:5)

Considerable effort has been expended in the attempt to solve the riddle of the Sabaoth name; a consensus on the matter, though, does not exist (see Excursus 20, "The Sabaoth Designation in Modern Biblical Scholarship"). An indication of the situation is the fact that Gerhard von Rad, one of the greatest biblical scholars in this century, despaired of our ever achieving clarity on the content of this divine name.[1]

Here we shall not attempt to hunt for various details that might support one or another of the available interpretations. Instead, I want to start at zero base: we shall work as if no one had previously tackled the Sabaoth problem. First, we shall attempt to determine in what setting in life the term was at home and what associations it awakened among the ancient Israelites by studying the contexts in which the term occurs. On the basis of the clues thus arrived at, we shall then attempt to determine the meaning of the word *ṣĕbāʾôt* itself. Our next step will be to study the understanding of God implicit in the Sabaoth theology; in this connection Isaiah and certain of the psalms will be the focus of our interest. Finally, we shall examine the likely milieu of origin of the Sabaoth name.

THE CONTENT OF THE DIVINE NAME

THE CONTEXT OF THE NAME: INDICATIONS POINTING TO THE TEMPLE

Botanists and zoologists speak of ecosystems: there is a reciprocal interaction between an organism and the milieu in which it lives. Something similar applies to language as well; it is usually quite informative to study a linguistic phenomenon in its milieu, that is, in its context. We biblical scholars may use the word "context" in two different senses. (1) We can speak of a word's *lexical context*, which includes the synonyms and antonyms that usually appear together with the word in question. Here, too, we find the connections that the word makes with other words in sentences. (2) We can also speak of a word's *situational context*, by which is meant the cultural milieu in which a given expression belongs. Essentially this is the phenomenon Hermann Gunkel called *Sitz im Leben* ("situation in life"). By study of the "situation in life" in which a given expression was typically used, we can to some extent make out what sorts of associations it brought to mind.

Here we shall investigate the situational context of the Sabaoth name; in the process we shall see that various tracks lead us to the milieu of the temple. At the same time we will also study the associative content of the term. Then we shall study the semantic content of the term "Sabaoth," narrowly construed; this will be mainly an investigation of the etymological origin of *ṣĕbāʾôt*.

124

Some Statistical Evidence

Some help in the effort to circumscribe the use of our term in the Old Testament is provided by statistics.[2] There are 284 occurrences of the name; of these, no fewer than 251 (i.e., 88 percent) are in the prophetic books. The 82 occurrences in the Book of Jeremiah represent a problem with which we cannot deal here.[3] However, one should note the frequency of the term in Isaiah 1—39 (56 times), Haggai (14 times), Zechariah (53 times), and Malachi (24 times). These prophets have one notable feature in common: *they represent a tradition closely associated with the Jerusalem temple. Is the name Sabaoth in some way contingent on this temple tradition?*

We know that the temple lay in ruins during the Babylonian captivity. How is "Sabaoth" attested in the literature of this period? A notable fact is that the term nowhere occurs in Ezekiel; and in Isaiah 40—66 it occurs only 6 times. Furthermore, the D-work (see Glossary) from late pre-exilic or, rather, exilic times comprises about 28 percent of the Old Testament text but contains only 15 occurrences of the Sabaoth name, 5 percent of the total sum of occurrences. These are mainly found in the source materials of the work. Thus, literature from the period of the exile contains disproportionately few attestations of the Sabaoth name.

In striking contrast, Isaiah 1—39 contains 56 occurrences of the Sabaoth name—20 percent of the total sum—although it comprises only 3 percent of the Old Testament text. Thus, a corpus from the heyday of the temple contains disproportionately numerous attestations of the Sabaoth name.

Thus we may conclude (*a*) that the period of the exile was something of a blank space in the historical distribution of the Sabaoth name, and (*b*) that it occurs with extraordinary frequency among the prophets, and particularly in the writings of those who, whether pre-exilic or post-exilic, were in some way associated with the Jerusalem temple. This causes us to pose the following question: *Was the Sabaoth name somehow specially associated with the temple, which, of course, was in ruins during the period of the exile?*

When was the first appearance of the Sabaoth name? If one reads the Old Testament from one end to the other, the first attestations of the name occur in 1 Samuel (1:3, 11; 4:4), where it appears in the context of ancient traditions associated with the Shiloh of the period of the judges. Note also that Shiloh contained a sanctuary, which was in fact the only sanctuary prior to the erection of Solomon's temple that was designated by the word *hêkāl*, "temple" (1 Sam 1:9; 3:3). Additionally, in the early materials the ark of the covenant is especially connected with the Sabaoth name (1 Sam 4:4;

2 Sam 6:2), and it soon took up its place in the temple of Solomon (1 Kings 8:6).

Now if the divine name in question played a special rôle in connection with the Jerusalem temple and, previously, in the sanctuary at Shiloh, then it is quite surprising to learn that it occurs only 15 times in the Psalter. This is one of the surprising features of the distribution of this designation. The 15 occurrences in the Psalter are concentrated in only 8 psalms: 24:10; 46:7, 11 [8, 12]; 48:8 [9]; 59:5 [6]; 69:6 [7]; 80:4, 7, 14, 19 [5, 8, 15, 20]; 84:1, 3, 8, 12 [2, 4, 9, 13]; and 89:8 [9].

It should be noted that Psalm 24 is often held to feature a procession in the course of which the ark was brought into the temple, and that Psalms 46, 48, and 84 are so-called Psalms of Zion (psalms with especially strong Jerusalem and temple associations).

What does this study of the distribution of the Sabaoth name in the Old Testament indicate? That we should be alert for signs pointing to a connection between Sabaoth and the temple milieu.

The Textual Evidence:
The Sabaoth Name, the Temple,
the Cherubim Throne

Unlike the other Israelite names for God, "YHWH Sabaoth" is connected with one particular geographical site: Jerusalem, and in particular Zion, the temple mountain.[4] Time and again "YHWH Sabaoth" is connected with Zion. In such passages the Lord Sabaoth "dwells on Mount Zion" (Isa 8:18), establishes his royal domain on Zion (Isa 24:23), and invites guests to a coronation banquet on the same mountain (Isa 25:6). In the Book of Zechariah, Mount Zion has been linguistically connected with "YHWH Sabaoth," and so has become "the mountain of YHWH Sabaoth" (Zech 8:3). One psalm calls Jerusalem "the city of YHWH Sabaoth" (Ps 48:8); this psalm is one of the Zion psalms, and it is especially in these that the Sabaoth attestations in the Psalter are concentrated (Pss 46:7, 11; 48:8; 84:1, 3, 8, 12).

Our study of the general distribution of Sabaoth in the Old Testament indicated that it had something to do with the temple. We have also noted the connection of Sabaoth with the temple mountain— Mount Zion. We therefore begin to suspect that it is more than coincidental that the name also occurs in the description of the call of Isaiah (chap. 6). The name "Sabaoth" figures in both the song of the seraphim (v 3) and in Isaiah's own confession:

126

Woe is me! For I am lost; for I am a man of unclean lips, and I dwell in the midst of a people of unclean lips; for my eyes have seen the King, YHWH Sabaoth! (Isa 6:5)

The Temple: God's Royal Palace

One thing literary scholars invariably watch for is the presence of fixed expressions and formulaic language in a given text. This is rewarding because in ancient Israel different groups and milieux had their own peculiar sorts of language. Sometimes one or another formulaic usage can provide an important clue pointing to some group behind a particular text or concept.

In fact, one special formulaic expression is associated with the Sabaoth name: "the one who thrones above the cherubim." We often encounter an extended divine designation. This occurs, for example, in connection with the ark: it is said to belong to "YHWH Sabaoth, who is enthroned on the cherubim" (1 Sam 4:4; 2 Sam 6:2; cf. also Isa 37:16). Psalm 80—"the one who is enthroned upon the cherubim" occurs in the beginning of the psalm (v 1 [2])—is essentially also a witness to this association, since the Sabaoth name occurs no less than four times throughout the psalm (vv 4, 7, 14, 19). (The credit of having introduced "the one who is enthroned upon the cherubim" into the discussion of the divine name "YHWH Sabaoth" belongs to Otto Eissfeldt.[5]) To what does this clue point, then? It provides yet another hint of connection with the temple.

At this point it is appropriate to turn for some help in the visual arts of the ancient Near East, where we find the cherubim as winged sphinxes with human faces. Three archaeological finds deserve especial attention in this connection.[6] A picture has been incised on the stone sarcophagus of King Ahiram of Byblos, on the Mediterranean coast; it depicts a king or deity seated on his cherubim throne (Figure 10). In a barely pre-Israelite stratum from Megiddo, on the northern side of Mount Carmel, excavators have found an ivory plaque about 26 cm long; it depicts a monarch on his cherubim throne (Figure 11). The same site has also yielded a small model in ivory of a cherubim throne (Figure 12); the throne seat itself is supported by two cherubim, the outer wings of which are entirely visible, while the inner wings seem to meet under the throne seat, supporting it.

We know that King Solomon had two mighty cherubim made and placed them in the Holy of Holies of the temple (1 Kings 6:23–28). Their bodies were parallel to one another, while their faces pointed

FIGURES 10–13
THE BIBLICAL CHERUBIM IN THE
LIGHT OF ARCHAEOLOGY

Figure 10. A ruler on his cherubim throne. The biblical cherubim were prob-ably shaped like winged lions, as we see in representations like the above. The motif here is a 33-cm-wide relief on the stone sarcophagus of King Ahi-ram (Hiram I) of Byblos, who was presumably a contemporary of David and Solomon in the tenth century B.C.E. (See Mettinger [1982 B, 21, note 10].)

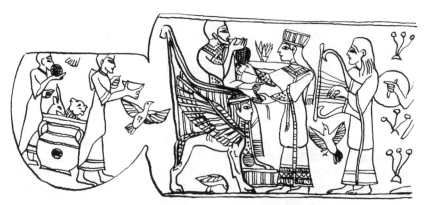

Figure 11. A ruler on his cherubim throne. This scene of courtly life recurs on the famous ivory plaque from Megiddo, which dates from ca. 1350–1150 B.C.E., that is, before the Israelite conquest of the city (cf. Judges 1:27 and 1 Kings 4:12). The total breadth of the plaque is 26 cm. (See Mettinger [1982 B, 21, note 11].)

128

Figure 12. Megiddo has also yielded a small
ivory model of a cherubim throne (2.6 cm
high). (See Mettinger [1982 B, 21, note 12].)

towards the entrance of the temple (2 Chron 3:13). Their total height
was about ten cubits (i.e., five meters). The outer wings of the figures
brushed the walls of the Holy of Holies; the inner wings probably
met on the horizontal plane and were in all likelihood soldered together (1 Kings 6:27; 2 Chron 3:12; cf. Ezek 1:23).

Although there is disagreement on this point, it was probably not
just for the sake of aesthetic effects that the cherubim were placed in
the temple. Rather, they also had a particular symbolic content, and,
more to the point, one that is illuminated by the archaeological finds
described above: *the cherubim in the temple of Solomon composed a
throne* (Fig. 13).

To human eyes the throne was empty, although this was only apparent, since *God was held to sit enthroned in invisible majesty in the Holy of
Holies of the temple.* The seat of the throne was formed by the conjoined inner wings of the two cherubim. Furthermore, the ark of the
covenant was the footstool of the enthroned God (cf. 1 Chron 28:2; Ps
132:7).[7] Taken together, these features communicate with visual ex-
plicitness an important insight: the temple was the palace of the invisible God. (There is a logical connection between the prohibition of
iconic representation of God and the fact that ancient Israel had no
concrete divine image in her temple, but only an empty throne.[8])

Summary. The Sabaoth name was connected with Jerusalem and
Zion. It was sometimes complemented by the "cherubim formula," so
that the combined divine name was "YHWH Sabaoth, who is enthroned above the cherubim." Therefore, we may conclude that the
Sabaoth name was at home in the milieu of the temple. After all, it
was in the temple that the two cherubim were placed which formed

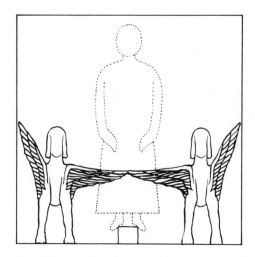

Figure 13. The cherubim in Solomon's temple may have looked like this (cf. 1 Kings 6:27); they formed the throne of the invisible God. In other words, the designation "YHWH Sabaoth, he who thrones upon the cherubim" has a very concrete background. On the cherubim in the tabernacle, cf. Exod 25:10–22 and see Mettinger ([1982 B]: 19–24, 87–88).

the throne of YHWH Sabaoth. It accordingly seems likely that the Sabaoth name was the designation used by the temple priests for God.

It should also now be noted that the milieu in which the Sabaoth name apparently made its earliest appearance was that of Shiloh during the era of the judges (1 Sam 1:3, 11; 4:4), where, of course, there was also a temple and likely a cherubim throne as well (cf. 1 Sam 4:4); it was probably destroyed later by the Philistines. Moreover, the ark of God was also located there. When, after many complications the ark was transferred by David to Jerusalem and ultimately was placed in the temple by Solomon, the Sabaoth name was also transplanted into this milieu. Thus the Sabaoth name became a central element in the praises of God that were sung in temple worship. The high frequency of the name in Isaiah (56 times), Haggai (14 times), and Zechariah (53 times) is then explained: the name belonged to the temple tradition which these prophets represented.

Furthermore, the theology promulgated in the Jerusalem temple focused on the idea of God as King. This conclusion is supported by the presence of the cherubim throne in the Holy of Holies and by the fact that the temple was designated by the word *hêkāl* (e.g., Ps 27:4;

Isa 6:1), a word which was also used of the palace of the earthly king (1 Kings 21:1; 2 Kings 20:18). Thus, if it was the case that the Sabaoth name belonged to this milieu, then we may surmise that its sphere of associations was enriched by the concept of the Lord as King. Here we are not dealing with the semantic nucleus of the name, but with its linguistic overtones or connotations. Thus we ask, Does the name "YHWH Sabaoth" occur in texts which show that it was rooted in a milieu in which God was represented as a King seated on his cherubim throne?

One thinks immediately of the words of Isa 6:5: "my eyes have seen the King, YHWH Sabaoth." But also Psalm 24 is explicit on the subject. It is conceivable that this psalm was originally used in connection with the consecration of the temple and later was used in the annual celebration of the autumn festival. The psalm describes unambiguously how God approaches his temple—his palace—in royal majesty. It is "the King of glory" (*melek hakkābôd*) who enters into his sanctuary, after which we hear: "Who is this King of glory? YHWH Sabaoth, he is the King of glory!" (Ps 24:10). Yet another indication in this direction is the formulaic expression "the King, whose name is YHWH Sabaoth" (Jer 46:18; 48:15; 51:57).

The Sabaoth designation had its home in the temple in Jerusalem. Its immediate reference is to the God who was held to sit enthroned invisibly upon the cherubim in the Holy of Holies of the temple. This explains the royal associations that a wide variety of texts associate with the designation YHWH Sabaoth.

The Temple: Meeting Place of Heaven and Earth

We must linger in the temple somewhat longer, since, in addition to the royal associations, there is yet another feature needing attention: the special understanding of space that the Israelites attached to the temple.

To the Israelites, the temple was the place where the boundaries were surpassed, that is, where the dimensions of space were transcended. At one point in all existence, heaven and earth intersected. In the space of the temple there was no absolute "either-or." Rather, *in the temple heaven and earth were thought to be one. The temple was the earthly part of the heavenly reality.*

This peculiar understanding of the temple was widespread in the ancient Near East.[9] We find it in Mesopotamia. For example, the god Enlil's cult center in ancient Nippur was called Dur-an-ki, "the bond between heaven and earth." In Egypt, too, we find temple names that express the same concept. Thus the temple in Heliopolis was called "the Heaven of Egypt," just as the complex in Karnak was called "Heaven on Earth." One particular ancient Egyptian term for temple means literally "the doors of heaven." Similarly, in Canaan we find the temple area in Sidon called "the Heights of Heaven."

This widespread understanding throughout the ancient Near East will scarcely have contained aspects that directly contradicted traditional Israelite faith. Thus everything suggests that ancient Israel embraced it, too. And indeed, this view is palpably present in Jacob's words after his dream in Bethel: "This is none other than the house of God, and this is the gate of heaven" (Gen 28:17). It is also expressed in Isaiah 6; here we have a heavenly vision that has been localized to the temple in Jerusalem. The shaking of the thresholds, the incense, and the glowing coals on the altar show that we are in the earthly temple, but at the same time the text contains other features that exceed the limitations of the earthly sanctuary. The closest parallel in formal terms is 1 Kings 22:19–23, which unambiguously takes place in heaven, as we there encounter the heavenly host gathered around the throne of God. In Isaiah 6, God speaks in the plural and asks, "Who will go for *us?*" In so doing, he is speaking on behalf of his heavenly "government."

But it is not only the temple, broadly conceived, which contains such heavenly symbolism. The same also applies to the arrangement of the throne—the place where YHWH Sabaoth is enthroned upon the cherubim. The description of the inaugural vision of the prophet Ezekiel contains a description of God's throne (Ezek 1:22–26). Here we are once again told that the wings of the cherubim meet one another (v 23). Moreover, they support some sort of surface which the text calls a *rāqîaʿ*. The same term is used of the "firmament" in Gen 1:6–8. Here, God is enthroned upon this surface. The cosmic symbolism is unmistakable. Moreover, in the Psalter the cherubim throne serves as God's heavenly cloud chariot (Ps 18:9–10; cf. 104:3 and 1 Chron 28:18).

It is against the background of this understanding of the temple as the point of intersection between heaven and earth that we are to read the following words from the Psalter:

The Lord is in his holy temple,
the Lord's throne is in heaven. (Ps 11:4)

Note that the two verses are linked by *parallelismus membrorum*, so that they provide variant expressions for one and the same phenomenon. What is decisive for the Israelite understanding of the temple is this basic fact: *the Lord is present. Where the Lord is present humanity encounters a new dimension where the heavenly world discloses itself.*

WHAT DOES THE WORD "SABAOTH" MEAN?

We now turn to the element ṣĕbā᾽ôt in the compound divine name.[10] A number of interpretations have been proposed. But we have already shown what direction our study of the Sabaoth name ought to take. In sum, we have determined its primary situation in life—the temple. In this connection YHWH Sabaoth served as a term for God—the invisible one who was enthroned on the cherubim throne in the temple. As for the conceptual world of the temple, we have made two observations:

1. The temple was God's royal site, and the cherubim formed his throne. God was depicted as King.
2. The temple was part of the heavenly world; here the boundary between heaven and earth ceased to exist.

Thus we have determined both the situation in life and the associative content of the Sabaoth name. The reference of the term was special: God is *the heavenly King* on the cherubim throne in the temple. YHWH Sabaoth, then, was the King on the throne in the temple.

Just as earthly monarchs have a court and a government, the King of kings had his court of advisers. (The concept of a God who reigns in splendid isolation is, incidentally, a projection of alienated modern man, as a Swedish theologian once appropriately remarked [B.-E. Benktson].) The God of the Bible is surrounded by myriads of heavenly beings, for whom the Hebrew language has a rich terminology. Thus we encounter such designations as "the sons of God," "the divine council," and "the divine assembly" (Ps 89:5–7).[11]

Among this terminology we also find the singular of ṣĕbā᾽ôt, namely, Hebrew ṣābā᾽, of which an occurrence appears in 1 Kings 22:19–23. Here the prophet Micaiah ben Imlah describes how he was momentarily granted a vision of the heavenly world, in the course of which he listened to the deliberations preceding a decision of the "heavenly government." He prefaces his description in the following manner: "I saw the Lord sitting on his throne and all the *host* of heaven standing beside him on his right hand and on his left" (v 19). The translation reads "host" where the Hebrew text reads ṣābā᾽. Yet another context is the description of the same heavenly host in Ps 103:19–21. Here, too, the text speaks of God as King: God "has established his throne in the heavens" (v 19). The myriads around the throne are characterized with a number of synonyms, one of which is God's "hosts" (v 21). Numerous other examples are easily cited in this connection (Josh 5:13–15; Ps 148:1–5; Isa 13:4; 40:26; 45:12; Dan 8:10–13).

If the Sabaoth name refers to God as the heavenly King, and the term *ṣābā'* in the singular is a common term for the heavenly host surrounding the throne, then it would be reasonable to conclude that the Sabaoth name is to be interpreted on the basis of this use of the word *ṣābā'* rather than on the basis of its application to Israel's mortal armies, or to the universe in general, or anything else. The Sabaoth name speaks of God as "YHWH of the heavenly hosts."

It is possible to test this conclusion by asking, Does the usage of "YHWH Sabaoth" as a name of God occur in texts in which God's heavenly council plays a role? The passages to be mentioned in this conjunction are few, but they are sufficient to answer the question in the affirmative.

In Isaiah 6, in which the presence of the heavenly council may be inferred, God says, "Who will go for *us?*" (v 8). God is here speaking on behalf of the divine government. The prophet confronts God within the circle of the heavenly government. It is hardly surprising that both the seraphim and the prophet here employ the Sabaoth name (vv 3, 5).

Psalm 89, which also contains the idea of God as King, uses various terminology to speak of the heavenly council. In vv 5–7 we find reference to "the assembly of the holy ones," "the heavenly beings," and "the council of the holy ones." And when the psalmist lifts his gaze to the speaker and director of this heavenly council, he naturally uses our terminology: "YHWH *'ĕlōhê ṣĕbā'ôt*, who is mighty as thou art?" (v 8).

Summary. Our argument has so far followed two different approaches. First, the Sabaoth name belongs to the temple milieu and refers to God as the heavenly King on his cherubim throne. Second, "Sabaoth" is linguistically related to the word *ṣābā'* which itself designates the heavenly host, God's divine council. It is important to recognize that these two lines actually converge. *The Sabaoth name designates God as the heavenly King, and the element ṣĕbā'ôt directs our attention to the heavenly hosts around the throne of God.* These heavenly hosts have multiple functions: they sing the eternal praise of

God in the heavenly sanctuary; they serve as members of God's heavenly government; and they carry out God's assignments on earth.

Here we need to comment on the syntax of the compound in question. Since *ṣĕbā'ôt* in YHWH Sabaoth contains a reference to the hosts around God's throne, it is natural to regard *ṣĕbā'ôt* as a concrete, nonabstract noun. This conclusion is supported by countless attestations of the noun *ṣĕbā'ôt*, with the simple meaning "armies," "military units." The compound *YHWH ṣĕbā'ôt* should be understood as a construct form. The inscriptions from Kuntillet Ajrud in eastern Sinai show that it was possible for the divine name *YHWH* to stand in the construct state, for we here find both *YHWH šomrōn*, "YHWH of Samaria," and *YHWH tēmān*, "YHWH of Teman" (Emerton [1982 A]). I prefer to allow the question of the grammatical nature of this construct relationship to remain open, although I feel that it could well be an adjectival, descriptive genitive.

THE UNDERSTANDING OF GOD IN
THE SABAOTH THEOLOGY

We may now abandon linguistic problems in connection with the Sabaoth name and proceed to the theological question: What aspects of an understanding of God come to expression when God is called "YHWH Sabaoth"? Here the previous linguistic study may be of some help, since we have concluded that the name refers to God as the heavenly King who reigns from the cherubim throne in the temple and as the chief of the heavenly council, *ṣābā'*. We shall now attempt to extend this analysis by examining the texts in which the Sabaoth name is the central divine designation (especially the Psalms of Zion and Isaiah).

THE PRESENT GOD

The cherubim throne in the temple gave tangible expression to a concept that must have been central to Israelite faith during the entire history of the Solomonic temple: the concept of God as the *Deus praesens*, the present God, the invisible one on the cherubim throne in the temple.[12]

It was in the Jerusalem temple that the prophet Isaiah had his vision of the Lord of Hosts on his throne (Isa 6). The same prophet characterized YHWH Sabaoth with a descriptive participle as "the one who dwells on Mount Zion" (Isa 8:18).

The same idea is also clearly expressed in the Psalms of Zion (Pss 46, 48, 76, 84, 87, 122). Jerusalem is "the city of YHWH Sabaoth" (Ps 48:8). We also read that "his abode has been established in Salem, his dwelling place in Zion" (Ps 76:2). Perhaps the most pregnant expression is to be found in Psalm 46, which formulates an important consequence of this divine presence: the present God also defends his city.

> There is a river whose streams make glad the city of God,
> the holy habitation of the Most High.
> God is in the midst of her, she shall not be moved;
> God will help her right early.
> The nations rage, the kingdoms totter;
> he utters his voice, the earth melts.
> YHWH Sabaoth is with us; the God of Jacob is our refuge.
> (Ps 46:4–7; [5–8])

The phrase "YHWH Sabaoth is with us" occurs twice in the psalm (vv 7 and 11) and serves as a refrain. The words have the force of a motto. Though the peoples may rage and kingdoms totter, yet Zion's security rests on a secure foundation: the presence of the Lord of hosts. Where the translation reads "the Lord of hosts is with us," the Hebrew has the compound ʿimmānû, "with us, in our midst."

The God of the Sabaoth theology is the present God, the one who sits enthroned in the temple as King. Here it is important to acknowledge that this idea of God did not mean for the Israelites that God was confined to the temple. The concept is by no means a naive idea of immanence. The texts make this fully clear by showing in a variety of ways that God extends beyond the limitations of the temple.

One such passage is Isa 6:1, where the RSV informs us that "his train filled the temple." The Hebrew word šûlîm, however, does not really mean a robe, but its lower edge, or hem. The suggestion is that the very hem of God's garment fills the temple; how much vaster God must be!

Note also Psalm 24. Here the gates are instructed to raise their heads so that the King of glory may enter. God is so great that the temple gates are too low for him! ·

THE REGNANT GOD AND GOD'S HEAVENLY COUNCIL

The Sabaoth theology is based on the enthroned God, who fills the temple with his divine presence. This, however, does not exhaust this particular understanding of God. In his capacity as YHWH Sabaoth the deity also acts: *he reigns.*

In the days of Isaiah, for example, Israel found herself being seriously threatened for the first time by a growing superpower. Thus, in a way that had never previously occurred, the Israelites were faced with the question of how far God's power extended. In 745 B.C.E. Tiglath-pileser III became the king of the Assyrian Empire (Map 3); this event introduced a period of Assyrian expansionism which was to last until the middle of the seventh century. We do not know in what year Isaiah received his call, though this most likely happened sometime between 742 and 735 B.C.E. It is tempting to suppose that Isaiah was called into service shortly after the accession of the Assyrian monarch and at this time was allowed to behold the Lord of lords and King of kings, the Lord of hosts on his throne in the heavenly world.

One might easily suppose that the heavenly King had heaven alone as his sphere of action; nothing, however, could be more wrong. The prophet Isaiah, the foremost exponent of the Sabaoth theology in

MAP 3
THE ASSYRIAN EMPIRE

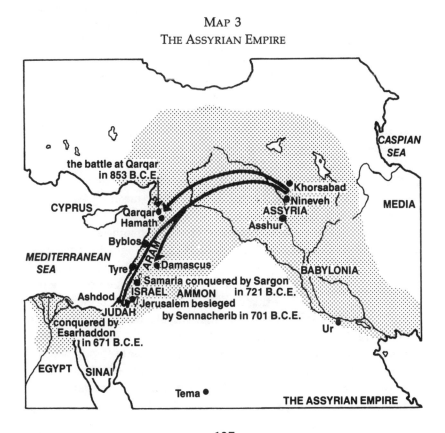

the Old Testament, proclaims the God who is extraordinarily interested in conditions on earth—God who is the Lord of history. Isaiah 6 depicts a vision of God as King on his heavenly throne. Apart from this vision, the Book of Isaiah contains almost nothing else of the sort. On the other hand, it speaks correspondingly more of God's activities on the earthly scene, in the realm of history.

The Immanuel Prophecy in Isaiah 7

Chapter 7 of Isaiah tells how the prophet was sent to proclaim the word of God in the midst of a military political crisis. The Arameans and North Israelites had declared war on Judah in order to force her into an anti-Assyrian coalition. This was the so-called Syro-Ephraimite War, which took place towards the end of the 730s B.C.E. (cf. 2 Kings 16). The invaders intended to replace King Ahaz of Judah with a more cooperative regent. At this time the Lord spoke to Ahaz through the prophet Isaiah and said, "Take heed, be quiet, do not fear" (Isa 7:4). Isaiah then summarizes the enemies' plans (vv 5 ff.) and announces, "Thus says the Lord God: 'It shall not stand, and it shall not come to pass'" (v 7). The plans of human beings are confounded by God's own intentions.

Ahaz, the somewhat ambivalent Judaean king, is subsequently offered a sign intended to confirm the word of God: "Behold, a young woman shall conceive and bear a son and shall call his name Immanu-el" (v 14). This name has caused scholars considerable problems, since it is unique among the Hebrew personal names.

We have already noted, however, that the prophet Isaiah belongs to the same theological tradition as that which is proclaimed in the so-called Psalms of Zion. The name Immanuel, meaning "with us is God," bears a striking resemblance to an expression we previously noted in one of those very psalms: "YHWH Sabaoth is *with us,* the God of Jacob is our refuge" (Ps 46:7, 11). The linguistic nucleus in the expressions both in Isa 7:14 and in the psalm in question is ʿimmānû, "with us," a prepositional phrase that has been conjoined to a divine name. In Isa 7:14 this name is ʾēl, the usual Hebrew word for "god," so that the child's name is "Immanu-el." In the psalm, on the other hand, it is "YHWH Sabaoth." Thus to the dispirited King Ahaz the name Immanuel serves as a prophetic reminder of the theology of promise and assurance of salvation expressed in the Psalms of Zion, and particularly in Psalm 46. This is theology formulated with paradigmatic conciseness!

God's Heavenly Decree

We have just seen how God sometimes thwarts human initiatives (Isa 7:5); the same theme is also attested elsewhere (e.g., Isa 8:9–10; 19:3). But the Book of Isaiah also contains some striking formulations that directly speak of the way YHWH Sabaoth enacts his own decisions on the historical scene; these passages speak of God's heavenly "decree."

The paradigmatic example of this phenomenon is Isa 14:24–27, a prophecy that is probably to be dated to 701 B.C.E. in the context of Sennacherib's invasion of Judah. The formal center of the section consists of a prediction that the Assyrian king will experience a fiasco in the arena of world politics: "I will break the Assyrian in my land, and upon my mountains trample him under foot" (v 25). This expression is framed by sentences that anchor this course of events in the decree of YHWH Sabaoth:

> YHWH Sabaoth has sworn:
> "As I have planned, so shall it be,
> and as I have purposed [*yāʿaṣ*], so shall it stand." . . .
> This is the purpose [*ʿēṣâ*] that is purposed
> concerning the whole earth;
> and this is the hand that is stretched out
> over all the nations.
> For YHWH Sabaoth has purposed [*yāʿaṣ*],
> and who will annul it?
> His hand is stretched out,
> and who will turn it back? (Isa 14:24, 26–27)

The terminology here consists of the verb *yāʿaṣ*, "counsel, purpose," and the noun of the same root, *ʿēṣâ*, "counsel, advice, plan," which sometimes has the sense of "a decision taken in council."[13]

Isaiah 14:24–27 may profitably be read against the background of Isa 10:5–15. In 10:5–15 the prophet proclaims his "woe!" over Asshur. God has used Asshur as an instrument to punish his people, but Asshur has exceeded instructions and conceived her own plans (10:7); these plans intend destruction where the Lord had merely intended a chastising judgment. Against the plans of this world power for the liquidation of the people of God, Isaiah announces YHWH Sabaoth's "decree" in chapter 14. And while the ruler of the world brags that "his hand found like a nest the wealth of the peoples" (10:14), the prophet says of the God who is about to realize his "decree" that "his hand is stretched out, and who will turn it back?" (14:27).

Thus the prophet Isaiah answers the question as to the extent of God's sphere of authority by the assertion that not even the great power of Assyria is exempted from it. At some point during the last part of the eighth century B.C.E. when Assyria was unquestionably the mightiest power in the world, a Judaean prophet pronounced God's judgment on this empire. The fate of Assyria was sealed by God's decree; the tyranny was destined for destruction.

The texts also speak of God's plan in relation to other peoples and nations. In Isaiah 19 it is Egypt's turn, once again with the same terminology as before. Thus we find reference to "what YHWH Sabaoth has purposed [yāʿaṣ] against Egypt" (v 12), just as we are told that the Egyptians will be frightened "because of the purpose [ʿēṣâ] which YHWH Sabaoth has purposed [yāʿaṣ] against them" (v 17). Isaiah 19 also emphasizes the contrast between God's decree and man's intentions: "I will confound their plans" (v 3).

The same terminology of divine decision and plan recurs in Isa 23:9, this time applied to the city-state of Tyre. Also, this arrogant state is subject to God's judgment, like the recently mentioned great powers: "YHWH Sabaoth has purposed it [yāʿaṣ], to defile the pride of all glory." Once again we note the occurrence of the Sabaoth designation. We find the same conception in the Book of Jeremiah, in which reference is made to God's decisions concerning Edom (Jer 49:20) and Babylon (Jer 50:45).

But it is, above all, in Isaiah that we find well-defined statements concerning God's decision and plan. It comes as no surprise that it was Isaiah who arrived at the following description of YHWH Sabaoth: "He is wonderful in counsel [ʿēṣâ] and excellent in wisdom" (Isa 28:29). And what is true of God is also predicated of the son who is to be born and who is predestined by the divine will to be the new ruler:

And his name will be called:
"Wonderful Counselor, Mighty God,
Everlasting Father, Prince of Peace." (Isa 9:6 [5])

This relationship between divine decree and human plans deserves our full attention. It is not the case that human plans by their very existence are a challenge to God; everything depends on the nature of the plans. There are, for example, situations in which human plans agree with God's. The prophet Isaiah no doubt knew that the Assyrian policy of expansion followed a carefully worked-out strategy. The inclusion of the Aramean kingdom and of North Israel with the Assyrian provincial system were pre-planned components of the foreign policy of the great power. Remarkably, we know of no condemnation by Isaiah of the Assyrians for having liquidated the Northern Kingdom. On the contrary, Isaiah maintains that this conformed to the task set out by the Lord (Isa 10:6). Thus, although the Assyrians were formally pursuing their own strategic ends, these happened to coincide with God's purposes.

In other words, the Assyrian power was in this instance commissioned to perform a particular task. Assyria was an instrument in God's hand; she was the tool God had chosen to punish his people. This is expressed through a number of different metaphors. Assyria is called "the razor," which God had fetched from across the river (Isa 7:20); but she is also called the "axe," the "saw," and the "rod" which God had set in motion (Isa 10:15).

This means that the Assyrian great power had a given task to perform, a task that went only so far and no farther. Thus when the Assyrian plans went even farther and became a policy of pure destruction aimed at both Judah and Jerusalem, God drew the line and required a requital (Isa 10:5–15, esp. vv 7–12). Human plans, then, can oppose those of God. They may for a period of time look as if they will be successful, but in the long run they will come to nothing if they are on a collision course with YHWH Sabaoth's intentions (cf. also Isa 7:5–7; 8:9–10; 19:3). What Isaiah represents is the calm assurance that earthly power will not have the last word.

The events on the scene of world politics, in which a great power step by step draws near to little Judah as part of a well-planned and executed strategy, mark off the external milestones in the life of the prophet Isaiah. The texts in the Book of Isaiah do not appear in chronological order, but we can follow the prophet all the way from the 730s, when he criticized the attempt to form an anti-Assyrian coalition (Isa 7), to the events in connection with the revolt led by King Hezekiah and the subsequent siege of Jerusalem in 701 B.C.E. Some of the texts we have already encountered belong to the latter context. However, the main events in this sequence are especially depicted in Isaiah 36—37, two chapters which have been long debated by scholars, and the historical source-value of which has been variously interpreted. Without choosing any particular side in this controversy, I contend that the understanding of God in these chapters is the same as that which we encounter in other Isaianic texts.

141

In the year 701, then, Jerusalem was surrounded by the Assyrians. King Hezekiah of Judah received a written Assyrian ultimatum. It looked as if it would be only a matter of days before he would have to capitulate to Sennacherib, the ruler whom the Assyrians themselves call "the great king" in our texts (Isa 36:4, 13). The expression reflects the official titulature of the Assyrian king; the title "great king," along with other titles, characterizes the Assyrian monarch as the absolute ruler of the world: "king of the world," "king of the four quarters," "king of the nations," "king of all princes," "king of all people," "the great king."

What does Hezekiah do? He takes the letter containing the Assyrian ultimatum and brings it to the temple. There he spreads it out "before the Lord" (Isa 37:14). We need hardly wonder where this takes place: at the feet of the cherubim throne in the Holy of Holies! Then Hezekiah prays, and his prayer opens with the appropriate address: "O YHWH Sabaoth, God of Israel, who art enthroned above the cherubim" (37:16).

To any outside observer, the natural result of the trial of strength between Judah and Assyria would have looked like a foregone conclusion. However, Isaiah 36—37 provides an entirely different point of view. Ranged against the Assyrian conqueror we find the heavenly King on the cherubim throne: YHWH Sabaoth. It is a thought-provoking fact that the Old Testament reserves the term "great King" for the Lord God of Israel (Pss 47:2; 48:2), and that this term is never adapted from the Assyrian royal titulature so as to apply to any mortal king of the Davidic dynasty.

The text subsequently describes how YHWH Sabaoth speaks through the prophet Isaiah (Isa 37:21–35); the actual reply to Hezekiah's prayer is in vv 33–35. The "Zion promise" of divine protection for Jerusalem is assured. Assyria had possessed the right to carry out certain plans (v 26), but no authority to conquer Jerusalem (vv 33–35). Sennacherib "shall not come into this city." We are then told of the divine intervention and of the retreat of the Assyrian army.

How Indelible Is the Divine Plan?

"YHWH Sabaoth" is a divine designation closely associated with belief in YHWH as the god who acts in history. Against all the intrigues of human endeavor, Isaiah opposes the heavenly decree of the Lord. That it is the Lord who gets the last word is among the absolute constants of Isaiah's proclamation. This prompts a question: Does Isaiah then mean that the course of history is according to a predetermined divine plan? It has been a general opinion in modern scholarship that Isaiah and other prophets actually thought in terms of a fixed divine plan for the course of world events from beginning to end. Note, however, that in his *History and the Gods,* Bertil Albrektson discusses this problem and concludes that Isaiah does not speak of a divine "plan" in the precise meaning of the term.[14]

Which interpretation of the matter is correct?[15] First of all, notice that the prophet Isaiah only speaks of God's "decree" (or "purpose": *ʿēṣâ,* 5:19; 14:26; 19:17; 28:29) in the singular. Thus, the prophet speaks of the Lord's "deed" and "work" in history; and when he does so, he uses the terms "deed" and "work" in the singular (*pōʿal* and *maʿăśeh,* 5:12, 19; 10:12; 28:21). He nowhere refers to a number of separate actions in history; we have a single divine act of guidance or direction.

Second, notice that Isaiah speaks of how God has shaped history in advance. Thus the prophet criticizes his fellow countrymen for thinking only of military precautions when confronted by the Assyrian threat: "But you did not look to him who did it, or have regard for him who planned it long ago" (Isa 22:11). There is no suggestion whatsoever of divine improvisation (cf. Jer 37:26).

Third, notice that the prophet sees the course of history moving in a particular direction; history has a goal (Greek, *telos*). And the goal (*telos*) of history is the final manifestation of the majesty of God and the establishment of God's sovereign rule. Thus, in his great description of the Day of the Lord (Isa 2:6–22) the prophet speaks of how "the Lord alone will be exalted in that day" (v 17).

In other words, this prophet does not describe God's historical actions as a series of improvised ad hoc interventions in the history of the people. Just as God is one and maintains his identity throughout history, so, too, God's historical actions are unified in a fundamental sense. But does this then mean that history, according to the Sabaoth theology which Isaiah represents, is predetermined?

In the kingdom of Judah from the days of David to the exile we discern a theology of promise with two foci. (1) According to the Davidic promise God will keep in power that royal line that has won his favor—the Davidic dynasty. David's line, his "house," will thus endure forever (2 Sam 7:16). (2) According to the Zion promise,

God will protect and defend the city in which he has his dwelling (e.g., Pss 46, 48, 76).

It is clear that Isaiah bases his proclamation on the secure foundation consisting of the Davidic promise and the Zion promise. It is remarkable, however, that he does not understand these promises as divine blank checks which will be cashed no matter what might happen.

1. *The Davidic promise.* There can be no doubt that Isaiah sees the future of his people as a future led by a descendant of David who has been chosen by God. Isaiah's pronouncements in chapters 9 and 11 are unequivocal. It is not obvious that Isaiah regarded the Davidic promise as conditional; this, however, does emerge from a close reading of Isaiah 7.

We recall that Isaiah 7 informs us as to how the kings of Aram and North Israel organized a campaign against Jerusalem in the 730s in order to force King Ahaz of Judah to join an anti-Assyrian coalition with them. When Ahaz is told of this, we read that "his heart and the heart of his people shook as the trees of the forest shake before the wind" (v 2). But the prophet then proclaims the word of the Lord that the enemies' plan will not succeed (vv 5–8).

We subsequently find the strange words which the RSV renders "If you will not believe, surely you shall not be established" (v 9). What does the prophet mean by this? For an answer, we must turn to the "charter document" of the Davidic dynasty: the prophecy of Nathan in 2 Samuel 7. Here we read that the house of David "shall be made sure forever" (v 16). The Hebrew text at this point consists of a passive form of the root '-*m-n*. This root also occurs in other texts that are related to the Nathan prophecy (1 Sam 25:28; 1 Kings 11:38; Isa 55:3; Ps 89:28 [29]). The root in question, '-*m-n*, has to do with "firmness," "stability"; of course, it also occurs in the word "amen."

As Ernst Würthwein has maintained,[16] Isa 7:9 actually plays on the wording of the Nathan prophecy. The Isaiah passage contains a pun on the same root as that which figures in the formulation of the dynastic promise. In the first half of the statement, "if you will not believe," we discover an active form of the root '-*m-n*; and in the latter half, "you shall not be established," we find a passive form of the same root. Many scholars have attempted to translate the passage so as to indicate the presence of the pun: "if you do not stand firm, you will not be made firm," or the like. However, it is clear that what the prophet actually means is "if you do not believe, you will not stand fast."

Isaiah's address to the Davidide Ahaz, then, contains a play on the Nathan prophecy. At the same time, however, something new has been added: the continued existence of the Davidic line is made contingent on their faith. As Hans Wildberger wrote on Isaiah's understanding of history, "The Nathan prophecy is here made subject to the *conditio* of faith."[17] Thus the promise is not on the order of a blindly functioning oracle; it is rather conditional in nature.

We have posed the question as to whether or to what extent the notion of the decree of the Lord presupposes historical determinism. Isaiah's way of adding a condition to the Nathan prophecy suggests an answer. God's action on behalf of his promise is not an autonomously functioning pre-program. Rather, God retains his freedom at all times and remains open to the complexities of historical reality.

2. *The Zion promise.* In the mighty "Ariel" prophecy (Isa 29:1-8), the prophet speaks of Jerusalem's distress, perhaps in connection with the siege of 701. Enemies have surrounded the city, the situation is desperate, but then the Lord of hosts intervenes and the enemy army disappears "like a dream, a vision of the night" (vv 6-8).

A different section, Isa 31:4-9, probably refers to the same historical situation. The metaphorical language of the text is expressive; here the Lord is likened to a lion that has captured its prey and intends to retain it. The prey is Zion. A multitude of herdsmen have appeared to deny the lion its prey. Of course, in the ancient Near East "shepherd" was a common metaphor for "king." Thus the description of the herdsmen who gather together refers to an attack on Jerusalem by enemy kings. However, the Lord refuses to give up Zion, his prey.

Then the author moves on to yet another metaphor. The lion metaphor is dropped in favor of one that pictures YHWH Sabaoth as a bird, most likely an eagle, which descends from the skies to defend the city on Mount Zion. In addition to these two texts, observe also Isa 17:12-14 and 30:27-33: both deal with God's protection of Zion. The Zion promise, too, is unshakable. But Isaiah does not regard the Zion promise, either, as an unconditional guarantee. A close reading of the "cornerstone pericope," shows that this is hardly the case (Isa 28:14-22). Here it is clear that for Isaiah the word of promise to Zion had no inherent automatic quality; it, too, was conditional in nature.[18]

This Isaianic prophecy is addressed to the leaders of Jerusalem (v 14). They are said to live in false security; they feel that the enemy's scourge cannot reach them (v 15). They are said to have enacted a covenant with "death" (v 15), which is probably an ironic reference to military alliances of doubtful worth, above all with Egypt (cf. 30:1–5; 31:1–3). Perhaps the leaders in question were appealing to the putative, absolute validity of the Zion promise.

The prophet addresses himself to these arrogant leaders. We begin with v 17. Here the prophet speaks of a "line" and a "plummet," tools one uses to determine whether a new or old building is aligned as it should be. But it is "justice" and "righteousness" that are to serve as plummet and line—the criteria for God's evaluation.

It is in this light that we must understand v 16, which speaks of "the precious cornerstone of a sure foundation." The stone in question is said to be a ʾeben bōḥan, a controversial expression which the RSV renders "a tested stone." But it is probably more accurate to understand it as a "stone of testing" (that is, one which is used to test the situation of the other stones, as the position of these to the cornerstone is of decisive importance).

The phrase about the cornerstone in v 16 is thus a parallel to what is said in v 17 about justice and righteousness as plummet and line, that is, as criteria for a test—God's testing of his people. Verse 16 also says of the cornerstone (stone-of-testing) that "he who believes will not be in haste," which recalls the expression in Isa 7:9 about believing in order to stand fast.

No doubt the concept underlying the idea of the cornerstone is that of the sacred bedrock of the temple mountain (cf. Ps 27:5). The rabbis spoke of the "foundation stone" with which God had blocked up the těhôm-deep. We might even interpret the "cornerstone" of this Isaiah passage as a symbolic expression for the prophetic proclamation, for the word of promise concerning God's own victory over the powers of this world. Whoever places his confidence in this promise "need not hasten away, flee."

Our text, then, speaks of two alternatives: either to place one's entire faith in the Lord and the Lord's promise or to secure human guarantees for Zion's continued existence with the help of military alliances. Jerusalem's leaders had chosen to rely on human guarantees, for which reason they come under the judgment. Then the events of the holy wars are rehearsed. Once long ago God himself had fought for Israel "on Mount Perazim" (cf. 2 Sam 5:20) and "in the valley of

Gibeon" (Josh 10:10ff.). God now proposes to reenact this drama, but with an important change of scenario: this time God will fight against the people of God! And yet, this, too, will be God's work, his "alien" work (Isa 28:21). Thus the text concludes that the prophet has heard "a decree of destruction" from YHWH Sabaoth (Isa 28:22).

We noted that the Davidic promise was supplied with a conditional statement. The same phenomenon repeats itself here; and here the terms of the condition attached to the Zion promise are confidence in God (v 16b), justice, and righteousness (v 17a). Once again, the word of promise retained its full validity, but was by no means a "pre-programmed missile." History is not determined by the word of promise.

It is usually supposed that it was in the period of the exile that the divine promises to David and Zion were supplied with conditions. It is correct that the era of Josiah and the D-literature represented an important development in this respect (Bright [1977]: 111–39). Now, however, we see from a close reading of two important Isaianic passages (7:1–9 and 28:14–22) that this development was anticipated by this prophet by a whole century.

And yet, there is an important difference between the conditions attached to the promises by Isaiah and by the D-literature. In Isaiah the conditions were "faith," (7:9; 28:16b), "justice," and "righteousness" (28:17a). In the later D-literature, however (Deut 11:26–28; 28:1, 15), the condition consisted in obedience to the Mosaic commandments; and both the Davidic promise (1 Kings 2:3–4; 9:4–5; Ps 132:12; cf. Mettinger [1976]:275–90) and the Zion promise (1 Kings 6:11–13) were subordinated to it.

In the proclamation of Isaiah we meet YHWH Sabaoth as the regnant God. This God's heavenly decisions determine historical events. Human plans and schemes are unable in the long run to achieve anything at all against God's will, although this did not mean for Isaiah that history was merely a predetermined program.

In a study of prophecy and fulfillment in the Old Testament, Bo Johnson concluded that fulfillment is never represented as the result of some blindly deterministic, automatic process; rather, it is always "a work by the living God, who always strives actively."[19] Our examination of the Book of Isaiah shows that this prophet's work is of a piece with this total picture. Thus we must finally insist on an ultimate ambivalence. The proclamation of Isaiah about the government and decree of YHWH Sabaoth present us with a dynamic dialectic between God's promise and human responsibility. History is both the realm in which God fulfills his promise *and* the courtroom in which God brings the culpable to account and demands responsibility.[20]

THE HISTORICAL ORIGINS OF
THE SABAOTH NAME

It should be perfectly clear that the Sabaoth name was specially associated with Solomon's temple in Jerusalem, especially in the Sabaoth theology in Isaiah and the Psalms of Zion from the period between Solomon and the exile.

It is nevertheless plain that the Sabaoth name had a history prior to its use in Jerusalem to designate God as the one enthroned on the cherubim of the temple. If we trace the name back through time, we arrive at Shiloh (approximately equidistant between Jerusalem and Shechem) during the period of the judges, the place where the young Samuel grew up. This divine name seems to have had its origin at Shiloh (1 Sam 1:3, 11; 4:4).

In Shiloh the Israelites worshiped the Lord as King.[21] The Lord had a sanctuary there; it was called a *hêkāl,* "palace, temple," like the temple in Jerusalem (1 Sam 1:9; 3:3). The indications are that there was a cherubim throne in Shiloh, too (1 Sam 4:4). It is also the likely case that the idea of God's divine council was entertained in this milieu. In all these respects there must have been considerable continuity between Shiloh and Jerusalem.

In other words, it must have been during the period of the judges that the Sabaoth name came into use among the Israelite tribes. Here we ought to recall our observations about "Gods and Myths in Canaan" (above, Chapter 4). The two main Canaanite gods were El and Baal. Baal was represented iconically and textually as a young warrior who battled against the forces of chaos, while El was the old enthroned monarch who determined destinies.

Our study of the Lord as "King" and as "YHWH of hosts" shows us what might be called Israel's "response": YHWH was held to be King rather than Baal. Israel adopted a Canaanite divine epithet. In conjunction with this we find biblical texts that display the ancient pattern of chaos battle-kingship-temple. This "chaos battle complex" is the Old Testament theological complement to the designation "King" with reference to the Lord—*the warring God.*

Something similar applies to the Sabaoth name. The name itself characterizes the God of Israel as the one who was present in the temple, enthroned upon the cherubim and surrounded by the hosts of heaven. Here the throne conception is the central theological motif: *YHWH Sabaoth is the enthroned and regnant God.*

Now, if the Lord as the warring God (i.e., the Lord as "King") was Israel's response to the stimulus of this Canaanite concept of Baal, corresponding lines may be drawn between the Lord as the enthroned God ("YHWH Sabaoth") and the Canaanite El conceptions (see Figure 14).

But what about the name itself, "YHWH Sabaoth, who is enthroned on the cherubim"; was it perhaps originally a Canaanite divine designation? The term "the one who is enthroned on the cherubim" is not attested anywhere in the Ugaritic texts. As for the "Sabaoth" element, scholars have pointed out that a single Ugaritic text refers to the god Resheph as *ršp ṣbi.* However, as I have demonstrated elsewhere, this means "Resheph of the sunset" rather than "Resheph of the host," as some have preferred.[22] Thus there is not the slightest indication that the Sabaoth name was adopted by the Israelites from the Canaanites. The Sabaoth designation apparently took its beginnings among the Israelites themselves. We can trace it back to the temple at Shiloh, but no farther back than that. We search in vain among the hundreds of names of Canaanite gods available to us; we will not find the Sabaoth designation among them. The Sabaoth name seems to be a unique Israelite divine designation.

The warring God and the enthroned, regnant God are one and the same God. Thus it is hardly surprising to discover that certain texts interweave the features of these two ideas of God, as if they are inseparable. A clear example of this occurs in Ps 89:5–18. Here we find both the enthroned God in the midst of his heavenly assembly (vv 5–8) and

FIGURE 14

THE UGARITIC TEXTS AND

THE OLD TESTAMENT

The Ugaritic Texts	*The Old Testament*
Baal and the chaos battle motif	YHWH as King in the battle with the forces of chaos
El and the idea of the divine assembly	YHWH as the enthroned God, i.e., as YHWH on his cherubim throne

Two important aspects of the Old Testament understanding of God may be seen as Israel's "answer" to certain Canaanite conceptions. Compare with Excursus 9.

the warring God who defeats chaos and creates the world (vv 9–18). And while the first section is rounded off with the Sabaoth designation (v 8), the text as a whole concludes by speaking of the Lord as King: "The Lord, he is our shield; the Holy One of Israel, he is our king" (as the NEB correctly translates v 18 [19]). Similarly with Psalm 24, where the warring God upon returning from the chaos battle (vv 1–2, 7–9) is called YHWH Sabaoth when he enters into his temple (v 10). Something like this also occurs in Psalm 29.

SUMMARY

Our study of the Lord as "King" and as "YHWH Sabaoth" has given us a better grasp of the monarchical understanding of God in the Old Testament. God is described in the Old Testament in hierarchical categories, since everything depends on power. Nevertheless, as we have seen, the biblical monarchical portrait of God is not about the arbitrariness and violence of an oriental despot, but about power exerted in the service of life.

1. When God is described as "King" (*melek*), the subject is God in confrontation with the chaotic power of the ultimate evil. And this confrontation is not once-and-for-all; rather, it stretches from the creation to the completion of all things. The warring King is the world's Creator and Judge.

2. When God is characterized as "YHWH Sabaoth," it is the enthroned God who reigns and determines the destiny of the world, as in the Book of Isaiah.

3. Norman K. Gottwald has specially emphasized the egalitarian ideals of early Israel.[23] This being the case, it is worth noting that the monarchical understanding of God, which is related to a hierarchical way of thought and to power relations, is also positively related to such egalitarian ideals. The monarchical understanding of God comes repeatedly to expression in texts whose background is political oppression and in which God appears as the liberator (e.g., Exod 15:17; Isa 52:7; Micah 2:13; 4:6–7; Zeph 3:14–20). Other texts that exemplify this understanding of God lay special weight on God's care for widows, orphans, and sojourners, that is, for those who are powerless (Ps 146:5–10; cf. Pss 5:1–6; 10:12–18).

We have previously examined both "the God of the fathers" and "YHWH." If we accordingly compare the monarchical understanding of God with our results pertaining to these two designations, our portrait of the God of Israel begins to take shape. Under the designations "the King" and "YHWH Sabaoth" the God of Israel has manifested himself in a way never previously seen. Israel came to see that *God is ubiquitous* with respect to both time and space. God's power is not confined either to individuals of the tribal group or to a particular territory. If God chooses to do so, he is able to use the empires of the world as his instruments. Furthermore, God is not merely confined to the present; both past and future are God's time as well. God is *omnitemporal.* Now both protology and eschatology become important theological dimensions. Now we see that God is "who is and who was and who is to come," to use the expression in Rev 1:8.

It is worth noting that Israel adhered to the monarchical understanding of God, not only when things went well (e.g., when the empire of David and Solomon was a significant power in the ancient Near East[24]) but also when external reality seemed to falsify objectively all belief in God as the warring King and as the Lord of the heavenly hosts. In this connection one of the lamentations from the time of the exile is unambiguous. In spite of the darkness and the gloom, and no matter what the Israelites' eyes might behold, they continued to confess to the God who, nevertheless, possessed all power:

> But thou, O Lord, dost reign for ever;
> thy throne endures to all generations. (Lam 5:19)

Moreover, there are also other texts from the time of the exile that formulate the confession of the Lord as the warring and regnant God (cf. Isa 52:7; Ezek 20:32–44; Pss 74:12–17; 89:5–18).[25] Thus we observe the important fact: for the believer it is far from always the external course of events which announces to what extent God is victorious. Rather, as an English philosopher of religion (D.Z. Phillips) has expressed it, it is the belief in the sovereign God that determines what is reckoned to be a victory and what is not.

The catastrophe of the exile and the destruction of the temple led to reformulations of the classical tenets of the Sabaoth theology. The concepts of God's name (*šēm*) and his glory (*kābôd*) became at this time central in the D-literature and in Ezekiel, respectively. This important development cannot be dealt with here. (See Mettinger, *The Dethronement of Sabaoth: Studies in the Shem and Kabod Theologies* [1982].)

151

EXCURSUS 18
WHERE DOES THE SABAOTH NAME OCCUR
IN THE OLD TESTAMENT?

	Occurrences
1–2 Books of Samuel	11
1–2 Books of Kings (in 2 Kings 19:31, following the Ketib)	4
Isaiah 1—39	56
Isaiah 40—55	6
Jeremiah	82
Hosea	1
Amos	9
Micah	1
Nahum	2
Habakkuk	1
Zephaniah	2
Haggai	14
Zechariah	53
Malachi	24
The Psalter	15
1–2 Chronicles	3
TOTALS	284

Note that the highest frequency of the occurrence of the name is in Isaiah 1—39, Jeremiah, and Zechariah. By contrast, the name is conspicuously absent in Ezekiel. The unevenness of the distribution in these texts requires an explanation, and we shall attempt to deal with it in our discussion.

EXCURSUS 19
GOD AS "THE HOLY ONE"

In the call narrative of Isaiah we read, "Holy, holy, holy is the Lord of hosts" (Isa 6:3). This passage plus Psalm 99, which likewise intones the holiness of God three times (vv 3, 5, and 9) allow us to suspect that a similar *trishagion* ("thrice holy") was a permanent ingredient in the temple liturgy. God's transcendence is most strongly expressed in those statements that describe him as "the Holy One" (*qādôš*): "for I am God and not man, the Holy One in your midst, and I will not come to destroy" (Hosea 11:9; cf. Isa 40:25).

Perhaps the matter is best expressed by saying that "the Holy One" designates God as unapproachable in majesty. Other references to the holiness of God also lead us to the theological milieu that speaks of God as King and Ruler (Isa 6:3; Ps 89:18 [19]; cf. above, pp. 98, 100–105; Ps 99:3, 5, 9, an Enthronement Psalm; cf. also 1 Sam 6:20). One cannot approach a sovereign in just any way. The word *qādôš* speaks of God as the supra-worldly and fearful power that compels respect and even subjection. We catch a glimpse of God as a devouring fire, a supernatural phenomenon that awakens terrified admiration in all who approach it—leaving us wordless.

The ark narrative tells us that many of the inhabitants of Beth Shemesh died for having looked into the ark of the Lord and so made themselves guilty of lese majesty. Confronted with such a God one can only ask, "Who is able to stand before the Lord, this holy God?" (1 Sam 6:20). A similar event is related in the Pentateuch when Aaron's sons attempt to bring "strange fire" before the Lord, so that fire comes from the Lord and devours them, after which we are told, "This is what the Lord has said, 'I will show myself holy among those who are near me, and before all the people I will be glorified'" (Lev 10:1–3; here v 3). Such passages provide some of the background against which Isaiah's reaction is to be understood when he has beheld the Holy One: "Woe is me! For I am lost; for I am a man of unclean lips, and I dwell in the midst of a people of unclean lips; for my eyes have seen the King, the Lord of Hosts!" (Isa 6:5). Whenever passages in Isaiah utilize "the Holy One of Israel" to refer to God, they usually refer to God's offended majesty. One does not approach God without risk.

In this connection the "Entrance Liturgies" are important, in spite of the fact that the holiness terminology does not occur in them. They typically speak of how the presence of the Holy One on Zion has certain consequences for visitors to the temple. Typical examples are Psalms 15 and 24:3–6. An introductory question as to whom will be allowed to ascend the mount of the Lord and to enter into his sanctuary is answered with a listing of the qualifications that the prospective visitor must possess in order to be allowed to draw near to God in this manner. This can only be done by "he who walks blamelessly," "he who has clean hands," "who does not slander with his tongue," and so forth. Isaiah 33:14–16 has the same structure, but in this text we do find a direct reference to the unapproachable majesty of the present God. The sinners on Mount Zion become alarmed and ask, "Who among us can dwell with the devouring fire? Who among us can dwell with everlasting burnings?" The answer is similar to the ones we met in the two aforementioned psalms: "He who walks righteously and speaks uprightly, who despises the gain of oppressions, who shakes his hands, lest they hold a bribe" (cf. also Ps 5:4–7; Jer 7:5–7; Ezek 18:5–9). Thus we are presented with a reciprocal relationship: the holiness of the present God requires the righteousness of the celebrant assembly.

This reciprocal relationship is also expressed in passages that contain the holiness element in both terms. The so-called Holiness Code (Lev 17—26) contains three examples of the statement "You shall be holy, for I the Lord your God am holy" (Lev 19:2; 20:26; 21:8). The acknowledgment of God's holiness is the basis and ultimate motivation of the demand for human holiness. The relevant specifications in the Holiness Code are then to be compared with the descriptions of the "righteous" in the previously mentioned texts.

God as both "the King" and "YHWH Sabaoth" are designations that imply majesty. But God is also referred to as "the Holy One" or "the Holy One of

Israel." Thus, in the Old Testament understanding of God (*a*) God's *majesty* and (*b*) God's *holiness* play central roles. To these two features a third crucial one should be added: (*c*) God's *exclusiveness*. That is, God does not tolerate any other gods alongside himself; God is a "jealous God," *'ēl qannā'* (cf. above, p. 74). Not unexpectedly, the ideas of God's holiness and jealousy are combined in a pregnant phrase when Joshua says to the people: "You cannot serve the Lord; for he is a holy God; he is a jealous God; he will not forgive your transgressions or your sins" (Josh 24:19).

In brief, God's majesty, holiness, and exclusiveness are the three most decisive characteristics of God in the Bible. One should always bear these three aspects in mind when one considers the biblical proclamation about God's love.

An attempt has been made by scholars to interpret Hebrew *qādôš* etymologically as if it meant "to separate, reserve," but this view is hardly tenable. The fact that the holy is nevertheless frequently distinguished from the profane no doubt lies in the nature of the matter; note the correspondence between "to sanctify" and "to separate" in Gen 2:3, Lev 20:26 (cf. v 24), and Deut 7:6.

Statistics: The new, standard lexicon contains 56 attestations of God's holiness in the Hebrew Old Testament (HAL 998a). Of these passages, there are many that include various names: "the Holy One," "the Holy One of Jacob," "the Holy One of Israel," and so on. The more important of these are as follows:

- "The Holy One," 5 times: Isa 40:25; 57:15; Hosea 11:9; Hab 3:3; Job 6:10
- "The Holy One of Israel," 31 times: 2 Kings 19:22; Isa 1:4; 5:19, 24; 10:20; 12:6; 17:7; 29:19; 30:11, 12, 15; 31:1; 37:23; 41:14, 16, 20; 43:3, 14; 45:11; 47:4; 48:17; 49:7; 54:5; 55:5; 60:9, 14; Jer 50:29; 51:5; Pss 71:22; 78:41; 89:18 [19] ("the Holy One of Israel he is our King").

We note that the latter designation occurs 12 times in Isaiah 1—39 and 13 times in Isaiah 40—66. It may well be a linguistic usage that derives from the prophet Isaiah, although the conception of God's holiness is, of course, very ancient.

Literature: Vriezen ([1956]: 124–35); W.H. Schmidt (1962); H.-P. Müller (*THAT* 2: 589–609); Wildberger ([1979]: 241–48); Bettenzoli ([1979]: 25–49); Weinfeld (1982); and Otto (1986). On the demand for righteousness as a criterion for admission to the temple, see Bo Johnson ([1985]: 101, 109).

Excursus 20
THE SABAOTH DESIGNATION IN MODERN
BIBLICAL SCHOLARSHIP

When scholars have discussed the name "Sabaoth" in modern times, mainly two problems have been central to the discussion: the obvious question as to the actual meaning of the element *ṣĕbā'ôt* and the grammatical relationship between the two elements in the name YHWH *ṣĕbā'ôt*. The properties of the Hebrew language seem to allow several answers to each question. But in addition to these two problems—the semantic and the grammatical—there is the religio-historical problem of the origin and background of the term. Is it a purely Israelite construction? Or was it inherited from the Canaanites? What follows are a few selective glimpses of the scholarly discussion (cf. the surveys of R. Schmitt [1972]:145–59 and Mettinger [1982 A]: 109–11, 127).

1. *The semantic problem.*
   a. Scholars have often held that the element ṣĕbāʾôt has to do with Israel's earthly armies. The connections between the divine name and the ark (1 Sam 4:4; 2 Sam 6:2) as well as passages like 1 Sam 17:45 (cf. Pss 44:9 [10]; 60:12) would seem to support such a conclusion. But the name is extremely well attested in the prophetic writings (251 out of a total of 284 occurrences in the entire Old Testament). The prophetic language is not notably militaristic.
   b. Other scholars have seen in the Sabaoth element a reference to God's heavenly hosts. The fact that the LXX uses the translation *kyrios tōn dynameōn* "the Lord of the powers" is usually mentioned in this connection. That the Sabaoth designation is a name for God in his capacity as Lord of the heavenly hosts is an old and well-established interpretation, but it has lost ground in this century in favor of other views. One difficulty with this view is that the Old Testament invariably uses the singular form, ṣābāʾ and never the plural (ṣĕbāʾôt) with reference to the heavenly hosts (e.g., 1 Kings 22:19).
   c. A third possibility is to advocate a "totality" interpretation of the Sabaoth element. In a few passages in the Old Testament the word ṣābāʾ is used comprehensively to refer to the whole of creation (Gen 2:1; cf. Isa 34:2). Wambacq (1947) has proposed the following compromise: while the Sabaoth element originally referred to earthly hosts—the people of Israel—in the course of time the term was expanded so as to include all of creation. Thus the divine name in question would refer to God as the Lord of creation and so in a sense imply God's omnipotence. A difficulty for this idea is, of course, that the "comprehensive" use of ṣābāʾ is extremely rare in the Old Testament.
2. *The grammatical problem.*
   The name "Sabaoth" raises more than just the question of the meaning of the word ṣĕbāʾôt. The grammatical structure of the composite term is a problem in itself: What is the grammatical relationship between the words YHWH and ṣĕbāʾôt? YHWH of course serves as a proper name for God. In Hebrew, proper names are already determined quantities; they usually do not have explicative complements. Thus one would not expect that YHWH would stand in a construct relationship to a subsequent genitive. This is a difficulty for the interpretation which holds that the composite means "Sabaoth's YHWH," that is, "YHWH of hosts."

An alternative avoids this difficulty by regarding the composite as a composite of the proper name YHWH and an apposition—giving us "YHWH, that is, Sabaoth." Naturally, our decision on these linguistic issues will determine our understanding of the matter. If we have a proper name plus an apposition, then YHWH and ṣĕbāʾôt are identical quantities, although this is not necessarily the case if we insist on the construct interpretation.

W.R. Arnold ([1917]:142–48) emphasized that ṣĕbāʾôt is indeterminate, and so understood the composite as an adjectival genitive compound of the same sort as, for example, har qōdeš, "mountain of holiness," or "the holy mountain." Here qōdeš, "holiness," cannot be separated from har, "mountain"; rather, it is a quality of the mountain in question. Correspondingly, in the composite YHWH ṣĕbāʾôt, the term ṣĕbāʾôt would then not be something separate from YHWH (such as heavenly or earthly hosts under his command), but would be one quality. Accordingly, the divine name in question would not mean "Yahwe of the Armies, whether Israelitish or celestial, but . . . the military Yahwe—Yahwe on the War-Path, Yahwe Militant" (143).

Eissfeldt ([1950/1966]:103–23) pursues the same line even further with the interesting complement to Arnold's suggestion that ṣĕbāʾôt may be an intensive abstract plural on the order of such plurals as dēʿôt, "full knowledge," and gĕbûrôt, "extraordinary strength." In this connection Eissfeldt could also have mentioned zĕmirôt, which is a divine name signifying "Guardian, Protector" in 2 Sam 23:1. Thus in Eissfeldt's view YHWH ṣĕbāʾôt signifies "Jahwe, der Zebaothafte," that is "YHWH, the Sabaoth-like." This would mean in turn that YHWH possesses to a high degree the quality that Eissfeldt holds to reside in the concept ṣĕbāʾôt; he determines this quality as "mass," "weight," "power." Thus the composite would ultimately characterize God as "YHWH the mighty." Eissfeldt's interpretation has been received with considerable enthusiasm in recent literature.

3. *The religio-historical problem.*

Victor Maag ([1950/1980]:1–28) has strongly emphasized the religio-historical aspects. The encounter between Israelite and Canaanite religion during the period of the judges meant that the former assimilated certain new elements into their faith. To Maag, the element ṣĕbāʾôt was a designation for the Canaanite nature deities who in the course of the process mentioned above lost their independent status and became subordinated to the Lord. Thus, for Maag, the Sabaoth designation was an illustration of the concept of omnipotence.

J.P. Ross (1967) proceeded on the basis of what he held to be the oldest attestations of the name Sabaoth in the Bible. He found these occurrences in the Books of Samuel and in the Psalter, mainly in contexts that spoke of God in royal categories. But in this connection Ross held it to be problematical to attempt to connect the divine name with the usual root ṣbʾ, as manifested in the noun "army" and the verb "to do service in an army." Ross saw a yawning chasm between the contexts of the divine name and the root that was usually associated with it.

I myself attempted a new synthesis of the Sabaoth problem (Mettinger [1982 A]). I anchored the divine name in a particular milieu—the context of the Solomonic temple. I further held that the temple's character as meeting-place between heaven and earth provides a clue to the understanding of the element ṣĕbāʾôt: it has something to do with the heavenly host (ṣābāʾ) around the throne. I also emphasized the importance of the milieu in Shiloh during the era of the judges for the emergence of the term. The arguments of other scholars to the effect that the Sabaoth name was Canaanite in origin prove, on closer examination, to be based on a misunderstanding of a pair of key passages in the Ugaritic texts.

8

God As "Redeemer," "Savior," "Creator": The Divine Designations As Used by the Prophet of Consolation

We have studied "the God of the fathers" and the various "El" names in the patriarchal texts. We have seen how the name "YHWH" came into use in connection with the Mosaic age and the drama of the exodus, and how the subsequent encounter with Canaanite religion led to the use of such new divine designations as "the living God," "the King," and "YHWH Sabaoth." We have further seen that the "Sabaoth" designation served as a catchword in the milieu of the temple in Jerusalem.

Now we shall visit the period of the exile—the time of the Babylonian captivity. At this time a new divine address was directed to the conquered and deported Israelites. The prophetic oracles of Isaiah 40—55 contain this address to the exiled Israelites. The temple lay in ruins (Isa 44:26–28; 51:3; 52:9); important elements within the population had been deported (42:22); the leading power was no longer Assyria, as in Isaiah's day, but Babylonia (43:14; 47; 48:14, 20). And, as it developed, the Persian king Cyrus, who was to prove too strong for Babylon, had begun his victorious progress (44:28; 45:1; cf. also 41:2; 45:13; 46:11; 48:14).

Isaiah 40—55, so-called Second Isaiah, is framed within two majestic expressions about the word of God. These chapters present a message of hope to the downtrodden Israelites. The prophet speaks of a God who brings liberation and new creation; his message is unambiguous, no matter how we tackle the problem of authorship. The theory about the existence of a Second Isaiah is and will remain a hypothesis, but as such it has considerable "explanatory power"; it solves more problems than it creates. Here we shall speak of this anonymous prophet from the time of the exile as the Prophet of Consolation; he was responsible for chapters 40—55 (and perhaps also chapters 35 and 60—62) in the Book of Isaiah.[1]

Having observed that the Sabaoth designation was the most important divine name for First Isaiah, one is naturally curious to see how the Prophet of Consolation talks about God.[2] In chapters 40—55, together "the Holy One" and "the Holy One of Israel" occur 14 times,[3] while the Sabaoth name occurs 6 times. These usages attest a degree of continuity with the work of First Isaiah (1—39). It is more rewarding, however, to investigate an idiosyncratic feature of the Prophet of Consolation: his peculiar use of descriptive participles as designations for God. Here are a few examples: "Thus says God, the Lord, *who created* the heavens and *stretched* them out, *who spread forth* the earth and what comes from it, *who gives* breath to the people upon it" (42:5). "Thus says the Lord, *your Redeemer, who formed you* from the womb" (44:24).

When one reads the Hebrew text, one quickly notices this special way of talking about God. The phrases printed in italics above are easily recognizable as participial forms of a number of different Hebrew verbs. One scholar has reckoned that 34 verbs are used in this special way in these chapters and that these "divine participles" occur 88 times in Isaiah 40—55.[4] In other words, we here have a phenomenon which is specific to these chapters.

We have previously emphasized the interaction between situation and theology. Our approach to the "divine participles" of the Prophet of Consolation will again lead us to reemphasize this feature. When the Prophet of Consolation proclaims his gospel, he does so by directing it into the darkest depths of historical catastrophe. The prophet speaks to a people who have been crushed by the wheel of history. The temple was in ruins, and the king and many key individuals had been deported. Several different biblical books provide us with concrete information about the disaster (2 Kings 25; Jer 39—44; 52; Lam 1—5).

One must recognize that this was a crisis which affected more than just the external and material facets of Israelite life (see Map 4). The catastrophe of the exile represented an intense test of faith.[5] In order to understand this we must look back into the past. The theology of the period of the monarchy may be defined as an ellipse with two

MAP 4

THE BABYLONIAN EMPIRE

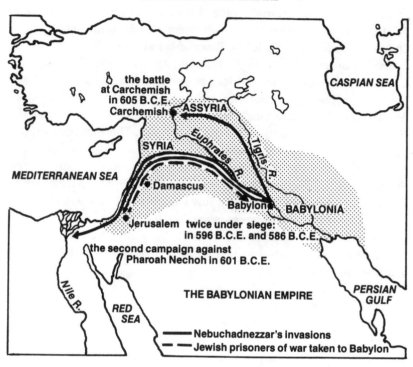

foci: the Zion promise and the Davidic promise.[6] The Zion promise was an assurance of God's presence in his temple on Mount Zion; its corollary was God's guarantee of the inviolability of Jerusalem (Pss 46:4–7; 48:3). In the exilic situation, however, the walls of the city lay in ruins, and the heathen had plundered God's dwelling—the temple on Zion (Lam 2:15; 4:12; 5:17–18; Ps 137).

The promise to David was the assurance that a descendant of David would always inherit the throne in Jerusalem (2 Sam 7:16; Ps 89:3–4). During the exile, however, the real situation was horribly different (2 Kings 25:5–8; Lam 4:20; Ps 89:38–51).

To Israel, the decades after 586 B.C.E. produced an enormous crisis of confidence as to the divine promises. Reality seemed to have delivered a massive disconfirmation of the content of the promises; the one-time gilt-edged securities had a market value of approximately zero in the wake of the disaster. As a result, the people experienced what we would call a crisis of faith: the experience of the absence of

God and of God's silence (cf. Pss 44:1–3, 9, 23–24; 74:1, 10, 22). Doubt flourished, although no one was then tempted to question God's existence. The God-is-dead theology was never to make any headway in ancient Israel. On the other hand, the Israelites did entertain doubts as to God's ability and willingness to help.[7] After all, was not the Babylonian victory a sign that the Babylonian gods were stronger? When the Prophet of Consolation speaks to his people, we note that he addresses himself to an openly formulated doubt as to God's power and concern; thus he quotes his people's doubts: "He [God] has no hands" (45:9*); "my way is hid from the Lord, and my right is disregarded by my God" (40:27); "the Lord has forsaken me, my Lord has forgotten me" (49:14).

This leads to an important insight: the message of the Prophet of Consolation in Isaiah 40—55 is to be understood as an answer to the desperate questions caused by doubt. These chapters are addressed to an Israel immersed in uncertainty.

It is important to bear two features of the message of the Prophet of Consolation in mind. First, to the Prophet of Consolation the exile was by no means a sign of God's impotence. His diagnosis was completely different, in that he concluded that the national calamity was instead the ultimate consequence of Israel's sin: "Who gave up Jacob to the spoiler and Israel to the robbers? Was it not the Lord, against whom we have sinned?" (Isa 42:24). The prophet repeats this message time and again (Isa 42:18–25; 43:22–28; 50:1–3), and it became one of the exilic period's most important insights (cf. Isa 57:17; 59:1–2; Lam 1:14, 18; 2:17; 5:7).[8] In this way the prophet defined the nature of the situation.

Second, the prophet held that the Babylonian captivity was not destined to be the ultimate goal of the people of Israel. The mission of the Prophet of Consolation was therefore to preach freedom to the captives. God had previously kept silent and concealed his face, but now he was about to intervene. On the gray cement walls of their prison, the prophet painted for his people a tantalizing fresco with colors of startling brightness. The remarkable aspect of this painting is that it provides a double exposure, or two motifs: the liberation from Babylon and the exodus from Egypt. The liberation repeats and even surpasses the exodus; once more God will split the rock and pour out water in the wasteland (Isa 48:20–21; cf. Exod 17:6). He who had once made "a way in the sea, a path in the mighty waters" will now prepare "a way in the wilderness" (Isa 43:16–21). The God of Israel will be both behind and ahead of his people when they set out, although this time it will not be a headlong flight (Isa 52:11–12; cf. Deut 16:3). In the proclamation of the Prophet of Consolation the typology of the exodus plays a major part.[9]

Thus the message of the Prophet of Consolation is a divine promise of liberation. When we turn to this prophet's use of the "divine participles," we shall see that these designations for God in themselves convey this central message. A study of the "divine participles" leads us quietly but surely into the prophet's theological *sanctum sanctorum*.

The statistics in Carroll Stuhlmueller's *Creative Redemption in Deutero-Isaiah* ([1970 A]: 268–71) allow us easily to review all 34 of the verbs employed as "divine participles." In the main, these verbs can be sorted into two classes. On the one hand, we have those verbs that speak of God as the Liberator and Redeemer. Most prominent among these are the participles *gō'ēl* (RSV: "Redeemer"), which occurs 10 times, and *môšîa'* (RSV: "Savior"), which occurs 5 times. On the other hand, we have a group of verbs that speak of God as Creator. Here the terminology is fairly varied, although it is easily recognized, nevertheless, by its resonance with other Old Testament creation texts. This group consists of participles of the Hebrew verbs signifying "to create," "to form," "to make," "to stretch out," and so on.

If, on the basis of the "divine participles" we were to describe the understanding of God of the Prophet of Consolation, we might say that he mainly emphasizes two different aspects of God's being: *God as Savior* and *God as Creator*. When we note this conjoining of salvation and creation, we naturally become curious: How did the Prophet of Consolation conceive of the internal relation between God as Savior and God as Creator?

GOD AS "REDEEMER," HEBREW *Gō'ēl*.

One of the two key words employed by the prophet to speak of God as Savior is *môšîa'*, a participle of the verb *yāša'*, meaning "rescuer, savior" (see Excursus 21). The other keyword is *gō'ēl*, which we shall now examine.[10]

In using the word *gō'ēl* the prophet has chosen a term deriving from Israel's juridical vocabulary. Its sense is associated with various types of ransom or redemptive purchase; the *gō'ēl*, then, is the person who carries out such an act (RSV: "Redeemer"). It happens to be the case that there are two different Hebrew verbs that mean "to redeem." In Deuteronomy we find the verb *pâdâ*, used to describe the way God "redeems" Israel from her captivity in Egypt (15:15; 21:8). It goes without saying that the Prophet of Consolation knew this verb (Isa 50:2; 51:11). He nevertheless prefers to use another verb, namely, *gāʾal* and its participial form, *gōʾēl*. Including all forms, our prophet uses this root 17 times (10 times as a participle, and 7 times in other forms).

But why does the Prophet of Consolation prefer the verb *gāʾal* (*gōʾēl*) to *pādâ* when he speaks of divine redemption? J.J. Stamm ([1940]:27–45) has concluded in a study of these two that both were derived from the juridical sphere but that they had different applications within this sphere. The verb *pādâ* was a neutral term used in business relationships. Against this, the verb *gāʾal* (and its participle, *gōʾēl*) was specific to family law. Thus, for example, when person *A* ransomed person *B*, he did so because of some already established kinship relation, which gave him not only the right but also the duty to do so. One might express the difference by saying that the verb *pādâ* places emphasis on the price to be paid in the course of a given transaction (cf. 1 Sam 14:45), whereas *gāʾal* underlines the blood tie linking the redeemer and the redeemed. A glance at the laws pertaining to *gāʾal*-redemption in the Old Testament shows how the kinship aspect is emphasized. This sort of redemption occurs in three sorts of cases:

1. Above all, there is the redemption of slaves. If an Israelite was forced to sell himself as a slave, it was the duty of his closest kin to "redeem" (*gāʾal*) him (Lev 25:47–55): "One of his brothers may redeem him, or his uncle, or his cousin may redeem him, or a near kinsman belonging to his family may redeem him" (v 48ff). In other words, the duty is incumbent upon male kin in the sequence brother, uncle, cousin, and so forth.

2. Another case has to do with the redemption of lands belonging to the kinship group (Lev 25:23–34). If poverty forced someone to sell off some of his kinship lands, then it was the duty of "his next of kin" (*gōʾēl*, v 25) to intervene and "redeem" the land in question.

3. A third case was the *gōʾēl*-redemption from widowhood. Admittedly, in this case the laws themselves use a different terminology (cf. Deut 25:5–10). But the narrative in the Book of Ruth, nevertheless, tells us explicitly how Boaz acts as the *gōʾēl* and, in doing so, thereby assumes the relative's duty to marry the widow and have offspring with her (Ruth 4).

Through its emphasis on kinship ties, *gāʾal* (and *gōʾēl*) has a warmer nuance than its linguistic cousin, *pādâ*. This is no doubt the main reason why our prophet chose as he did. Implicitly, when God acts as the *gōʾēl* and redeems his people from their Babylonian captivity, he is acting like one who intervenes in a case on behalf of his kinsman.[11] Thus it is hardly surprising that one and the same verse can describe God as both "Father" and "Redeemer" (Isa 63:16).

Among the writings of the Prophet of Consolation, two texts in particular are important for our purposes. One of these is Isa 43:1–7. Here the *gōʾēl*-liberation of slaves lies in the background. Of course the deported Israelites were just such a collection of slaves. But then God addresses the captives and says, "Fear not, for I have redeemed [*gāʾal*] you; I have called you by name, you are mine" (Isa 43:1). The juridical language is also evident in v 3: "I give Egypt as your ransom, Ethiopia and Seba in exchange for you."

We also need to pay attention to the literary genre of the section.[12] For the best perspective on this matter, we must turn to the Psalter. Any worshiper who came to the temple to pray was able to make use of developed formulas which we usually call "Psalms of Lament." Of these, Psalm 13 is a typical example. It is introduced by *(a)* a complaint about one's situation (vv 1–4), followed entirely without preamble by *(b)* a statement expressing the applicant's certainty of salvation (v 5). This structure is typical of these psalms. Scholars have suspected that between *(a)* and *(b)* a priest or cult prophet pronounced a divine promise of assistance, more or less as during our communion service when the minister pronounces the general absolution to the congregation on God's behalf in response to the general confession of sin. This divine promise of salvation (i.e., "oracle of salvation") is the corollary of the individual psalm of lament in the Psalter (cf. 1 Sam 1:17).

Scholars think they have found such oracles of salvation in the Prophet of Consolation (Isa 41:8–13; 41:14–16; 43:1–7; 44:1–5). Here we often find divine assurances such as, "Fear not, I am with you." For our purposes, note that the "oracle of salvation" typically addresses itself to the isolated individual; it corresponds to the individual psalm of lament. But in the writings of our prophet this kind of text works in a new way, as is clearly the case in Isa 43:1–7, a typical example of the genre. In formal terms, the oracle is addressed to an individual ("you"). But this individual, however, is the people of Israel (v 1). The oracle of salvation is here directed to the people of God, Israel. These seemingly trivial observations about the genre of the text open our eyes to the profundity of the thought in it: God speaks to his people Israel as if they were a single individual, and he speaks of himself as if he were this individual's close kin, its *gōʾēl!*

The second significant text is Isa 54:1–10, where we twice find the word *gōʾēl* (vv 5, 8). Here, however, there is no question of the *gōʾēl*-liberation of slaves; the underlying metaphor deals with something else:

> Fear not, for you will not be ashamed;
> be not confounded, for you will not be put to shame;
> for you will forget the shame of your youth,
> and the reproach of your widowhood you will remember no more.
> For your Maker is your husband,
> the Lord of hosts is his name;
> and the Holy One of Israel is your Redeemer [*gōʾēl*],
> the God of the whole earth he is called. (Isa 54:4–5)

Using a poetic metaphor, Israel's exile is described as her widowhood. Israel's sons had let their blood on the battlefield, so that Israel was like a childless widow. In ancient Israel, the childless widow was in a difficult situation, since the ordinary form of social security in the land consisted of the woman's husband and of the children whose duty it was to care for her in her old age.

In the verses cited above, a connecting thread links the word "widowhood" in v 4 to *gōʾēl* in v 5. The Lord intervenes and effectuates a sort of *gōʾēl*-liberation from widowhood (see above, item 3). The well-known use of the metaphor of bridegroom and bride to characterize the relationship between the Lord and Israel here undergoes an interesting variation. The Lord is not only the bridegroom but also the *gōʾēl*. The Lord saves Israel from a situation which, without his aid, would be absolutely hopeless. The Lord gives new life, new children, and a new future to his ravaged people. And this fact provides the ultimate motivation for the hymnic introduction of the text (vv 1–3).

If we look back over Second Isaiah as a whole (i.e., Isa 40—55), we see that Israel had complained about being forgotten and abandoned by her God. "My way is hid from the Lord," as 40:27 says. Further along we read, "The Lord has forsaken me, my Lord has forgotten me" (49:14). To this God is said to reply with the metaphor of a mother who cannot forget her child and with that of the lover who draws the name of his beloved in the palm of his hand (49:15–16). In Isa 50:1–3, God once again counters the notion that he could have abandoned Israel; the divorce, or so we read, was only temporary, a formal decree had not been published.

We may describe this situation thusly: against Israel's complaints of having been forgotten by her God, the Prophet of Consolation offers the portrait of a God who engages himself deeply. And the metaphorical language used by the prophet is more trenchant than that which we otherwise encounter elsewhere in the Old Testament: the picture of the mother who cannot forget her child, of the lover, and of the *gōʾēl*. This last metaphor unites feelings to actions. It speaks of the way kinship solidarity forces one to act in a situation of oppression and need. The result in this case is God's own intervention; this leads to liberation from slavery and hopelessness.

This presents us with an important problem: if the *gōʾēl* usually only acts on the grounds of an existing kinship relationship, what is the nature of this tie with respect to the Lord and Israel? Here we are automatically led to examine the other major group of "divine participles" in the Prophet of Consolation—those which speak of the Lord as Creator.

EXCURSUS 21

GOD AS "SAVIOR"

In the writings of the Prophet of Consolation, the Hebrew word *môšîaʿ* occurs 5 times. It is a form of the verb *yāšaʿ*, "to save, rescue"; to be precise it is a Hiphil participle with the meaning "he who saves, rescues."

A number of important Old Testament theological terms derive from the realm of juridical language. This is the case with Hebrew *běrît*, "covenant," a word that had a "profane" usage in contract law. Something similar applies to *môšîaʿ*. When an Israelite chanced to be the victim of assault, robbery, or some other injustice, he or she had the possibility to let out a "cry," and whoever heard it was obliged to intervene. The terminology for this cry was the verb *ṣāʿaq* and the noun *ṣěʿāqâ*. This usage is attested in Deuteronomy 22:24, 27 and in Job 19:7, among other passages. Specifically addressed to the reigning king, this "juridical cry" occurs in 1 Kings 20:39; 2 Kings 6:26; 8:3, 5.

This is where the *môšîaʿ* comes into the picture, because whoever hears such an outcry and intervenes is called the *môšîaʿ*, "the savior." It is used of *human beings* in similar sorts of contexts in Deut 22:27; 28:29, 31; and in certain passages in the Book of Judges (3:9, 15; 10:10–14; cf. also Isa 19:20 and Neh 9:27). However, the term is also used to characterize *God* as the one who intervenes and saves in response to the "juridical outcry" of the victim of violence or injustice. The occurrences in the Prophet of Consolation (Isa 40—55) are more numerous than in any other book in the Bible, as the following survey shows:

- Isaiah 40—66: Isa 43:3, 11; 45:15, 21; 49:26; 60:16; 63:8
- Remaining prophets: Jer 14:8; Hos 13:4
- The Psalter: Pss 7:10 [11]; 17:7; 18:41 [42](= 2 Sam 22:42); 106:21
- Prose literature: 1 Sam 10:19; 2 Sam 22:3

Literature: Boecker ([1964]: 61–66).

EXCURSUS 22
GOD AS "REDEEMER":
THE RELEVANT PASSAGES

One of the most important divine designations employed by the Prophet of Consolation (Isa 40—55) is *gōʾēl*, by means of which God is described as Israel's "Redeemer." The term itself has a juridical background (see above pp. 162–63).

The word *gōʾēl* is a participle of the verb *gāʾal*, "to redeem, ransom"; in its participial form it means something like "the ransomer, redeemer" (RSV: "Redeemer"). The Prophet of Consolation uses this terminology frequently, 17 times in all:

- The Prophet of Consolation uses the participle *gōʾēl* 10 times: Isa 41:14; 43:14; 44:6, 24; 47:4; 48:17; 49:7, 26; 54:5, 8.
- The Prophet of Consolation uses other forms of the same verb in connection with God 7 times: Isa 43:1; 44:22, 23; 48:20; 51:10; 52:3, 9.
- The distribution of the word *gōʾēl* outside of Isaiah 40—55 is as follows: Isa 59:20; 60:16; 63:16; Jer 50:34; Pss 19:14 [15]; 78:35; Job 19:25; Prov 23:11.

Although certain of these passages may date from the preexilic period (e.g., Prov 23:11), it is clearly in the work of this prophet that *gōʾēl* is used intensively as a divine designation. The prophet uses this terminology to speak of the way God is about to liberate Israel from her Babylonian captivity—a new exodus. Notice that other texts that characterize the first exodus, that is, the exodus from Egypt, make use of the verb *gāʾal:* Exod 6:6; 15:13; Isa 63:9; Pss 74:2; 77:15 [16]; 78:35; 106:10.

Literature: The statistics used here are based on the study of Stuhlmueller ([1970 A]: 268–71, 273–78).

GOD AS "CREATOR"

Here of course we have no intention of presenting a general treatment of the idea of creation in the Old Testament. Instead, we shall deal with the topic as to how God is characterized as Creator through the use of a variety of participles in Isaiah 40—55 and what this entails for an understanding of God. Our investigation focuses on the way the Prophet of Consolation speaks of God (1) as the Creator of humankind *and* (2) as the Creator of the *world*. Here we shall pay special attention to the important insights of Rainer Albertz ([1974]: esp. 1–53).

EXCURSUS 23
GOD AS "CREATOR"
ACCORDING TO THE PROPHET
OF CONSOLATION

The Prophet of Consolation uses participial forms of a number of different verbs to designate God as Creator:

- The verb *bārā'*, "to create," is immediately recognizable because of its occurrence in Gen 1:1, 21, 27, and 2:4. It is used in the Old Testament with God alone as subject, and no material is ever mentioned from which he creates. The prophet uses the participial form of this verb in connection with God 7 times: Isa 40:28; 42:5; 43:1, 15; 45:7a, 7b, 18.
- The verb *yāṣar* is actually a potter's term signifying "to form, fashion, shape" (Jer 18:2, 4, 6). In connection with the creation the verb occurs in Gen 2:7–8, 19. The prophet uses the participial form of the verb in connection with God 9 times: Isa 43:1; 44:2, 24; 45:7, 9a, 9b, 11, 18; 49:5.
- The verb *'āśâ* is a simple verb meaning "to do, make." The prophet uses the participle of this verb in connection with God 8 times: Isa 43:19; 44:2, 24; 45:7a, 7b, 18; 51:13; 54:5.

If we examine the materials in question thematically, we discover that the prophet speaks of God both as the Creator of men (i.e., Israel) and as the Creator of the world. These two themes occur repeatedly in two different sorts of texts:

- God is described as the Creator of humankind above all in texts that contain the promise of his salvation ("salvation oracles"): Isa 43:1, 7; 44:2; 54:5.
- God is described as Creator of the world particularly in texts whose aim is polemical ("disputations" and "trial texts"): Isa 40:12–26; 45:9–13; 48:12–15. An important text of a somewhat different character is 44:24–28.

This connection between theme and text type will prove to be an important key when we attempt to elucidate the prophet's proclamation about God as Creator.

Literature: For the statistics and a survey of the materials, see Stuhlmueller ([1970 A]: 268–71). For the relationship between theme and text type, see Albertz ([1974]: esp. 7–53).

THE CREATION OF MAN AND
GOD'S CARE

"But now thus says the Lord, he who created [*bārā'*, ptc.] you, O Jacob, he who formed [*yāṣar*, ptc.] you, O Israel" (Isa 43:1)—such "divine participles" repeatedly speak of God as the Creator of human beings in the writings of the Prophet of Consolation (cf., e.g., Isa 44:2; 45:9, 11; 49:5; 51:13; 54:5).

But what theological function do these creation expressions have in the Book of Consolation? Once again, there is help to be found in the comparative materials offered by the psalms of lament. As supplicants have done for thousands of years, so also the men and women of ancient Israel entered into controversies with their God. God was besieged with arguments as to why he should intervene in a given situation. In the national and collective psalms of lament it was common to use historical retrospects for this purpose: one pointed back to the ways God had dealt with his people in times past (Pss 44:1–3; 80:8–11). In the individual psalms of lament we find another sort of argument being used to force God to acknowledge his responsibility: the supplicant relates how he or she personally was created by God and was accordingly wholly dependent (Pss 22:9–10; 71:5–6; cf. Job 10:3, 8–12, 18).

In the work of the Prophet of Consolation we find no psalms of lament, but there is one literary feature related to these psalms—the "oracle of salvation" (which corresponds to the assurance of salvation that the priest ordinarily communicated to the supplicant). It is, above all, in such sections that the prophet speaks of God as the Creator of humankind (Isa 43:1, 7; 44:2; 54:5).

When a supplicant communicates desperation to God, she finds the ground of security to reside in one single fact: she was created by God; on this fact she can rely. And the converse is also true: when the prophet attempts to console his suffering people, he speaks from the perspective of God's relation to the people: "I have created you; this is the guarantee that I, God, will ultimately intervene."

The final implication is obvious: when the Prophet of Consolation speaks of God as "the one who created you," he is speaking of the God who from the very beginning had a special relationship to his work: God cared about and felt responsible for his creation. It is on this basis that God acts when God serves as Israel's *gō'ēl*.

169

We should keep one linguistic feature in mind. Several times we meet the expression *yōṣēr mibbeṭen* (Isa 44:2, 24; 49:5). The question is, what is the precise significance here of the preposition *min?* The compound expression has sometimes been translated "who formed you in the womb." In other words, it has been interpreted as if it dealt with a once-and-for-all action that took place in the past. It is more properly translated so as to convey an ongoing, durative sense: "the one who forms you from the womb and onwards."[13] All of human life, from the very beginning to the end, is encompassed by God's creation. The Old Testament does not distinguish, as the modern world is inclined to do, between God's creative and maintaining activity; the God who once initiated human life is also the one who through continuous exercise of his creative power maintains it.

In formal terms, the expressions in the work of the Prophet of Consolation that deal with God as the Creator of human beings seem to be directed to an individual; in point of fact, however, they are aimed at a whole people, Israel (cf. "he who formed you, O Israel," Isa 43:1). To Israel, the disaster at Jerusalem (586 B.C.E.) and the subsequent exile were a real crisis in life but also a crisis of confidence in the divine promises (i.e., of the Zion promise and the Davidic promise). Thus we observe in this prophet a strategic retreat on the theological level. He does not argue on the basis of these old promises but retracts to his ultimate stronghold: the fundamental fact of the creation. It was here that Israel was to find the new Archimedean fulcrum for her faith.

THE CREATION OF THE WORLD AND
GOD'S POWER

I have chosen to place the emphasis on the twin themes of the creation of humankind and the creation of the world.[14] In a sense these two themes belong to two different sorts of texts, and in the message of the texts they have different functions.

The creation of humankind is generally emphasized in the psalm of lament and its corresponding oracle of salvation. Its subject is God's care—his will and duty to intervene once more.

But what sort of text speaks of the creation of heaven and earth—the creation of the world? Of course we find this theme in the primeval history (Genesis 1). But the creation of the world plays an important role in other texts as well and, above all, in the Psalter. If we examine the psalms closely, we discover that they are mainly hymns (e.g., Pss 24; 104; 146; 148; Jer 10:12–16; etc.) in which the key aspect of God's being is God's power. When the Prophet of

Consolation speaks of God as the Creator of the world, it is this aspect of God which is highlighted.

Gerhard von Rad[15] once spoke of the way that faith in creation in the work of the Prophet of Consolation serves the proclamation of salvation. The prophet speaks of God's power as Creator of heaven and earth in order to create a firm foundation for his proclamation of liberation from captivity. Thus the writings of the prophet endow the motif of creation with a soteriological function: God brings salvation (*sotēria*).

This observation is both correct and important. Rolf Rendtorff[16] has added yet another useful observation. Von Rad had contrasted the proclamation of the Prophet of Consolation with that in Psalm 136. This psalm consists of two main parts: the first part (vv 4–9) speaks of the creation of heaven and earth—the world—and of the way God positions the great heavenly bodies in the firmament. The second part (vv 10–25) proceeds to something new: here we hear about God's past actions—the exodus from Egypt, the miracle at the Sea of Reeds, and the conquest of Canaan. Thus the psalm combines creation theology and salvation history.

The same combination is to be found in the work of the Prophet of Consolation, but Rendtorff has pointed to an important distinction. The distinction can be recognized when we compare Psalm 136 with one of the prophet's important texts (Isa 44), a creation text which begins:

Thus says the Lord, your Redeemer,
who formed you from the womb:
"I am the Lord who made all things,
who stretched out the heavens alone,
who stretched out the earth—Who was with me?" (Isa 44:24)

This is the introduction to the piece. But how long is the section itself? We can answer the question by noting a subtle literary detail in Israelite compositional practice: identical or similar phrases at the beginning and end of the text ("inclusio"). The words "who made all things" in v 24 recur in the text at 45:7. In addition, the entire section is framed by short hymns, consisting of 44:23 and 45:8.

Thus the complete section runs from Isa 44:24 to 45:7. The same combination of motifs occurs in this Isaiah text as in Psalm 136. After a presentation of the creation motif, the text proceeds immediately to salvation history. And here the previously mentioned distinction is evident. All indications are that Psalm 136 is a late composition, perhaps from the period of the exile. However, the psalm allows the history of salvation to conclude with Israel's entrance into Canaan. Salvation history is understood as something touching the distant past; the psalmist's own present, then, stands outside of the process.

We find something quite different in our prophetic text. Here the Lord makes fools of false prophets and diviners while he vindicates his own prophetic word (Isa 44:25–26), as we are informed by a couple of verses that briefly characterize God's salvific action in history. In this context the focus of God's activity is concentrated exclusively on the present: "[I am the Lord] who says of Jerusalem, 'She shall be inhabited,' . . . who says to the deep, 'Be dry, . . .' who says of Cyrus, 'He is my shepherd, and he shall fulfill all my purpose'" (44:26–28). The text then proceeds to describe how God is installing the Persian king in the office of shepherd.

This is the point of the text's special combination of two different units: first, a series of participles that describe God as Creator (44:24–28); second, a section in which God empowers Cyrus (45:1–7). The ascent of King Cyrus to power is an event that takes place on the stage of world history, but this event is seen from a special perspective: it is the result of the activity of the creator God. The event is made possible by the God who determines the fate of the world from its creation onwards.

For the people of God it was always a temptation to try to limit the salvation-historical perspective to the distant past, to the exodus from Egypt and the conquest of Canaan. When the Israelites glanced into the past, they saw only the great and long-gone events from which the river of time mercilessly separated them. Here, however, the Prophet of Consolation awakened the people to new insight: God not only reigns over the present but also the future! This is powerfully emphasized in Isa 43:16–21 where the prophet speaks of the liberation from Babylon as a reenactment of the first exodus. However, Israel's task is not merely to look back in time toward God's ancient intervention:

Remember not the former things,
nor consider the things of old.
Behold, I am doing a new thing;
now it springs forth, do you not perceive it?
I will make a way in the wilderness
and rivers in the desert. (Isa 43:18–19)

172

Thus the idea of God as the Creator of the world plays its own special part in the message of the Prophet of Consolation. The emphasis is upon a God who possesses power. According to the prophet, this power extends into the present as well as into the future.

We also find the same basic pattern of Isa 44:24—45:7 elsewhere in the Book of Consolation. It consists of (a) a description of God as world-Creator directly followed by (b) a characterization of the present historical events. In Isa 45:9-13 there is a "disputation," a text in which God refutes Israel's objections and doubts. The text contains several quotations of Israel's various complaints to her God (vv 9–10). But God counters these doubts via a statement about his power as Creator: "I made the earth, and created man upon it; it was my hands that stretched out the heavens" (v 12). This creation pronouncement is followed immediately by an account of what God is bringing about in the present—the work being accomplished through the Persian king Cyrus: "I have aroused him in righteousness, and will make straight all his ways; he shall build my city and shall set my exiles free" (v 13). The same pattern is repeated in 48:12–15 (cf. 40:12–26).

Finally, we need to consider one more important aspect of the creation motif. The Prophet of Consolation has something to say about the instrument through which God expresses his creative activity: God creates through his word.[17] The book is framed within two majestic statements about God's creative word. In the prologue we are told that "the grass withers, the flower fades; but the word of our God will stand for ever" (40:8). In the book's conclusion the word of God is compared with objective meteorological phenomena whose effects are well known to humankind—the rain and snow which water the earth so that it can bear fruit: "So shall my word be that goes forth from my mouth; it shall not return to me empty, but it shall accomplish that which I purpose, and prosper in the thing for which I sent it" (55:10–11). In the end of the book we have come full circle to its beginning.

God's creative word also plays an important role in Isa 44:24ff. Here we find three important formulations: "[I am the Lord] *who says* of Jerusalem, 'She shall be inhabited'"; "*who says* to the deep, 'Be dry'"; and "*who says* of Cyrus, 'He is my shepherd'" (44:26–28). The Hebrew involves a participle of the verb "to say," *hāʾōmēr*, which lends solidity and poignancy to the formulations. These formulations reveal divine commands that are immediately realized. The divine fiat—"let there be . . ."—in Genesis 1 immediately comes to mind—the primeval beginning.

Summary. We are now able to summarize our exegesis of the Prophet of Consolation who describes God as Creator (through the use of participles). (1) On one hand, the prophet proclaims God to be the Creator of humankind. With this theme the Prophet of Consolation urges faith and confidence in God: since God is Israel's Creator, he has had an obligation towards his people from the very beginning. This, too, provides the basis for God's *gōʾēl* actions towards Israel; the Redeemer (*gōʾēl*) was, after all, the close kinsman who had both the right and the duty to intervene in the event of trouble. (2) On the other hand, the prophet speaks of God as the Creator of the world. This motif occurs especially when the prophet attempts to awaken Israel to an awareness of God's potency and power. Time and again the history of salvation is brought up to date so as to include not only the present, but the future as well.

In the beginning of this book I mentioned that Claus Westermann highlighted two foci in the Old Testament understanding of God. One is the saving God who intervenes from time to time more or less "directly from above" (i.e., the "senkrecht von Oben" of Karl Barth), the God who is active in salvation history. The other focus is the creating God, the one who by his blessing manifests himself "horizontally" in the world, immanently in the course of events from one generation to the next. The former aspect is emphasized in the historical literature of the Old Testament, while the latter is exemplified by the hymns of the Psalter. In this study of the "divine participles" in the work of the Prophet of Consolation we have beheld a portrait of God in which both of these aspects are unified in such a way as to render the picture multidimensional. The central message of the Prophet of Consolation is the liberation from the bondage of the exile—salvation. This assurance of salvation, however, is guaranteed by the care and power that God has demonstrated as Creator—again and again.

9
Job and His God

Our study of the ideas of God in the Old Testament has focused on the various divine names. In this final chapter we will depart from this approach by concentrating on the way in which different views of God confront one another in the Book of Job. As such, this chapter will serve as the *fermata* for our presentation.

The Book of Job contains the most daunting poetry in all of the Old Testament. For anyone who reads the Bible, the Book of Job looms like Mount Everest. It is of course a proverbial challenge to the biblical scholar as well.[1] In each successive chapter in which Job speaks the reader has to deal with adamantine blocks of expressions about a God who destroys both the evil and the good with equanimity and who even scorns the desperation of the innocent (9:22–24). Throughout the book one often encounters sublime descriptions of the majesty of God and the insignificance of human life.

When the reader at last achieves the plateau on top of the mountain, those chapters at the end of the book in which God speaks to Job from out of the whirlwind, still new surprises are in store for her or him. The Job who has raged in his desperation against both God and humankind is answered by the deity in a form much like a two-hour lecture on major subjects of natural history and science. Thus in chapter 38 God relates how he once laid the foundations of the earth, has preserved both snow and hail in storehouses, and has bound the chains of the Pleiades. In chapter 39 God's speech resembles an inventory list from a museum of natural history, plus commentary. A God who seems to be uninterested in the needs and pains of human life speaks to Job of various animals—the hind, the wild ass, and the ostrich. In chapters 40 and 41 there is a description of two even more peculiar creatures from the animal kingdom—the hippopotamus and crocodile, which the text refers to as Behemoth and Leviathan.

175

What are these speeches, then, but an admission by God of the correctness of Job's charge. That is, they are conclusive proof of the sovereign disinterest of the deity, who in pastoral conversation with a desperate Job uses precious minutes to discuss the impressiveness of the crocodile (41:1–10) or the way the hippopotamus holds his tail (40:17)! Can such a God be taken seriously?

Nevertheless the astonished reader discovers that, in the conclusion of the book, Job seems to think that he has received some kind of answer. He has seen God "with his own eyes" (42:1–6), glimpsed that deity who elsewhere calls himself "I am" (Exod 3:14).

The Book of Job, a literary work dealing with the desperate struggle of an individual, has produced much grist for scholarly debates, journals, and commentaries. All too easily does one forget that the book concerns a mortal who wrestles with the question of God in the face of the ultimate challenges of human existence. How does that God look to the suffering and tormented human individual, Job, when he stands face to face with that God? This is the question for which we seek an answer in the Book of Job.

First of all, we will recapitulate the main features of the Book of Job.[2] The first two chapters of the book comprise a prose prologue. The Accuser (*haśśāṭān*) gets God to accept the famous bet, the purpose of which is to show whether any man exists who fears God "for nothing," rather than because of possible advantages inherent in such an attitude (1:9). Thus Job is abandoned to the hand of the Accuser and is deprived of property, posterity, and health. Job's reaction to these disasters occurs in his two confessions:

Naked I came from my mother's womb,
and naked I shall return;
the Lord gave, and the Lord has taken away;
blessed be the name of the Lord. (Job 1:21)

The good we accept from God,
should we not accept evil as well? (Job 2:10*)

This poetic work is then framed by a final narrative section, 42:7–17, where the sorely tried Job is restored by the Lord. The two prose sections (Job 1—2 and 42:7–17) thus frame a book in which the exposition exploits the expressive possibilities of Hebrew poetry to the full—the so-called dialogue section (2:11—42:6). It is introduced by a song of lament (chap. 3), in which the basic structure of the song is punctuated by the question "Why?" (vv 11 and 20). Here tormented Job curses the day of his birth: "Let that day be darkness!" (v 4).

Job's friends join in subsequently: first Eliphaz, then Bildad, and finally Zophar give a speech, each of which is answered by Job in turn. The first round is completed in chapters 4—14; the two subsequent rounds consist of chapters 15—21 and 22—31. After Job's concluding plea (31:35), a fourth friend, Elihu, appears rather surprisingly on the scene (chaps. 32—37). The friends have spoken. Job has had his say.

Then suddenly God, the subject of all previous discussion, begins to speak. He addresses Job twice "out of the whirlwind" (38:1ff. and 40:6ff.). In each case God's speech deals with subjects that on first inspection appear to have nothing to do with the disagreements between Job and his friends in the dialogue section.

The scheme of the Book of Job

1:1—2:10	*Prologue of the narrative frame*
2:11—42:6	*Dialogue section*
Chapter 3	Job curses his birth
Chapters 4—14	First round
Chapters 15—21	Second round
Chapters 22—31	Third round
Chapters 32—37	Elihu's speeches
38:1—42:6	God's two speeches
38:1—40:5	God's first speech
40:6—42:6	God's second speech
42:7-17	*Epilogue of the narrative frame*

At the risk of oversimplification it may be said that three quite different understandings of God compete with each other in the Book of Job. It is possible to speak of the "God of the friends," that is, the idea of God that emerges from the addresses of the three friends to Job. One may speak of a "God of Job," if a label is to be found for the understanding of God that can be glimpsed through Job's anguished expostulations. Finally and most significantly, there is the "God of the whirlwind," the view of God that emerges from the mysterious divine speeches in the conclusion of the book.

THE GOD OF THE FRIENDS

If one is to speak of the understanding of God in a particular biblical book, one should not draw conclusions on the basis of isolated quotations plucked out of context. Instead, it is essential to construct for oneself an overarching perspective.

One might therefore ask what the real theme of the Book of Job is. Scholars have offered numerous answers. It has been suggested that the book attempts to explain the problem of suffering: suffering is God's punishment visited upon the sinner (the view of Job's friends); it is God's pedagogical chastisement of humans (thus Elihu); or it is God's test of the seriousness of purpose of the righteous (cf. the prologue, esp. 1:9). Some have felt that the book attempts to prescribe the correct attitude for a believer who is confronted with suffering (cf. 1:21 and 2:10). Still others have maintained that the fundamental problem of the book has to do with the origin of suffering. Above all, scholars have been concerned with the role played by God in connection with human suffering: how can we harmonize the sufferings of the just with God's righteousness and goodness? Thus the American dramatist Archibald MacLeish has formulated the dilemma of the Book of Job with these alternatives: "If God is God He is not good, if God is good He is not God." Either a good God who is powerless or an almighty God who lacks love—these seem to be the alternatives.

For the moment, we will suspend our quest for the overarching theme of the book and confine ourselves to the dispute between Job and his friends (chaps. 3—37). Here the subject of the dispute seems to be the meaning of Job's sufferings. The comforters have an answer at their fingertips: Job's suffering bears witness to his sinfulness. Job himself rejects this answer out of hand.

A characterization of the God of the friends could perhaps be "Lord of retribution."[3] In this sense God's main function would consist of enforcing the law of retribution. God would be the merciless engineer of the mechanisms of divine retaliation. One scholar has termed this teaching about punishment "the theology of the natural man."[4] As such, its logic has the simple form of act and consequence. It should be noted that, in this view, retribution has a dual nature in the sense that God is thought to punish the sinner but also to reward the righteous. The duality of such retribution is expressed, for instance, in Psalm 18: "With the loyal thou [i.e., God] dost show thyself loyal . . . and with the crooked thou dost show thyself perverse" (v 25).

The understanding of Job's friends of both God and reality presupposes this principle—the act-consequence relationship. And they illustrate it with metaphors drawn from agriculture, as in the following reference to sowing and reaping:

As I have seen, those who plough iniquity
and sow trouble reap the same. (Job 4:8)

In the Hebrew text we read in Job 5:7 that man is born to trouble. In its present context this expression seems peculiar, but by retaining the consonantal text and merely altering the vocalization of a single word the passage can be taken to mean that "man begets evil." It is a result of retribution; catastrophe is the result of man's own actions:

Indeed, misfortune does not come forth from the ground,
nor does evil sprout from the earth.
It is man who gives birth to evil,
as surely as the sparks fly upward. (Job 5:6–7*)[5]

That this is the correct interpretation is supported by a passage later in the book:

They conceive mischief and bring forth evil,
and their heart prepares deceit. (Job 15:35)

Job's friends emphasize that the teaching on retribution is not their own invention; indeed, they describe the law of sowing and reaping as the conclusion of generations of experience. They repeatedly maintain that this is the result of time-honored experience and the sum of the wisdom of the fathers. Consequently, two other passages dealing with the teaching on retribution are introduced with reference to the fact that it is part of the legacy of the fathers: "consider what the fathers have found" (cf. 8:8–22; 15:17–35).[6]

The part played by this teaching in the argumentation of the friends is transparent. When Eliphaz speaks for the first time, he practically assumes that the teaching on retribution will serve to comfort Job. Job's piety was apparent both to Job himself and to others. Thus Eliphaz believes that Job has only to consider further: should not Job's piety give occasion for confidence even when an innocent man is punished (4:6–7)? Here Eliphaz argues from cause (Job's piety) to effect (Job's ultimate success).

Elsewhere, however, the tone becomes sharper as Job's friends begin to realize that his sufferings in reality are punishment for secret sins. Already in his second speech Eliphaz claims that Job is "doing away with the fear of God" (15:4). And when he resumes his discourse in his third speech, Eliphaz launches a series of accusations against Job, the burden of which is, among other things, that he must have required surety from his brother and plundered widows and orphans (chapter 22). Here Eliphaz argues from effect (Job's suffering) to a cause (Job's alleged sins).

Seen in the wider context of the total biblical message, there is something to the assertions of Job's friends concerning the laws of life—the connection between sowing and reaping. A person has responsibility for his life; thus one cannot act against all reason and simultaneously believe that in a given case God will annul the relationship between act and consequence. But in the reasoning of Job's friends one mistake is evident: they elevate the principle of retribution to a universal principle and, accordingly, in the case at hand they reason backwards from the pattern. Thus from the fact of Job's suffering they deduce that he has committed some sort of sin, even if its nature is unknown.

A close inspection of the Old Testament shows that this chain of reasoning is defective; much suffering is related in the Bible which cannot be accounted for by the simplistic pattern of the teaching on retribution. Consider Abel, the righteous man who was the victim of the first fratricide (Gen 4); Uriah, the husband of Bathsheba (2 Sam 11); or the account of Naboth's vineyard (1 Kings 21). And concerning Job, everyone who has read the prologue knows that his righteousness was unstained.

It would be appropriate to conclude concerning the God of the friends that his is a cynical calculus which metes out reward and punishment on earth according to an inflexible tariff.

To this we should add that the God of the friends is in principle a marionette, since the pattern is simply one in which humans act and God re-acts. God's activity becomes rationally intelligible; indeed, in principle it is predictable. Thus the God of the friends is in reality the prisoner of the system; this God is no longer sovereign. For this reason Job fittingly describes his friends as people "who bring their god in their hand" (12:6).

One positive thing may be said concerning the theology of Job's friends: theirs is a well-ordered world. There is one single pattern or structure permeating all existence. There is no room for chaos. Their God is the highest judge (5:8–16), with the wisdom of a judge. Thus in his first speech Zophar speaks of God's inscrutable wisdom (11:5–12), a wisdom which makes God the judge who "knows worthless men" (v 11).

THE GOD OF JOB

We shall now turn to those chapters in the dialogue section (2:11—42:6) in which Job is the speaker. Here we find the naked cry of despair, an uncensored expression of the existential experience of an individual who is possessed by the deepest angst. This is a significant aspect of the greatness of the Book of Job: questions as to the nature of existence are allowed to be posed; no effort is made to mute the shriek of desperation. Job gives voice to the whole of humanity's despair. For this reason the Book of Job has a message for each new generation; it retains its relevance. In saying this, we have also said that Job's expressions about God are to be seen in the light of Job's situation; the speeches of Job express the interpretation of existence as seen by suffering humanity.

1. God is a criminal. Job's friends argue on the basis of the pattern described by the teaching on retribution. Job's sufferings lead them to the conclusion that Job must be a sinner. Surprisingly enough, Job shares the point of departure with his friends; he seems to maintain that the teaching on retribution ought to function (see 6:24; 13:23). Job suffers but is unaware of having committed any sin. Thus the principle has failed and Job's world is reduced to a world with no functioning moral order; good is no longer repaid with good. The principle of act and consequence has gone haywire.

Because of Job's sufferings his friends conclude that he is a sinner. Job, however, draws a different conclusion. He knows that he is innocent, just as he knows that he suffers. Thus he arrives at the conclusion that God is a criminal who does violence to the law. Job says this unambiguously and, in saying it, knows that he is expressing something unheard-of:

> It is all one; therefore I say,
> the blameless and the wicked he destroys alike.
> When disaster brings sudden death,
> he mocks the plea of the innocent.
> The earth is controlled by a criminal,
> who covers the face of her judges.
> If not he, then who is guilty? (Job 9:22–24*)

This is the first characteristic of suffering Job's concept of God: God is a criminal (cf. 19:6 and contrast 34:12, 18). Job knows himself to be on the verge of blasphemy, as we learn from two other passages. First, in chapter 13, Job says to his friends:

Let me have silence, and I will speak,
and let come on me what may.
I will take my flesh in my teeth,
and put my life in my hand. (Job 13:13–14)

It is clear that Job has chosen his ground; he speaks of a legal trial between himself and God, in which he himself will emerge victorious (vv 18ff.). The last stichos in the quotation, which runs *wĕnapšî ʾāśîm bĕkappî*, has often been translated "I will put my life in my hands." We now know that this expression has its counterpart in Near Eastern legal procedure. In Babylonian legal texts we find the expression *napištam lapātum*, "to touch one's throat," "to seize one's neck," as a synonym for self-cursing.[7] As is well known, Hebrew *nepeš* may also mean "throat." Accordingly, our passage should be translated as referring to this gesture of self-imprecation. Job touches his throat. He is determined to speak, even if it should cost him his life.

Second, there is Job's lengthy oath of innocence in chapter 31. As Sheldon Blank has maintained, chapter 31 diverges from the usual pattern of Hebrew oaths.[8] In principle, the structure of an oath is composed of two elements: *(a)* if I do such and such, *(b)* may such and such a disaster strike me down. In the Old Testament, the usual form only has the first element clearly expressed; the second element goes unstated and remains implicit. Presumably the swearer would avoid mentioning the punishment to which one would be liable in the event one broke the oath. Thus in the Hebrew Old Testament we generally find phrases of the type "If I do such and such . . .," where the expression more or less hangs in the air. Such phrases are oath formulas in which the second clause (the one concerning punishment for breach of oath) is simply understood. They are generally translated "I have certainly not done such and such."

Thus the actual mention of the punishment in question would be a rare exception (cf. Pss 7:3–5 [4–6]; 137:5–6). Nevertheless, this is precisely what happens in Job 31. Job repeatedly breaks with the standard pattern and dares to express the punishment that will affect him if he actually has committed the transgression in question. Look, for example, at 31:7–8: "If my step has turned aside from the way . . . then let me sow, and another eat." Or 31:9–10: "If my heart has been enticed to a woman . . . then let my wife grind for another." The same structure recurs in 31:19–22 ("then let my shoulderblade fall from my shoulder") and 31:38–40 ("let thorns grow instead of wheat").

In brief, we observe how Job throws all caution to the wind and directly expresses the second element (the self-curse) in his protestations of innocence. His intention is thus clear: he will force God either to kill him or to admit his innocence.

Thus all the dialogues between Job and his friends focus on Job's personal suffering and the applicability of the teaching on retribution. This logic requires Job's friends to conclude that he is a sinner; the same logic requires Job to conclude that God is a criminal.

Where the friends paint a picture of God as the ice-cold mathematician who enforces the principle of retribution, the understanding of God promulgated by Job is that of an omnipotent tyrant who does violence to his own creation (10:3). At this point it is important to recall that the dialogues between Job and his friends do not represent the author's last word. Rather, this is spoken when God himself begins his address in the majestic conclusion of the work.

2. God is the absent God. Yet another feature of suffering Job's concept of God should be noted: the God of Job is an absent deity. One aspect of Job's suffering is the awareness of having been abandoned by God himself: "Why dost thou hide thy face, and count me as thy enemy?" (13:24). God has absented himself; Job's world is a world "emptied" of God: "But I go to the east and he is not there; to the west and I do not perceive him" (23:8*).

Of course, it is well known that our understanding of God and our experience of reality are interdependent; indeed, our understanding of God and of reality are two different facets of our interpretation of life. This realization leads to a third conclusion concerning Job's understanding of God.

3. God has created a world void of meaning. The world of the friends was characterized by order and system; existence revealed a fundamental pattern: the self-evident principle that good is rewarded with good and evil with evil. Their God is a God of order. Job is unable to follow them on this point. Indeed, for Job the world is without meaning, God is not a God of order, creation conforms to no moral pattern, and existence itself has no structure.

There is one passage in the Book of Job which exemplifies this view of Job's better than any other, namely, the one in chapter 3, in which Job curses the day of his birth. This text is to be read with the creation narrative in the back of one's mind.[9] The process of creation begins with the divine word of power, "Let there be light!" (Gen 1:3). In Hebrew this is *yĕhî 'ôr*. In the RSV Job's curse reads, "Let that day be darkness! . . . Let gloom and deep darkness claim it" (3:4–5). In the Hebrew text Job's first phrase is *yĕhî ḥōšek*, "Let there be darkness," unmistakably a play on the "let there be light" of the creation narrative. It is here that Job voices his nihilistic credo: if the world is like this, then it may just as well return to chaos.

Moreover, Job is also able to describe the God of his experience as his personal enemy and opponent:

> He has walled up my way, so that I cannot pass,
> and he has set darkness upon my paths. . . .
> He breaks me down on every side, and I am gone,
> and my hope has he pulled up like a tree. (Job 19:8, 10)

> Thou hast turned cruel to me;
> with the might of thy hand thou dost persecute me.
> Thou liftest me up on the wind,
> thou makest me ride on it,
> and thou tossest me about in the roar of the storm.
> Yea, I know that thou wilt bring me to death,
> and to the house appointed for all living. (Job 30:21–23)

What astonishes us here is not the fact that we find someone in the Bible who speaks of darkness and despair, for we often encounter these features in the Scriptures. No, what is astonishing is that this anguished cry of desperation takes the form of a charge against God. And it is even more astonishing that this accusing shriek of despair is allowed to stand bleak and uncensored. This, however, is a feature of the greatness of the Bible. The musical score contains other elements than just hymns to the Creator. We encounter here the appalling dissonances within the suffering creation.

These dissonances are rhetorically expressed in *ironical allusions to traditional faith*. One example of this pertains to the idea of God's care of man. The psalmist said: "What is man that thou art mindful of him, and the son of man that thou dost care [*pāqad*] for him?" (Ps 8:4 [5]). Job makes a clear allusion to this but at the same time twists the words to mean the opposite:

> What is man, that thou dost make so much of him,
> and that thou dost set thy mind upon him,
> dost visit [*pāqad*] him every morning,
> and test him every moment? (Job 7:17–18)

Where the psalmist speaks of the caring Creator, Job speaks of the fault-finding Controller. The irony is made possible by the ambiguous meaning of the word *pāqad,* "to care" and "to visit." Another example is connected with the traditional notion of the impossibility of escaping God, as in Ps 139:7–12 ("if I take the wings of the morning"). What Job says in chapter 23 about the impossibility of finding God represents a thematic inversion of this: "If I go east, he is not there; if west, I cannot find him; when I turn north, I do not descry him; I face south, but I see him not" (Job 23:8–9*). The above-mentioned reversal of the divine "let there be light" found in Job 3:4 also falls neatly into this line of examples.

Thus Job's picture of God includes the following characteristics: God is a *Deus absconditus.* God is a fearful and arbitrary despot. It remains to be seen that this understanding of God does not go un-contradicted in the Book of Job. In the last instance the reader is not compelled to choose between the cynical teaching on retribution of Job's friends and the diabolical tyrant depicted by Job. There is reason to believe, however, that Job has seen one aspect of the problem correctly. When Job accuses his friends of being people "who bring their god in their hand," this implies Job's prior presupposition of God's sovereignty. Job realizes that God is not to be manipulated: at all times God remains sovereign.

THE GOD OF THE WHIRLWIND

We have spoken of the "God of the friends" and of the "God of Job." Up to this point in the Book of Job (chap. 38), the One about whom everything is finally concerned has remained silent. But now God speaks; both Job and his friends fall silent. Twice we read, "Then the Lord answered Job out of the whirlwind"; both divine speeches begin with precisely these words (38:1; 40:6). But what does it mean that God speaks "out of the whirlwind"? The word "whirlwind" (*sĕ'ārâ*) connects the divine speeches in Job to a number of other contexts which all have something in common: they refer to a majes-tic revelation of the presence of God.[10]

The prophet Ezekiel relates such an experience. Ezekiel was among those who were victims of the first Babylonian deportation (597 B.C.E.). In his exile the prophet was cut off from Jerusalem and more precisely from the temple, the locus of God's especial Presence. But Ezekiel discovers that the God whom he once had experienced in the Jerusalem temple is also present among the deported captives. One day at a site by the river Chebar, where the Jews may have had a place of prayer (cf. Acts 16:13), Ezekiel experiences a manifestation of the presence of God:

> As I looked, behold, a stormy wind [sĕʿārâ] came out of the north, and a great cloud, with brightness round about it, and fire flashing forth continually, and in the midst of the fire, as it were gleaming bronze. (Ezek 1:4)

Both here and in similar passages God approaches humans from the midst of the whirlwind.

"Then the Lord answered Job out of the whirlwind." In this fashion these texts bear clear witness to the majesty of God's presence. This aspect is anticipated already in the conclusion of Elihu's speech, where we read:

> And now men cannot look on the light
> when it is bright in the skies,
> when the wind has passed and cleared them.
> Out of the north comes golden splendour;
> God is clothed with terrible majesty. (Job 37:21–22)

This depiction of the arrival of God accompanied by cloud and whirlwind allows us to assign the divine speeches in question to the Old Testament *theophanies*. In this connection I use the word "theophany" in a narrow sense, as a designation for passages which describe *(a)* the advent of God and *(b)* such accompanying phenomena as storm, lightning, fire, and so forth (cf., e.g., Judges 5:4–5; Pss 18:7–15; 97:1–5; 144:5–6; Isa 19:1; 64:1–3; Micah 1:3–4; Nah 1:3–5). The expressions in such passages clearly derive from the terminology for meteorological phenomena such as rain clouds, whirlwinds, and lightning.

In short, when we read that God speaks to Job "out of the whirlwind," we are to understand that the hidden God emerges from concealment and reveals himself. God manifests his presence, and this in such a way that it cannot be questioned. In other words, the absence and silence of God are not the last word of the Book of Job. Ultimately, the book deals with the *Deus praesens*, the near and present God who speaks out forthrightly in a particular situation.

THE LEGAL METAPHOR

Before we proceed to discuss the contents of the two divine speeches, it is necessary to underline an important thread in the warp and woof of the Book of Job. The book repeatedly plays on the metaphor of a legal confrontation between Job and God. Job announces again and again during his addresses to his friends and erstwhile comforters that he intends to take God to court in order to prove his innocence with respect to God. This is especially prominent in chapter 13 (vv 3, 18, 22ff.). Thus it is hardly surprising that Job's final plea after the third round concludes as follows:

> Oh, that I had one to hear me!
> (Here is my signature! Let the Almighty answer me!)
> Oh, that I had the indictment written by my adversary!
> (Job 31:35)

The conclusion is inescapable that in the Book of Job there is a *juridical pattern* of sorts, as above all Othmar Keel and Veronika Kubina have clearly demonstrated. Both of the divine speeches play on this basic pattern in the dialogues between Job and his friends.[11] Therefore, the second divine speech begins as follows:

> Then the Lord answered Job out of the whirlwind:
> "Gird up your loins like a man;
> I will question you, and you declare to me.
> Will you even put me in the wrong?
> Will you condemn me that you may be justified?" (Job 40:6–8)

Job, it must be remembered, had launched *two accusations* against God. According to one, God is a criminal (*rāšā'*) in his dealings with the world (9:24). Thus God takes up this challenge in the speech cited above, as he quotes Job with the words "Will you condemn me?" that is, "declare me to be a criminal [*rāšā'*]?" In short, Job discovers that his opponent takes the floor to defend himself.

This is the situation already in the first of the divine addresses, which is introduced in a similar fashion. Job had admitted the truth of creation but additionally claimed that God had made a world without order or meaning. Thus Job says that the day of his birth might just as well revert to the primal chaos (3:4). In this manner Job questions God's plan of creation. Accordingly, in the introduction to the first divine address God "quotes" this accusation. One should perhaps translate this passage so that the reference is plain. The RSV speaks of God's "counsel" (38:2), but the *'ēṣâ* of the Masoretic text is more correctly rendered by "world design," "creation plan":

> Then the Lord answered Job out of the whirlwind and said,
> "Who are you to call my world plan ['*ēṣâ*] darkness,
> speaking thus without insight?

187

Gird up your loins like a man:
I will question you, and you shall answer me." (Job 38:1–3*)

In other words, the Book of Job is internally coherent; the divine speeches refer back to Job's accusations and deal with them:

Speech 1: deals with Job's charge that the world is meaningless; Job has described God's plan of creation as darkness (Job 38:2; cf. chap. 3).

Speech 2: deals with Job's charge that God is a criminal (Job 40:8; cf. 9:24).

This means that the divine speeches are to be understood as God's defense pleas in the trial to which Job has summoned God. God answers! It is therefore interesting to observe how Job reacts to the divine speeches. Each of them is concluded by Job's again taking the floor.

After the first divine speech Job confesses *qallôtî*, "I am too unworthy" (40:4). The basic sense of the verb *qālal* is probably "to be light." I personally think that the verb is here used with the conscious intention to express a distinction between human beings and God; mention is made in a number of theophanic contexts of the "glory" of God. The word *kābôd* is used to this end, a word which is derived from the verb *kābēd*, "to be heavy." Such use of *kābôd* in theophanic contexts is attested in a variety of contexts (Exod 33:18–23; Pss 29:3; 97:6; and Ezek 1:29 [28]). Thus, confronted with the presence of God, which is to say, with the "glory" (*kābôd*) of God—although this term nowhere appears in the divine speeches in Job—the sufferer announces his *qallôtî*, "I am too light, too unworthy." Job realizes that he is teetering on the edge of the abyss that divides a human being's insignificance from the majesty of God.

Job adds a few more words to his confession:

I lay my hand on my mouth.
I have spoken once, and I will not answer;
twice, but I will proceed no further. (Job 40:4–5; cf. 42:5–6)

In short, after God's defense speech, Job declines to press his accusation; he "abandons the floor." After God has spoken, Job has nothing more to add.

These observations give rise to an important conclusion: *Job feels he has indeed been answered by God*. If this supposition is correct, then the divine speeches in the Book of Job are of crucial significance for our understanding of the book in its entirety, since it is at this point that Job realizes how the pieces of the puzzle of existence unexpectedly fit together and form a meaningful pattern. Moreover, it is here

that the reader of the Book of Job arrives at a corresponding realization, that the book begins to cohere as a meaningful whole.

Of course, some scholars have regarded the divine speeches as
additions to the Book of Job, that is, as poetic ornaments of some
beauty but with no significant content. This notion will now be seen
to be absurd. The juridical thread running through the book is so
pervasive that the divine speeches have an obvious and original
place within the ensemble; indeed, they provide the "answer" to the
riddle of the book: God's intentions in responding to Job's address.
The exegete who closes her or his eyes to the divine speeches and
regards them as mere poetic digressions, or else as later additions to
the book, has thus effectively renounced the possibility of forming, if
only at the surface level, an impression of "the book of the ways of
God."

What Do the Divine Speeches Tell Us about God?

In my introduction to the Book of Job, I likened it to an imposing
mountain which confronts the would-be climber with practically in-
surmountable obstacles. We have at length reached the top: the divine speeches of the Book of Job, the sublime highpoint of the work.
Thus we are in a position to say what these divine speeches tell us
about the God of the whirlwind, or, more precisely, how they serve
to answer the pleas of Job uttered in the course of the dialogues with
his friends. After all, Job does receive an answer to his addresses; the
question is, what answer? It is essential to recognize that this is the
decisive question confronting any serious attempt to deal with
the message of the Book of Job. If one goes off course here, then one's
orientation in relation to the book as a whole is seriously skewed.
The reverse is also true, in that a meaningful answer to this question
provides a point of departure from which a panoramic view of the
book can be formed.

At the outset the reader is shocked, since the divine speeches have a
rather surprising content. The answer God returns to Job is by no
means a simple and univocal explanation of the mysteries of existence;
there is no obvious "solution" to the problem of Job's suffering. Instead, God provides what has been called "drei Stunden Naturkunde
für Hiob," that is, a three-hour lecture on natural science to Job. God
treats the despairing sufferer to a lengthy exposition on geology, as-
tronomy, and zoology. But this is precisely the point! We have to deal

with a theology of creation. Here it is impossible to examine all the peculiarities of the two divine speeches. It is instead preferable to discuss their central character, if we are to arrive at an understanding of their message, that is, to understand what Job seems to have experienced as a "divine answer" in the deepest sense of the phrase.

The First Divine Speech:
The Divine Order of Creation

Job had concluded that in the last analysis human existence is without meaning. In the darkness of his suffering he felt himself to be more closely related to chaos than to God's creation (chap. 3). Thus the sufferer had indirectly characterized God's plan as darkness, as God implies when, by way of introduction, he starts from Job's discourse and more or less cites Job's accusation (38:2).

Accordingly, if we read the first divine speech attentively, we discover that it in fact does offer an answer to this charge of Job: our world is not possessed by chaos and darkness because in the last analysis it rests in the palm of its Creator. As Robert Gordis has maintained, the author here draws *an analogy between the natural and the human worlds.* On this analogy, the natural world is characterized by beauty and order; this is correspondingly true of the moral universe of humankind.[12]

In Job 38:4–7 God describes the creation as a well-planned structure. God has laid both the foundation and the cornerstone of the earth; he has determined the measurements of creation. Thus to the eye of the reader the creation emerges as an architectural masterpiece of which God himself is both architect and engineer:

> Where were you when I laid the foundation of the earth?
> Tell me, if you have understanding.
> Who determined its measurements—surely you know!
> Or who stretched the line upon it?
> On what were its bases sunk,
> or who laid its cornerstone,
> when the morningstars sang together,
> and all the sons of God shouted for joy? (Job 38:4–7)

Against Job's experience of existence as fragmentation and chaos, God opposes the architecture of the creation. God has determined the measurements of the earth, established the paths of the planets, and formulated the laws of nature (cf. 38:33). The world God has bequeathed to human beings has both pattern and meaning.

The next section, chapter 38:8–11, is one of the most important segments of the first divine speech. Its theme is captured with the phrase "God subdues the sea." Among the ancient neighbors of Israel we frequently encounter the conception of a divine battle with the forces of chaos, where the latter bear such designations as sea, stream, dragon, and so forth (see above Chapter 6). This motif occurs in the Babylonian creation narrative and in the Canaanite Baal myth, known from the finds at Ras Shamra/Ugarit on the Syrian coast (see Chapter 4). In the poetic literature of the Old Testament, and not least in the psalms, we often find a corresponding chaos symbolism in which the waters of chaos play a major part as God's opponents. In all cases we encounter expressions that describe the majesty and might of God by drawing a contrast with chaos. A single example will suffice here:

> Yet God my King is from of old,
> working salvation in the midst of the earth.
> Thou didst divide the sea by thy might;
> thou didst break the heads of the dragons on the waters.
> Thou didst crush the heads of Leviathan. (Ps 74:12–14)

Unsurprisingly, this description of a chaos battle transmutes into a song of praise to God as Creator:

> Thine is the day, thine also the night;
> thou hast established the luminaries and the sun. (Ps 74:16)

In Psalm 74 we encounter such designations as "the sea," "the dragon," and "Leviathan"; however, God's opponent also bears such other titles in the Old Testament as "the serpent" (Isa 27:1) and "death" (Isa 25:8). Furthermore, the passages that refer to this struggle between God and his opponents are legion; thus the conception of the battle between God and the forces of chaos was well known to the author of the Book of Job (7:12; 9:8, 13; 26:5–14; cf. 3:8).

The section in the first divine speech (Job 38:8–11) deals with the sea as a symbol for the power which is hostile to God; Job is informed that God has closed "doors" upon the sea and that he has marked off "bounds" for the waters. God is even able to speak of a time when he

> prescribed bounds [*ḥōq*] for it,
> and set bars and doors,
> and said, "Thus far shall you come, and no farther,
> and here shall your proud waves be stayed." (Job 38:10–11)

Here creation is no unorganized chaos; rather, God has set limits to chaos. Here we glimpse an important theme which is in fact the structural foundation of the theology of creation presented in Old Testament wisdom literature: God's limits and laws, the divine ordinances of creation.[13]

The passage in question employs the word *ḥōq* to describe the limit set for the waters by God in order to protect the creation. The word *ḥōq* is in general most at home among the juridical vocabulary of the Old Testament, where it usually signifies "law," "statute" (Gen 47:26; Exod 12:24). The same usage occurs in several other passages in which mention is made of the order of creation. Like Job 38, a number of passages speak of setting limits to the waters:

> when he assigned to the sea its limit [*ḥōq*],
> so that the waters might not transgress his command. (Prov 8:29)

> I placed the sand as the bound for the sea,
> a perpetual barrier [*ḥōq*] which it cannot pass. (Jer 5:22)

It would be appropriate to compare these passages with the beginning of Psalm 104, in which the earth is threatened by the *tĕhôm*-deep (v 6) until God sets a boundary against the waters (here: *gĕbûl*), so that they will be unable to threaten the earth again (v 9).

But the word *ḥōq* meaning "law" or "statute" designates not only the boundary set by God against the waters, but also the laws describing and regulating the movements of the heavenly bodies. Psalm 148 contains a good example. The psalm is introduced by an injunction to the sun, moon, and stars to praise the Lord. We subsequently read,

> And he established them for ever and ever;
> he fixed their bounds [*ḥōq*] which cannot be passed. (Ps 148:6)

The Book of Jeremiah provides us with two more examples. In Jer 31:35 we read that God "gives the sun for light by day and the fixed order of the moon and the stars for light by night." The following verse describes this arrangement as "this fixed order"; here the text uses the plural of *ḥōq*. A closely related word occurs in Jer 33:25, where we find a reference to God's covenant with day and night as "the ordinances of heaven and earth." In this context the word for "ordinances" is *ḥuqqâ* in the plural. God's ordering of the universe is also referred to in Job 38:

> Do you know the ordinances [*ḥuqqâ*, pl.] of the heavens?
> Can you establish their rule on the earth? (Job 38:33)

Thus, in spite of all of Job's complaints, a principle of divine order does in fact permeate all of creation; human beings are not left alone as helpless prey of the chaotic powers of darkness and the waters. As long as the earth shall endure, a bright ray of hope will continue to penetrate the darkness, one that is also visible in the blessing of God upon all that grows and sprouts:

While the earth remains, seedtime and harvest, cold and heat, summer and winter, day and night, shall not cease. (Gen 8:22)

Yet another perspective emerges from the biblical references to the order of creation; human sin tilts this divine order out of balance. Thus human sin is represented as an attack upon the vital nerve of creation itself. Jeremiah 5 contains a passage which describes God as the one "who gives the rain in its season, the autumn rain and the spring rain, and keeps for us the weeks appointed for the harvest." The text then continues,

Your iniquities have turned these away,
and your sins have kept good from you. (Jer 5:25)

It would be appropriate to compare this passage with another, whose import is ultimately eschatological; I am thinking of a passage in the "Isaiah apocalypse" (Isa 24—27). The content of this passage has been much discussed; however, I am personally inclined to think that it describes how mankind in its sinfulness does violence to the divine order of creation, that order which otherwise provides divine protection against the forces of dissolution:

The earth mourns and withers,
the world languishes and withers;
the heavens languish together with the earth.
The earth lies polluted under its inhabitants;
for they have transgressed the laws,
violated the statutes, broken the everlasting covenant.
Therefore a curse devours the earth,
and its inhabitants suffer for their guilt;
therefore the inhabitants of the earth are scorched,
and few men are left. (Isa 24:4–6; cf. vv 19–20)

Summary. A number of Old Testament passages describe how God has built his ordinances into the creation. In such passages the Hebrew text generally uses *ḥōq*, a word associated with juridical usage and whose basic meaning is "law," "statute." It is used to characterize God's laws directing the movements of the heavenly bodies. The word is similarly employed in Job 38:10 of God's "boundary" against the threatening chaos-sea.

Thus the first divine speech in Job clearly speaks of God, a God who created the world just as an expert engineer erects a structure according to precise calculations (Job 38:4–7). Moreover, this is a God who has been engaged ever since the beginning of the world in a struggle with the anti-divine powers who despise God's creation (Job 38:8–11). There are, in other words, anti-divine forces, but God is not a passive observer of their ravages. Against the distorted picture entertained by Job in his desperation—according to which God is an omnipotent despot who scorns suffering humanity—the divine speeches reveal the concept of a God who set bounds and statutes already at the creation. This Creator God provides the cosmos with a bulwark against chaos. The Creator God is a God who subdues and at last expels the powers of darkness.

The same theme is also visible in the following section of the divine speech. Suffering Job had voiced an ambivalent attitude toward the world. On the one hand, Job's world was one in which he could never be certain that he would not be attacked, as he thought, by God. On the other hand, this presumably hostile God was strangely intangible and evasive. Job attempted to summon God to appear in court but could not find him; thus Job's world was, so to speak, "emptied" of God. The first divine speech offers something of an antithetical image of this conception. When everything is regarded from the perspective of the creation, it is immediately obvious that God is everywhere evident. Moreover, the sovereignty of this ever-present God emerges against the dark background of the existence of an anti-divine evil. God's opponent, however, can never be sure that he will remain untroubled by this ever-present God; the power of darkness has no protected haven. Thus God is able to enquire of Job:

> Have you entered into the springs of the sea,
> or walked in the recesses of the deep?
> Have the gates of death been revealed to you,
> or have you seen the gates of deep darkness? (Job 38:16–17)

God's creation may rest secure in the knowledge that the power of God extends even as far as the gates of the underworld: "Sheol is naked before God, and Abaddon has no covering" (Job 26:6; cf. Prov 15:11; Deut 32:22). This same certainty resounds in Psalm 139:

> Whither shall I go from thy Spirit?
> Or whither shall I flee from thy presence?
> If I ascend to heaven, thou art there!
> If I make my bed in Sheol, thou art there!
> If I take the wings of the morning
> and dwell in the uttermost parts of the sea,
> even there thy hand shall lead me,
> and thy right hand shall hold me.
> If I say, "Let only darkness cover me,
> and the light about me be night,"
> even the darkness is not dark to thee,
> the night is bright as the day;
> for darkness is as light with thee. (Ps 139:7–12)

Accordingly, the first divine speech has to do with the God who from the moment of creation is involved in a struggle with the powers that are hostile to him. This implies that there are some aspects of existence that are not actually, or not yet, subject to the Lord. But in Job 38:23 there is the suggestion of a viewpoint which assures us of God's ultimate victory; when this verse refers to what God has reserved "for the time of trouble, for the day of battle and war," it points forward to that final day when God will reduce the power of death to nothing forever (cf. Isa 25:8; 27:1).

The Second Divine Speech: Behemoth and Leviathan

If the foregoing observations are correct, then the first divine speech plays an important role in the work as an answer to Job's accusation against God that the world behaves as if it were a meaningless chaos. Accordingly, we turn now to the second divine speech (40:6—42:6) to see whether this speech, too, has a meaningful function within the compass of the book.

We begin with the introduction to the speech where God asks Job,

Will you even put me in the wrong?
Will you condemn me that you may be justified? (Job 40:8)

Already here God responds to Job's charge that he is a criminal (9:24); the main purpose of the whole second divine speech is to demonstrate the unreasonableness of this charge.

What does God have to say in his defense? Strangely enough, God speaks of two animals, two monstrous beasts designated Behemoth and Leviathan, respectively. If one carefully reads the description of these creatures in the Book of Job, then one readily concludes that the hippopotamus and crocodile were the models for the portraits of Behemoth and Leviathan (see Figure 15). It is also evident that this description does not merely intend to inform the reader of a number of zoological details, since, like the first divine speech, the second also has a deeper dimension.

We turn first to the hippopotamus, Behemoth. The name itself is a plural form of the Hebrew word *běhēmâ*, "creature." We here have an intensive plural signifying "the beast par excellence." We may assume that we are confronted in this creature with an Old Testament prototype of the beast in the Book of Revelation (Rev 13, Greek *thērion*). But why was the hippopotamus, of all creatures, chosen as a

FIGURE 15
SCENES FROM THE TEMPLE
OF EDFU

Job 40—41 speaks of how God subdues both Behemoth and Leviathan, that is, the hippopotamus and the crocodile. Egyptian temple reliefs offer a good explanation of the choice of these two animals in particular. In Egypt they represented the forces of chaos. We see above two scenes from the temple in Edfu. The god Horus (towards the middle) and the king (flanking) pursue both the crocodile (left) and the hippopotamus (right), that is, the same combination of animals as the one in the Book of Job! (From E. Chassinat, *Le temple d'Edfou*, vol. 3 [Cairo, 1928] fig. 82.)

model for Behemoth? Eberhard Ruprecht and Othmar Keel have tendered an interesting answer.[14]

It seems that in the Egyptian narrative of the battle between the god Horus and the evil god Seth the latter becomes transformed into a hippopotamus. The narrative ends when Horus harpoons his opponent and is subsequently proclaimed king. All of these events are related in Papyrus Beatty no. 1; yet another text, inscribed on the walls of the huge temple of Horus in Edfu, depicts the cultic drama enacted at this sanctuary. This cultic drama was performed on the sacred lake in Edfu. In the course of the drama, Horus harpoons Seth, who was symbolized for ritual purposes by a hippopotamus-shaped cake. After his triumph Horus becomes king of Egypt.

As far as I can see, these texts strongly imply that in the second divine speech Behemoth stands for the same chaos powers to whom allusion is already made in the first divine speech. Thus the question addressed by God to Job, "who can catch him . . . who can pierce his nose with a snare?" is purely rhetorical. Job is forced to recognize that even if no human is able to deal with the forces of darkness, there still exists one who is able to do so: God.[15]

The remainder of the second divine speech (41:1ff. [40:25ff.]) deals with Leviathan. This name is constructed from a Semitic verb whose basic sense is "to twist," "curl," "coil." Superficially at least, the description has to do with the crocodile. But in order to understand this part of the second divine speech, it is important to recall that Leviathan is the name of a monster that figures in several Old Testament descriptions of the battle between God and the forces of chaos (see esp. Ps 74:14 and Isa 27:1; cf. also Job 3:8; Ps 104:26). Accordingly, when God mentions Leviathan in the course of his second address to Job, there are echoes of the description of how God subdues the sea in 38:8–11. The diabolical aspect of Leviathan is expressed in the description of him as a fire-spouting dragon (41:18–21). Furthermore, the text in 41:25* [17] says quite literally, "When he raises himself up, the gods are frightened." God further says to Job of this unconquerable monster,

Will you play with him as with a bird,
or will you put him on a leash for your maidens? (Job 41:5* [40:29])

Of course, Job is unable to do this, but again the question is a rhetorical expression of the fact that God is able to do so; God is the one who is able to play with Leviathan. The same expression recurs, for example, in Ps 104:26; where the NEB correctly translates, "Leviathan whom thou hast made thy plaything."

If this understanding of the second divine speech is correct, then this speech propounds the same message as the first. It emphatically depicts the monstrous and diabolical character of evil. The hippopotamus and crocodile have been chosen as appropriate symbols to express this aspect of existence. The existence and activity of the dark forces is thus underlined by means of a symbolic language that is ultimately realistic with respect to the bitter facts of existence. Nevertheless, the center of gravity in this speech does not reside in the trial of strength aspect, but in the relationship between forces: Behemoth and Leviathan are employed as frightening symbols for

the sinister powers of existence.[16] But in the last analysis human beings are not subject to these threats to the creation, since God is
represented as the most powerful.

I perceive that the Behemoth and Leviathan designations in Job are
used in a broad sense. Similar designations of the chaos-monster
are used elsewhere in the Old Testament as code-names for the great
political powers in the contemporary life of the biblical author (e.g.,
Isa 30:6–7; Ezek 32:2; Ps 68:30 [31]).[17] This is probably not the case in
Job, where these designations more likely refer to the ultimate reality
of evil. That is, they serve as symbols for the anti-divine power that
manifests itself at various times and in various ways and that underlies all of the various concrete manifestations of evil.

SUMMARY

We encounter three quite different portraits of God in the Book of
Job. Job's friends paint a picture of God as the ice-cold engineer who
enforces the steely mechanisms of retribution. To Job's friends the
world is an ideal and just arrangement; they do not seem to be conscious of the reality of the dark powers.

Job himself, by way of contrast, has something different in mind.
Like his friends, he regards evil as something sent by God. But since
Job knows that he is righteous, his suffering is proof of pure capri-
ciousness on God's part. Suffering Job understands God as a devilish
tyrant who scorns the extremity of his creation. However, Job, too,
seems not to be conscious of the perspective revealed by the divine
speeches.

Seen from the vantage point of the divine speeches, we realize that
both portraits of God are fallacious; and when Job is confronted face
to face with God, he discovers that God is different from what he
had imagined. Faced with the "God of the whirlwind," Job is compelled to learn two lessons which, taken together, make up an Old
Testament gospel. In the first place, the fact of evil is not to be de-
nied; the author of the Book of Job is a realist in this respect. In
the second place, the evil present in the world is not an aspect of the
nature of God. God is, to the contrary, the good Creator who defends
his creation against the threats of the powers of chaos. The Creator is
on the side of his creation; the cosmos is by no means abandoned to
the ravagers.

In my opinion one should avoid the simplistic alternatives dualism and monism (see Glossary) when discussing the theology of the Book of Job.[18] Indeed there are several features pointing in different directions. The prologue to the work in fact contains two expressions that at first sight might be taken to imply monistic understanding. One of these is the phrase, "The Lord gave and the Lord has taken away; blessed be the name of the Lord" (1:21); the other is, "The good we accept from God, but should we not accept evil as well?" (2:10*). These words bear witness to the exemplary attitude of righteous Job when exposed to suffering; they are in reality a confession of the sovereignty of God. As Frederik Lindström has recently maintained, it would be absurd on the basis of these two expressions to conclude that the Book of Job promulgates a monistic theology, that is, that God is behind all the evils of existence.[19] As we have contended, the entirety of the Book of Job is to be evaluated in the light of the divine speeches—they provide us with the "answer" of the book. This answer deals with the God who created the world and who does not abandon it to the unlimited ravages of evil forces.

In Old Testament creation theology we find a continuum. At one end stands the full-fledged combat motif in Psalm 74, at the other Genesis 1 with its idea of creation through an unchallenged word of God. The divine speeches in Job take a place somewhere in between. In the first speech God "closes" doors upon the sea, marks off "bounds" for the waters and visits the gates of death. In the second he subdues Behemoth and Leviathan, who have the dimensions of mythic monsters. The theology is thus antagonistic. God is depicted in his trial of strength with the sinister forces. At the same time it is said expressly that Behemoth is a created being (Job 40:15, 19; on Leviathan cf. 41:33 [25]). Nevertheless, it seems clear that God as the preserver and protector of his creation has a more important place in the author's agenda than the question of the ultimate origin of evil.

The question may be posed as to whether it would be possible to reduce the understanding of God in the Book of Job to a simple formula. If we reexamine the prologue (chaps. 1—2) and the divine speeches, we discover a profound connection between them with respect to their understanding of God. The two scenes in heaven in the prologue describe how the "sons of God" approach the Lord; that is, God is in the midst of his heavenly council. In an extended sense, God figures as *King* in these two sections. We happen to know that God is described as King in the Old Testament in many ways. He is not always described as a king sitting on his throne (on the enthroned God, see Chapter 7); rather, we repeatedly find the picture of God as *the warring King* (i.e., the chaos battle motif; see Chapter 6). For our purposes, note that it is precisely this aspect which is expressed in the divine speeches. Thus we conclude that while they speak of God in quite different ways, the prologue and the divine speeches fundamentally express the same monarchic conception of God. It is of no account that God is not expressly designated "King," since he is King nevertheless in the Book of Job. Therefore, the understanding of God expressed by the Book of Job is intelligible in the light of the rest of the Old Testament.

We have reached the end of our peregrination through what is perhaps the most singular book in the Old Testament, one which relates how Job is liberated from his fallacious conceptions of God, from his fearful nightmares, so that he is at last able to exclaim,

I had heard of you by hearsay,
but now my own eyes have seen you. (Job 42:5*)

10
Concluding Reflections

The God of the Bible is the one who cannot be confined to the material form of a cast or graven image and who cannot be named except in figures of speech. Symbolic language is the mother tongue of faith (Gustaf Aulén), and the various divine names are symbols. What does this mean? I shall use an illustration to show what I mean. The human ear is able to perceive sounds ranging between 20 hertz (the low register) and up to about 20,000 hertz (the highest tones). As we grow older, our tone scale decreases somewhat; we gradually lose our ability to perceive the highest frequencies where, for example, the singing of the cicadas is to be found. Let us imagine that we constructed an electronic instrument capable of producing tones in the range from 60,000 to 80,000 hertz and we then composed music for this instrument. A concert of such music would be inaudible to the human ear; the music would be nonetheless real, but it would remain beyond the capacities of our senses to perceive. In order to make the music accessible to people, it would be necessary to transpose it to frequencies which we could hear.

What occurs in the Bible's metaphorical language is a similar kind of transposition of "the heavenly music." The biblical names of God are symbols. On the pump-organ of human language, these symbols perform the music that speaks about God. The symbols are not a direct reproduction of the original tones, but are a downward transposition with a supposedly analogical relationship to them. The symbols are names that speak of the Ineffable through categories deriving from the world of human experience.

We have seen how "the God of the fathers" designates God as a close associate and relative, as the head of the family, who wanders with his people and who accompanies them with his protective presence. Here human relations at the level of the family have provided the model. Such familial relationships also come into play when the exilic Prophet of Consolation calls God the "Redeemer" (*gō'ēl*).

Certain other designations were ultimately borrowed from the background of the national administrative and executive hierarchy. This is the case when God is called "the King" or when God is conceived of as YHWH Sabaoth who is enthroned upon the cherubim.

In our introductory chapter we defined the concept of God as consisting of God's (a) qualities, (b) actions, and (c) radius of action. Our study of the most important divine names in the Old Testament shows that the ancient Israelites reflected only slightly about God's *qualities*. God's *actions*, however, were much more important to them. God wages war against the powers of chaos; seizes power as King and reigns; and rules as YHWH Sabaoth. God intervenes as the Redeemer and so liberates his people. God leads his people and accompanies them.

If we inquire into the radius of God's activity, it is clear that this extended from the individual and her or his life ("the God of Abraham") to the nation, then to the entire earth, and, finally, to the universe—here the latter dimensions are encompassed by such designations as "the King" and "YHWH Sabaoth." The activity of God in nature is only visible in God's creation battle, although this concept is also expressed differently in other parts of the Old Testament (e.g., Hosea 2). Then there is God's activity in history. This aspect is important in connection with several of the divine names, above all with "the Lord Sabaoth" and the conception of his divine decree; but it is also significant in connection with "the King" and "the living God."

In our study of the understanding of God, two matters deserve further comment. First, there is the matter of divine *immanence* versus divine *transcendence* (see the Glossary). In the Old Testament God's proximity to the world is never such that one could speak of immanence in the narrow sense. God does not dwell in the sun, the stars, the rain, or the wind. Not even the passages that expressly speak of God's dwelling in the temple on Zion (1 Kings 8:13; Pss 24:7–10; 132:13) describe an unsophisticated or undifferentiated concept of immanence. On the contrary, the Old Testament emphasizes God's exaltation above worldly matters—transcendence. Of all the divine names, perhaps "the Holy One" best expresses this aspect; it is not for nothing that this title is related to the conception of God as a royal sovereign, as expressed in names like "the King" and "YHWH Sabaoth."

Certain names emphasize God's exaltedness and sovereignty. By the same token, other names stress God's nearness and personal engagement: for example, "the God of the fathers," "the Redeemer" (gōʾēl), and "the Savior" (môšîaʿ). Especially these last two names speak of how God intervenes in his world. The Old Testament opposition to deistic notions is clear: the emphasis on transcendence never transmutes into the notion of a God who in exalted dispassion leaves the world to its fate. Rather, God reveals himself and periodically intervenes in world affairs.

Second, there is the matter of *dualism* versus *monism*. It is evident that a dualistic tendency is present in the New Testament (God versus the satanic powers). Some scholars have maintained that the Old Testament understanding of God is monistic—the Israelites are supposed to have held that both good and evil came from God. However, Lindström's analysis (1983) of the Old Testament passages that have usually been taken to point in this direction (e.g., Isa 45:7; Amos 3:6) shows that this conclusion is untenable. Our own study of the divine names shows that a strongly dualistic tendency manifests itself here, too. We have noted that God, conceived of as "the King," is the warring God who struggles against the forces of chaos. This concept was especially associated with one of Israel's most central institutions—the temple—so that it cannot be dismissed as a marginal phenomenon.

The divine names are indeed symbols. The inventory of symbols changed from time to time in a continuous dialogue with the challenges of experience. Israel's own social existence was among the important contributing factors in this process. This seems to have been the case in connection with the God of the fathers. Similarly, the situation of the exilic captivity no doubt contributed to the Prophet of Consolation's choice of "the Redeemer."

The conceptual world of the Canaanites has also been a catalyst for important developments in Israelite religion. A number of Canaanite texts provide us with important and suggestive hints about the background of such divine names as "the living God" and "the King." At the same time, our knowledge of Canaanite literature and culture provides us with a much clearer idea of which religious developments are specifically Israelite. The arguments in Chapter 4 indicate that one should avoid the temptation to oversimplify the problem of "Israel versus Canaan" by forcing a choice between unbroken continuity and stark contrast. In spite of the fact that the traditional solution to this problem has emphasized the distinctiveness of the two cultures and their corresponding conceptual worlds, the evidence suggests a more complicated picture of the religious development of ancient Israel. One must be careful not to disregard, for example, features of the period of the judges and early monarchy which clearly suggest continuity (as is indicated by the personal names compounded with "Baal"), while at the same time, it should be recognized that subsequent historical developments in Israel's faith display an increasing tendency toward contrast.

One final reflection on the nature of Israelite faith is in order. The study presented above suggests a historical reality that is in many ways parallel to the emergence and development of Christianity. While Christianity took root as a Jewish sect (continuity), it soon acquired a distinctive identity of its own (contrast). In the same way, the faith which would eventually become uniquely Israelite broke away from its original West Semitic religious moorings. If one examines all of the extant literature and archaeological evidence with the help of currently available critical tools, it is difficult to avoid the conclusion that the essential characteristics of the faith of Israel did not suddenly appear in full form. The distinctive features of Israel's confession of faith around the time of the exile are, in fact, the result of a sculpting process which spans several centuries. Of course, those who believe that the God of the Bible is the Lord of history may well have some inkling of who has wielded the sculptor's hammer and chisel.

EXCURSUS 24:
GOD-LANGUAGE AND GENDER

Ancient Israel was a patriarchal society. This fact certainly helps to explain why the God-language of the Hebrew Bible is male oriented (i.e., androcentric). In a language that possesses two genders of nouns, pronouns, and verbs, the masculine form is invariably used of YHWH. Furthermore, the metaphors applied to God are also androcentric: God is denoted as the King on his throne, as the divine Warrior, as the Shepherd, the Father, and so forth. What does this imply for our understanding of the Israelite concept of God?

In order to answer this question intelligently we must make a distinction that is hard to express in English terminology: the distinction between *the mental concept* of God ("Gottesvorstellung") and *the express form* in which this concept is communicated in texts, iconographic representations, rituals, and so on ("Gottesbild"). Take an example from Egyptian religion: the goddess Hathor may be depicted as a woman, a cow, a lion, or as a woman with a bovine head. These are different symbolic representations of the mental concept of the goddess; we must not ascribe to the Egyptians the idea that Hathor was a woman with a cow's head. Similarly, when the Old Testament texts mention God's "hands" or "eyes," we designate this as an anthropomorphic (i.e., human-like) representation. However, such representations may be symbolic adumbrations of a *Gottesvorstellung* (mental concept) that is much more sophisticated than this. This may be seen in Ezekiel's report of his inaugural vision. Here the prophet makes clear that there is no one-to-one relationship between the elements in his vision and those in his report. (Note the use of the word *dĕmût* in the approximate sense of a comparative preposition in Ezek 1:5, 10, 16, 22, 26, 28; this usage is also found in Ps 58:4 [5]; Isa 13:4; and Dan 10:16.)

So far we have devoted our attention to the symbolic representations of the God of Israel. Now, however, the issue of sexual politics requires us to pose the question of the relation of androcentric God-language to the *Gottesvorstellung* behind these various representations. This problem will not somehow go away if we simply characterize the metaphors about God as "mere symbols." Symbols are semantically active; they call to mind numerous ideas and project upon the primary subject numerous associations and implications.

In the ancient Near East, particularly in Mesopotamia and Canaan, the various deities were often depicted as active sexual beings. In this connection it is sufficient to point to such couples as Dumuzi and Inanna, Tammuz and Ishtar, Baal and Anath. In these mythologies the sexuality of these gods is one of their most notable characteristics. In Israel, by way of contrast, matters were different. Whatever we conclude about the date of the emergence of Israelite monotheism, it is nonetheless difficult to prove that *official* Yahwism ever had room for the idea of a divine couple, that is, for the idea that YHWH had a consort. In fact, it seems to have been the case that when the tension between Yahwism and Baalism increased, the result was merely a heightened awareness of the fact that the God of Israel is one. And in the Priestly creation narrative (Gen 1:1—2:3), when this one and only God creates human beings "in the image of God," this formulation is immediately followed by the statement that God created them "male and female" (Gen 1:27). Being created in the image of God is not regarded as a privilege that is restricted to the male half of humanity. The logical implication of this would seem to be that God was conceived as standing above the genders of the created world, that is, that God was held to be asexual. In passing, one should be aware that the notion that the Israelites may have imagined God to be androgynous is entirely without foundation.

What are we then to say about the presence of androcentric language about God? By way of analogy I will use a handy distinction in current linguistics. In linguistic studies, it is common to speak of semantic entities as "marked" or "unmarked." For example, the word "tigress" is marked in that it denotes the feminine individual of a certain species. The corresponding word "tiger" may be used in opposition to the feminine "tigress," in which case it then denotes a male individual of the same species and may be said to be "marked" from the point of view of gender. However, "tiger" may also be used of any member of the species, whether male or female, and in this connection the word is unmarked as to its gender. Thus the word may be either marked or unmarked.

Although the analogy offered here may not be perfect, we must raise the question as to whether certain scholars have not unduly neglected the possibility that superficially androcentric metaphors may be used without any underlying intention to make a statement about the gender of the deity. Such metaphors may be thematically neutral with respect to gender.

Thus when God is denoted as "father" in such passages as Jer 3:19 or 31:7–9, the metaphor does not seem to be oriented towards the issue of divine gender, but towards the role that God plays in such texts. When God liberates his people from bondage and allots them their inheritances, he is acting like a father.

This use of the word "father" may be compared with a feature in certain Northwest Semitic inscriptions. In one of these, King Azitawadda says that "Baal made me a father and a mother to the Danunites" (KAI 26 A I 3, ANET, p. 653), after which the text proceeds to tell about his care for his people. In another text King Kilamuwa says that "I, however, to some I was a father. To some I was a mother. To some I was a brother" (KAI 24:10–11, ANET, p. 654), as a result of which the people were disposed towards him "as an orphan is to his mother." In a third text we find a proper name that means "Baal is my mother" (KAI 155). In these texts the terms "father," "mother," "brother," and "orphan" are metaphors, and in the present contexts they are clearly neutral as to gender. Otherwise, we should be forced to conclude that the two kings in question were hermaphrodites.

A similar observation may be apropos of Second Isaiah's language about God. The use of the male metaphor of the Divine Warrior is a prominent feature in this corpus (cf. Isa 51:9—52:12; see Mettinger [1986]). However, the very same prophet also uses female language of God: "Can a woman forget her sucking child, that she should have no compassion on the son of her womb? Even these may forget, yet I will not forget you" (Isa 49:15). Moreover, just after one of the Divine Warrior passages, God says that "now I will cry out like a woman in travail" (Isa 42:14).

One might also consult the Song of Moses in Deuteronomy 32. Here we find a number of androcentric metaphors for God; God is represented as "father" (v 6), as the supreme King, who allots portions to his people (vv 8–9), and as the Divine Warrior (vv 22–23, 40–42). On the other hand, the same poem applies the thoroughly feminine metaphor of birth pangs to God: "You were unmindful of the Rock that bore you (*yĕlādĕkā*), and you forgot the God who suffered travail to bring you forth (*mĕḥōlĕlekā*)" (v 18*). Neither set of metaphors seems to lend itself to any generalizations about the poet's understanding of the divine gender.

Concluding Reflections

For obvious reasons, it is impossible to interview the psalmists and prophets to whom we owe the biblical texts. Were we able to do so, however, the more reflective of them would probably tell us that God is neither male nor female, that God is above and beyond that distinction, and that the divisions of gender belong to the created world. What is at stake in texts that use metaphors of the sorts mentioned above is not divine gender. Rather, the point is the necessity to express certain aspects of God's being, such as his care, protection, compassion, and so forth. Some of these traits are best expressed by metaphors deriving from human females, others by metaphors derived from males of one and the same humanity.

Since it is clearly idolatrous to attempt to confine God to the material form of a cast or graven image, so it would also be idolatrous to try to confine God with human, gender-related language. God is above and beyond; the images and symbols should remain what they are: not solid prison walls, but the fragile stained-glass windows of transcendence.

Literature: P. Trible (IDBSup: 368–69; and 1978); Ph.A. Bird (1981); P.D. Hanson ([1982]: 83–106 and 136–47); F.R. McCurley ([1983]: 74–123); R.R. Ruether ([1983]: 47–71); and U. Winter (1983).

Notes

CHAPTER 1. THE DIVINE NAMES: MILESTONES IN SALVATION HISTORY

1. Black (1962). Cf. also McFague (1983) and esp. Martin Soskice (1987).

2. When discussing notions of God, we should always be aware of the difference between the mental ideas (the actual beliefs) of a certain individual or group and the representations of them in texts, rites, and artifacts. Anthropomorphic representations may stand for notions that are much more sophisticated than has commonly been held. Cf. Olsson (1983) and, below, Excursus 24.

3. For two other recent attempts to find a structure for the presentation of an Old Testament theology, see Sæbø (1977) and Veijola (1983). For a thorough discussion of various contributions to the current debate, see Reventlow (1985).

4. Note Anderson (1962 B), who also makes a selection.

5. ANET (60–61) and NERT (82).

6. McBride (1969: 73).

7. On names and the symbolism of names in the OT, see Grether (1934: 1–58), Fichtner (1956), Barr (1969), and van der Woude (THAT II: 937–39). Cf. also Gerhardsson (1958: 15–22) and Kjær-Hansen 1982: 100–105).

8. The name Nabal has been discussed by Barr (1969: 21–28) and Stamm (1980: 205–13).

9. See de Vaux (1978 vol. 1: 199) and Thompson (1974: 43).

10. For the following, see Mettinger (1982 B: 124–32 and 32–36 with literature).

11. The asterisk throughout indicates the author's translation of a biblical citation.

12. See Weiser (1950).

13. Galling (1956).

14. On the expression "in the name of Jesus," see Hartman (1973).

CHAPTER 2. THE GOD WHO SAYS "I AM": THE RIDDLE OF THE NAME YHWH

1. For surveys of research, see Mayer (1958) and Kinyongo (1970). Some recent studies with particularly good grasp of both sources and secondary

literature are those of de Vaux (1978 vol. 1: 338–57) and Freedman—O'Connor (the article on YHWH in TWAT/TDOT).

2. On name redactions in the OT see Delekat (1971: 37–55). The substitution of "Elohim" for "YHWH" in Pss 42—83 is made clear by a comparison of Ps 14 and Ps 53.

3. On the treatment of the name "YHWH" in the Qumran texts, see Howard (1977) and Fitzmyer (1979: 126f.). On the role of kyrios in the original Septuagint, see Pietersma (1984).

4. On the role of the divine name in early Judaism, see among others Dalman (1898: 146–91) and Marmorstein (1968: 17–145).

5. On this general attitude of utmost reverence towards the divine names, see the literature in note 4.

6. See Cullmann (1959: 195–237), Hahn (1974: 67–132), and Fitzmyer (1979: 115–42).

7. On the oldest Christian confession, see, e.g., Kelly (1960: 1–99) and Gerhardsson (1985).

8. See the literature mentioned in note 6. On the Septuagint, see note 3.

9. On Exodus 3 and 6 see esp. Childs (1974), W.H. Schmidt (1974: 100ff.), and Terrien (1978: 106–19).

10. On these personal names, see Noth (1928 = 1980: 101–14) and Norin (1986). The names of Moses' mother, Jochebed (Exod 6:20), is a debated but by no means impossible case.

11. See, for instance, W.H. Schmidt (1977: 123–29).

12. Zimmerli (1969: 11–40).

13. See Budde (1905: chap. 1). There is now an extensive literature on this issue; cf. de Vaux (1978: 330–38) with references. A sober discussion is found in Axelsson (1987: 48–65).

14. See now esp. Axelsson (1987: 48–65).

15. See Emerton (1982 A).

16. For the texts, which are from the temples in Soleb and Amara West, respectively, see Giveon (1971: 26ff. and 74ff.). For the grammatical construction see Görg (1976 :10f.).

17. For a different opinion, see Astour (1979).

18. See Görg (1976).

19. On Moses and Midian, see de Vaux (1978: 330–38). The present writer is less hesitant than de Vaux towards the Kenite-Midianite hypothesis.

20. On Exod 18:12, cf. Cody (1968).

21. For references to previous research, see esp. Mayer (1958), Kinyongo (1970), and de Vaux (1978: 338–57).

22. For references, see M. Weippert (1980: 249 b). On the patristic material, see also Rose (1978: 6–16) and Freedman—O'Connor (1982: 542).

23. See Huffmon (1965: 64, 72).

24. Rose (1978).

25. At this stage the three letters of the name were all consonants, according to Rose (1978: 30).

26. See Jaroš (1982) and Zevit (1984).

27. See Emerton (1982 A) and Dever (1984).

28. The final *he* is a *mater lectionis* (vowel letter) and was not part of the name from the beginning. As we shall see, this name is made up by a form of the verb for "to be." This interpretation, however, has been questioned by, for instance, Delekat (1971) and Sæbø (1981). For a survey of the epigraphic occurrences, see Freedman—O'Connor (1982: 536–39). The occurrence on the Moabite Stone may be irrelevant to the question as to whether the long or short orthographic form is the more original one; see Rose (1978: 27–30 with note 98).

29. For references, see de Vaux (1978: 344).

30. References in de Vaux (1978: 345f.). Cf. Knauf, VT 34/1984: 467–72. Knauf assumes a basic sense "to blow."

31. Cf. the Septuagint, which reads: *kai egō ouk eimi hymōn.*

32. See von Soden (1964), de Vaux (1978: 346–57), and H.-P. Müller (1981).

33. See Huffmon (1965: 64, 72) and de Vaux (1978: 348).

34. See Cross (1973: 60–71) and Freedman—O'Connor (1982: 545–48).

35. See note 33.

36. On Exod 3:14, see most recently Wambacq (1978) and esp. the survey by Caquot (1978).

37. On this stylistic figure, which is to be regarded as an *idem per idem* construction rather than as a case of paronomasia in the strict sense of the word, see Vriezen (1950), Wambacq (1978), Lundbom (1978), and Kilwing (1979).

38. See Shild (1954), Lindblom (1964), and de Vaux (1978: 349–57). Cf. Eissfeldt (Kleine Schriften 4/1968: 193–98). This interpretation was suggested already in the nineteenth century by A. Knobel and E. Reuss; see Lindblom (1964: 9).

39. Cf. the remarks made by Hidal (1985: 54f.).

40. See Albrektson (1968).

41. See McCarthy (1978: 316f.).

42. Hebrew *kî* is usually used in such passages in order to introduce the explanation; cf. Exod 2:22, etc.

43. See Delitzsch (1905: 50).

44. See Hehn (1913: 242). Cf. also von Soden (1964: 178).

45. See H.-P. Müller (1981, esp. 317–27).

46. See Euting (1891: nos. 156 and 472). This Nabatean name seems to have the same grammatical structure as the above-mentioned name from Ebla. It is the merit of Cazelles (1978: 43f.) to have called attention to this name. According to Cazelles, however, the element in question in such Nabatean names has got nothing to do with a Semitic verb for "to be." Cf. Knauf (1984).

47. For other observations supporting such an identification, see Hammond (1980).

48. For such divine names in pre-Islamic Arabia, see esp. M. Weippert (1980: 251). From ancient Greece we know of an *EI*, which can mean, among other things, "you are"; it was inscribed at the entrance of the Delphic temple of Apollo. See Plutarch, De EI apud Delphos, Moralia III.

49. See von Soden (1964: 179, 182f.) and Müller (1981: 314).

50. Note "Horeb" in v 1 (cf. Deut 1:2, 6, 19; 4:10, 15; etc.), "a land flowing

with milk and honey" vv 8 and 17 (cf. Deut 6:3; 11:9; 26:9, 15; etc.) and "a good (and broad) land" v 8 (cf. Deut 1:35; 3:25; Josh 23:16). Such features indicate that the tradition behind Exodus 3 was handed down by Deuteronomistic circles; see W.H. Schmidt (1974: 135–44).

51. For a survey of the question of Israelite monotheism, see Lang (1981: 47–83). Lang dates the definitive breakthrough to monotheism to the exilic era (73–78).

52. Cf. also such instances as Gen 2:5 and Prov 13:19.

53. Cf. also Isa 48:12; 51:12; 52:6; and Deut 32:39. In Isa 45:18–19, it is the formula *ʾănî YHWH* that is being rendered with *egō eimi*.

54. See G. Klein (1902: 31–56), Stauffer (1957: 130–46) and Zimmermann (1960).

55. See the passage *mâ ništannâ* at the very end.

56. See *m. Sukka* 4–5.

57. The change of *ʾănî hû'* into *ʾănî wĕhû'* was probably a deliberate variation made to protect the holiness of this formula of revelation. Compare the custom of "swallowing" the divine name YHWH (*b. Qidd* 71a), which has been taken as an attempt to avoid the precise pronunciation.

CHAPTER 3. THE GOD OF THE FATHERS:
DIVINE DESIGNATIONS IN THE
PATRIARCHAL NARRATIVES

1. For surveys of research, see Weidmann (1968), Westermann (1975, esp. 94–123), McKane (1979: 195–224), and Wenham (1980). Of works that give overall presentations of the religion of the patriarchs, see esp. Cazelles (1966: 142–55), de Vaux (1978: 161–287, esp. 267–87), W.H. Schmidt (1983: 10–27), and Axelsson (1987: 105–12). Note also Koch (1988: 9–31) and M. Köckert, Vätergott und Väterverheissungen. Eine Auseinandersetzung mit Albrecht Alt und seinen Erben (FRLANT 142). Göttingen 1988 (Vandenhoeck).

2. See, for instance, Wenham's discussion (1980: 177–83).

3. With the "patriarchal period" I refer to a real period which we cannot date in absolute terms, but which falls before the definite settlement of the tribes in the country; cf. Westermann (1981: 74).

4. See Thompson (1974: 17–51).

5. Thompson (1974: 43).

6. See de Vaux (1978: 200–209). Note also Otzen's fine discussion (1977: 68–95).

7. Alt's important paper from 1929 is easily accessible in Alt (1953: 1–78, German version) and Alt (1966: 3–77, English version).

8. Maag (1980: 111–44, 150–57, and 258–67).

9. See Noth (1928: 66–82) and Albertz (1978: 71–77).

10. Thus Müller (1980: 120). Several scholars have assumed the sense of "relative," "kinsman," in this divine name. For criticism of that contention, see Hillers (1972).

11. A comprehensive monograph on the idea of the personal god in the ancient Near East is available in Vorländer (1975, on the religion of the

patriarchs, 184–224). On the personal god, cf. also Hirsch (1966), Cazelles (1966: 142f.), Ringgren (1969: 20), and Jacobsen (1976: 145–64).

12. Albertz (1978: 77–91). Cf. Blum (1984: 499–501).

13. Cf. Galling (1928), Hoftijzer (1956), Tengström (1976: 102–62), Rendtorff (1977), and Blum (1984).

14. Alt (above note 7) and Westermann (1976 A: 92–168 and IDBSup 690–93).

15. Westermann (1976 A: 18–26).

16. Maag (1980: 260–61).

17. For such curse-rites, see Mettinger (1976: 222–23) with references to texts and literature.

18. On this promise, see esp. Preuss (1968) and Vetter (1971). Cf. also Albertz (1978: 81–87).

19. On the motif of blessing, see Blum (1984: 349–59).

20. See Miller (1984).

21. Cf. Lewy (1934: 50–56).

22. See de Vaux (1978: 191, cf. 199).

23. See, for instance, de Moor (IDBSup 928–31) and Kinet (1981), both with references to relevant literature.

24. Cross (1973: 1–75). Note esp. Cross's emphasis on the double character of El as not only king but also patriarch (41).

25. For a study of "El Elyon," see Lack (1962), who stresses, however, Israel's autonomy in its use of this name (58, 64).

26. Alt (above note 7) and Schmidt (1983: 15–20).

27. Cross (1973: 1–75).

28. See Roberts (1972), Cross (1973: 13–14), and Edzard (1976).

29. Here I should like to call attention to some circumstances, which do not seem to have been noticed in this connection: the relation between the use of "El" as a theophoric element in certain proper names and the use of a kinship term in the same function (see above p. 56). Names containing a kinship term and names with El/Il(u) are analogous insofar as (a) these theophorous elements are connected with the same predicates and (b) the charts depicting the chronological development of these two groups of names are strikingly similar: they show an early floruit, possibly at the presedentary stage of the clan group, and then a gradual decrease in frequency. Cf. Noth (1928: 66–101, on point *a* esp. 69 and 92, and on point *b* esp. 88, 90, and 93). Such observations seem to indicate proximity or even the identity of the worship of the God of the fathers and the El piety that we find in sources outside the OT.

30. On El Shadday, see esp. Cross (1973: 52–60), Weippert (1976 A), Koch (1976), de Vaux (1978: 276–78) and Knauf (1985).

31. See Cross (1973: 53).

32. For a survey, see Weippert (1976 A).

33. See Bertram (1959).

34. See, for instance, Cross (1973: 52–56) and Weippert (1976 A: 877–78). For a different interpretation that derives the element *šadday* from a West

Semitic word for "field," viz. Ugaritic *šd* and Hebrew *śādeh* respectively, see Loretz (1980 B) and Wifall (1980).

35. The presence of *šdyn* (a plural meaning "Shadday-beings") in combination 1 line 6 in the Deir Alla inscriptions has been understood along these lines. See McCarter (1980: 57) and Hackett (1984: 85–89). Note the same plural in Job 19:29.

36. See Bailey (1968) and cf. Ouellette (1969) and de Vaux (1978: 277). The latter two scholars understand "El Shadday" as "El of the plain," "El of the fields."

37. See esp. Koch (1976, esp. 316–32).

38. The question of how we are to understand the historical connections between the worship of the God of the fathers and that of YHWH has been discussed by Hyatt (1955) and Rendtorff (1975: 161–65).

39. Weippert (1976 B: 131) notes these specific features and adds: "This allows us to assume that we are dealing with a divinity of the Hadad; or if you will, the Baal type" (my translation).

40. Thus Roberts (IDBSup 257 b).

CHAPTER 4. SOME BACKGROUND:
GODS AND MYTHS IN CANAAN

1. Cf. above Chap. 3 note 23. The standard edition of the Ugaritic texts is now Dietrich—Loretz—Sanmartin, Die keilalphabetischen Texte aus Ugarit (KTU). A handy tool is Gibson (1978), where one finds text and translation arranged in parallel columns. Selections of texts in translation are to be found in ANET (129ff.) and NERT (185ff.). For presentations of Canaanite religion, see Gese (1970) and Ringgren (1973: 124–76). The people of Ugarit do not seem to have used the term "Canaanites" of themselves. Nevertheless, it seems justified to see the Ugaritic texts as representing the Canaanite world of ideas. For the above presentation of the myths, I follow the arrangement of the tablets suggested in KTU.

2. See esp. Koch (1979). Cf. also Schmidt (1961) and Mullen (1980: 1–110).

3. See esp. Schmidt (1963) and de Moor (1971). Cf. also Gibson (1984). Barstad's argument on the dying and rising god in the ancient Near East (see Barstad 1984: 148–51) is hardly convincing in reference to Canaan.

4. Mendenhall (1962), Gottwald (1979). Ahlström (below note 5), and Lemche (1985) talk of evolution. For a discussion marked by critical distance towards Mendenhall and Gottwald, see Halpern (1983: 47–63).

5. Particularly Ahlström has stressed this aspect in a number of studies. See most recently Ahlström (1984: 10f.; and 1986).

6. Fritz (1987). According to Fritz, "the objects of the early Iron Age indicate complete dependence on the culture of the Late Bronze Age" and "this continuity is best explained by intensive prolonged contact with the Canaanite culture" (97). On the other hand the architecture of these early Iron Age settlements shows a clear break over against the LBA settlements to an extent that makes it impossible to believe that the population derived from

certain groups from the cities (97). Tadmor (1982) has drawn attention to another important case of discontinuity. Among the numerous finds of clay plaques with the image of a naked woman she finds two separate groups. One of these displays a reclining woman and depicts a *human* figure. This group shows a continuity from the Late Bronze Age into the early Iron Age. The other group depicts a woman standing upright with turned-out feet and with symbols of Canaanite religion (the genuine "Astarte plaque"). This group seems to have been discontinued from the period of the Israelite settlement on (171).

7. Note, however, Miller (1985: 212).

8. On the background of the veto on images, see now Dohmen (1985: 237–77) and see also Mettinger (1979).

9. KTU 1.5.V.18–22 (Gibson 1978: 72). Cf. also KTU 1.10–11 (Gibson 1978: 132f. and Kinet 1981: 83f.). For the *hieros gamos* motif in connection with El, see KTU 1.23 (Gibson 1978: 123–27).

10. On the whole complex of problems, see U. Winter (1983).

11. On the notion of man as the image of God, see among others Mettinger (1974) and Bird (1981). On the rôle and status of the woman in the primeval history, see Mettinger (1978). On these two topics see now G.A. Jónsson, *The Image of God. Genesis 1:26-28 in a Century of Old Testament Research* (ConB OT Series 26). Stockholm 1988 (Almqvist).

CHAPTER 5. "THE LIVING GOD"

1. Schmidt (1983: 156–63) is a welcome exception. Some important contributions are those of Kraus (1967) and the comprehensive monograph by Kreuzer (1983).

2. During the time down to the exile, Israel counted the beginning of the year from the great festival in the autumn.

3. KTU 1.5.VI.9–10 (Gibson 1978: 73).

4. KTU 1.6.II.30–37 (Gibson 1978: 77).

5. KTU 1.6.III.20–21 (Gibson 1978: 78).

6. See Excursus 11. Text and translation in Attridge and Oden (1976). Note esp. § 6. On the Baal epithet *adn* in the Ugaritic texts, see Loretz (1980). For a survey of Phoenician religion, see Gese (1970: 182–203). Against Barstad (1984: 150) I consider Baal to be a dying and rising god. The contrast between life and death is basic to the myth.

7. Widengren (1955: 62–79).

8. See the text-critical apparatus in Biblia Hebraica.

9. I regard Hosea 1:10—2:1 [2:1–3] as an introductory summary of 2:2–23 [2:4–25].

10. Cf. above Chap. 5, the first section, and see KTU 1.6.III.8–9 (Gibson 1978: 77).

11. See Kraus (1967: 182). On the sleeping God, see now also Batto (Bib 68/1987: 153–77).

12. See von Soden (1964: 181).

13. See Kreuzer (1983: 356–70). In an attempt to trace the lines back to Egypt rather than to Canaan Kreuzer emphasizes that the OT oath "by the life

of God" has a counterpart in Egypt (300–14) but none in Ugarit (326). Note, however, that the OT hints at an oath by (the life of?) Baal; see Jer 12:16.

CHAPTER 6. THE LORD AS 'KING':
THE BATTLING DEITY

1. I have borrowed the term "root metaphor" from the philosopher Pepper (1942: esp. 84–114). Cf. also the special issue of the Journal of Mind and Behavior (vol. 3 no. 3, summer 1982), and note Black (1962: 239–41) and McFague (1983: 23–29).

2. Of previous discussions of the subject, note esp. Mowinckel (1922), Eissfeldt (1928), Alt (1953: 345–57), Gray (1956 and 1961), Schmidt (1961), Lipinski (1965), Gray (1979), Dietrich (1980), Mettinger (1985), and Jörg Jeremias (1987). For a thorough discussion of the whole complex of questions related to Mowinckel's theory of a festival celebrating the enthronement of YHWH, see Cazelles (1960).

3. See Rost (1960).

4. See Mettinger (1982 A: 128–35).

5. Maag (1980: 11–28).

6. Thus Schmidt (1961: 22).

7. KTU. Cf. above Chapter 4, note 1.

8. See esp. Stolz (1970: 66; and 1982: 85).

9. The relevant passages in *Enuma Elish* are I.71–77 and VI.57–72 (ANET 61f. and 68f.), where temple building follows upon theomachy. For the similarities between Enuma Elish and the Baal cycle, see Kapelrud (1960). The question of a possible historical connection is problematical; see Day (1985: 11f.). On this mythopoetic pattern, see esp. Cross (1973: 162f. This line of research goes back to Mowinckel (1922; NB before the discovery of Ugarit!) with an important supplement in Gray (1961). A popular presentation is available in McCurley (1983). Extensive discussions of the motif of God's battle against chaos are found in Stolz (1970: chapters 1–2), Day (1985), and Kloos (1986). Neither of these last-mentioned scholars seems to be quite aware of the importance of the configuration of battle-kingship-temple.

10. KTU 1.5.I.1–2 (Gibson 1978: 68). Cf. KTU 1.3.III.38–45 (Gibson 1978: 50), where the "dragon" is also mentioned. The Ugaritic counterpart of Hebrew *liwyātān* ('Leviathan') seems to have been vocalized *litānu*; see Emerton (1982 B).

11. See Ringgren (1981) and Metzger (1984). Some scholars are hesitant to assume a connection between battle and creation in the OT, namely, McCarthy (1967), Vosberg (1975: 24–57), and Saggs (1978: 53–63). This is a position that I cannot share. Some studies of OT creation theology that again stress the role of the battle motif in this context are those of Anderson (1967) and Hermisson (1978, now reprinted in Anderson's collection of essays on creation 1984: 118–34). Hermisson contrasts the wisdom literature (with its conviction that chaos has been eliminated once and for all by God's victory at creation) with the psalms of the temple literature (which reflect the experience that chaos is constantly threatening to overwhelm the creation).

12. For a study of *gāʿar*, "to rebuke," see Caquot in TWAT/TDOT.

13. Note also the beginning of the same psalm (Ps 104:5–9) and see Mettinger (1985: 35).

14. On the question as to whether there is a connection between the battle motif and creation already in the Ugaritic texts, see now esp. Cross (1976: 333f.) and Grønbæk (1985). This is still a moot point.

15. On this theology, in which the temple is the institutional center and the idea of YHWH as King is the ideological focus, see esp. Keel (1978 A: 111–76), Mettinger (1982 B), and Levenson (1984 and 1985: 89–184).

16. Cf. Roberts (1973) and Kraus (1979: 94–103).

17. See Mowinckel (1922), Schreiner (1963), Roberts (1982), and Mettinger (1982 A and 1982 B).

18. See, for instance, KTU 1.101.1–3. On Mount Zaphon and Baal, see Clifford (1972: 57–79); and on Zion and Zaphon, see ibid. (131–60).

19. Cf. Ps 29:3–9 (YHWH's seven thunders) and Ps 18:13–15 [14–16]. On Ps 29, see Day (1985: 57–61).

20. For a study of this motif, see Bach (1971).

21. For a discussion of this issue, see Stolz (1970: 72–101), Roberts (1973: 337f.; and 1982: 102), and Day (1985: 125–40).

22. On the background and implications of this fairly late development (the time around the exile), see Mettinger (1982 B: 67–77, esp. 72ff.). For a minute discussion of exodus texts containing the battle motif, see Norin (1977) and Day (1985: 88–101). For a study that compares the different OT presentations of the exodus miracle, see Scharbert (1981).

23. In Isa 51:9–11 the chaos battle points forward to the proclamation of the kingship of YHWH in 52:7. Both passages belong to the same composition, viz. Isa 51:9—52:12. See Mettinger (1986).

24. See von Rad (1962 vol. 2: 133–37, German; English version 1975 vol. 2: 119–25).

25. See Mowinckel (1922) and, for a modern study in English developing this perspective, Gray (1974).

26. For the following see, above all, Wildberger's commentary (1978), the paper by the same author (1979: 274–84) and Day (1985: 142–51).

27. See 1 Enoch 60:24; 2 Baruch 29:4; and the Fourth Book of Ezra 6:52.

28. See Wildberger (1979: 274–84) and Greenspoon (1981).

29. See Hanson (1983: 369–401).

30. Kee (1968). See also Caquot's article on *gāʿar*, "to rebuke," in TWAT/TDOT.

31. See esp. Beskow (1962: 67–70).

CHAPTER 7. "THE LORD OF HOSTS":
THE REGNANT GOD

1. von Rad (1962 vol. 1:32, German; English 1975 vol. 1:19). In the following presentation, I build upon my previous works, Mettinger (1982 A and 1982 B), where the reader will find ample references to literature.

2. Mettinger (1982 B: 11–17).

3. On the occurrences in Jeremiah, see Mettinger (1982 B: 62–66).

4. On the connection between the Sabaoth name and the temple with its cherubim throne, see Mettinger (1982 A: 111–23; and 1982 B: 19–37). Of the previous contributions to the iconography of the temple, that of Keel (1977) should be singled out for particular mention. Among recent works on the temple theology, note Levenson (1984; and 1985: 87–184). An extremely valuable discussion of the representations of thrones in ancient Near Eastern art is that by Metzger (1985).

5. Eissfeldt (1966: 116–19).

6. See now Mettinger (1982 A: 113–16 with literature) and Metzger (1985 vol. 1: 259–79).

7. A different interpretation is advanced by Metzger (1985 vol. 1: 309–67), whose opinions on this point I am unable to share. According to Metzger the cherubim in the temple are standing on their hind legs, carrying a (not represented) plate, on which there is a (not represented) throne (cf. Ezek 1:22–26). My above interpretation is based on the closely related Canaanite material, while Metzger builds on more remote parallels.

8. See Mettinger (1979) and Dohmen (1985: 236–77, esp. 245–51).

9. For the following, see Mettinger (1982 A: 121).

10. See Mettinger (1982 A: 123–28).

11. On the heavenly council, see Miller (1975).

12. See Mettinger (1982 B: 19–37).

13. On this terminology in Isaiah, see Fichtner (1951).

14. See Albrektson (1967: 68–97).

15. For what follows, see esp. Wildberger (1963 = 1979: 75–109), an important paper that was overlooked by Albrektson. Cf. also Dietrich (1976), Saggs (1978: 64–92), and, on the Israelite conception of history in general, van Seters (1983: 237–48). Note also Hermisson (1985).

16. Würthwein (1954: 58–63).

17. Wildberger (1963: 101 = 1979: 93), my translation.

18. My discussion of the cornerstone passage is based on Wildberger's commentary (1982: 1063–82). See now also Roberts (JBL 106/1987, 27–45).

19. Johnson (1972: 49), my translation.

20. Cf. Wildberger (1963: 108 = 1979: 100).

21. On the milieu that Shiloh offers, see Mettinger (1982 A: 128–35).

22. See Mettinger (1982 A: 134ff.).

23. See Gottwald (1979 esp. parts 9–11).

24. On the theology of the Davidic-Solomonic empire, see Roberts (1976 B).

25. See the discussions in Klein (1978) and Veijola (1982).

CHAPTER 8. GOD AS "REDEEMER,"
"SAVIOR," "CREATOR":
THE DIVINE DESIGNATIONS AS USED BY
THE PROPHET OF CONSOLATION

1. Introductions to the situation and theology of the Prophet of Consolation are available; see Preuss (1976) and Whybray (1983), with ample references to

literature. On those passages in Isaiah 42, 49, 50, and 53 that for almost a century have been singled out for special treatment as so-called Servant Songs, see Mettinger (1983), where I explain why I find the theory of "Servant Songs" unnecessary and impossible. Among the more outstanding recent commentaries are Westermann (1966 in German and 1969 in English) and Bonnard (1972).

2. For a survey of the various divine names in the Prophet of Consolation, see Bonnard (1972: 499ff.).

3. In this figure I include some cases of the suffix form.

4. Stuhlmueller (1970 A: 48). A special investigation of the "divine participles" is available in a Dutch dissertation by Dijkstra (1980); see the review by Whybray (Bibliotheca Orientalis 38/1981, 677–79). I was not aware of Dijkstra's work when I wrote the present chapter. Our approach seems fairly different, although we agree in our basic conclusions.

5. On the theology of the exilic period, see esp. Klein (1979) and Raitt (1977).

6. For a fine study of these promises and the crisis due to the exile, see Bright (1977).

7. See the paper by Kapelrud (1977).

8. See esp. Lindström (1983: 178–99 and 214–36).

9. See Anderson (1962 A) and Stuhlmueller (1970 A: 59–98).

10. On $gō'ēl$, see esp. Stamm (1940: 27–46) and Stuhlmueller (1970 A: 99–131).

11. The personal relation comes to the fore in the fact that in nine cases out of ten in the Prophet of Consolation the word $gō'ēl$ carries a suffix, usually in the second person: "your redeemer." See Stuhlmueller (1970 A: 277).

12. In studying the Prophet of Consolation, it is particularly important to pay attention to the various genres (*Gattungen*). For a first orientation about these, see the works by Westermann, Preuss, and Whybray, mentioned in note 1 above. One of the most important contributions to this issue is that by Melugin (1976). Note also Dijkstra (1980).

13. See Albertz (1974: 45).

14. For the following discussion of God as the cosmic Creator, see above all Albertz (1974: 1–53). For the question of a connection between God as cosmic Creator and God as King in the Prophet of Consolation see Rosenberg (1966), Stuhlmueller (1970 B), Ludwig (1973), and esp. Mettinger (1986).

15. von Rad (1961: 136–47, originally published in 1936; English version 1966: 131–43).

16. Rendtorff (1954).

17. On creation through the word of God in the Prophet of Consolation, see Stuhlmueller (1970 A: 169–92) and Zimmerli (1982).

CHAPTER 9. JOB AND HIS GOD

1. Among the more recent commentaries on Job, I would like to single out for particular mention Lévêque (1970), Gordis (1978 B), Janzen (1985), and

Habel (1985). Among other contributions to Job, note Gordis (1978 A) and, on the notion of God in Job, Lindström (1983: 137–57).

2. On the literary structure of Job, cf. Westermann (1978 in German, 1981 in English) and, on the structure of the speeches of God, Kubina (1979).

3. On the idea of retribution, see Rankin (1936: 77–97), Towner (IDBSup 742–44), and Blenkinsopp (1983: 41–73).

4. Preuss (1977: 342).

5. In Job 5:7 it seems preferable to read *yôlid* (Hiph.) instead of *yûllād* (Pual).

6. See Habel (1976).

7. See Pope (1974: 99). Cf. 1 Sam 19:5; 28:21; Ps 119:109.

8. Blank (1951). On Job 31, also cf. Dick (1979 and 1983).

9. See Fishbane (1971).

10. Cf. Isa 29:6; Jer 23:19; 30:23; Ezek 1:4; Zech 9:14. On the motif of theophany in the OT, see Mettinger (1982 B: 32–36, 103–6, 116–34 with literature), and on this motif in Job, see Preuss (1977: 330–43).

11. See Keel (1978 B) and Kubina (1979: 115–43), two contributions that beautifully supplement each other. On the legal metaphor in Job, see now also Habel (1985: 54–57 with literature).

12. Gordis (1978 A: 191); cf. Habel (1985: 57).

13. See Sæbø (1971) and Hermisson (1978).

14. Ruprecht (1971) and Keel (1978: 127–41). Day (1985: 75–87), however, refers to "El's calf Atik" as the possible background of Behemoth. For the Papyrus Beatty no. 1, mentioned below, see ANET (14–17).

15. A special problem for this interpretation of Behemoth may seem to be raised by the formulations about Behemoth as a being created by God (Job 40:15, 19). Does the text thereby say that the world began with a chaos created by God, and personified here as a monster that God created and then overcame and subdued? Cf. Ps 104:6–7 and cf. below.

16. Thus I cannot agree with Gammie (1978), who takes Behemoth and Leviathan to be didactic images for Job himself, an understanding that is dimly visible also in Kubina (1979: 154). I must also dissociate myself from Tsevat (1966: esp. 98 and 102), who takes the Book of Job to end with the idea of the amoral character of the created world.

17. Certain scholars have taken the second divine speech to refer to God as the Lord of history. The names Behemoth and Leviathan have then been taken to be ciphers for the historical powers on the political scene. Thus Westermann (1978: 108–24) and Kubina (1979: 122f., 144–46, 159).

18. Brenner (1981) makes some interesting observations. The point on which I find it difficult to agree with her is when she assumes a monistic theology in Job. She locates the conflict between good and evil within the godhead and finds in Job "the two-sided Godhead" (131) and a God who is "the ultimate source of both good and evil" (132).

19. Lindström (1983: 137–57). On the issue of God, chaos, and order see most recently Levenson (1988).

Glossary

Anthropomorphism (noun), **anthropomorphic** (adj.), used of conceptions of God that employ analogies and comparisons drawn from human characteristics in their God-language. Cf. the Greek *anthrōpos*, "man."

Chaos, the formless and randomly ordered condition that is the antithesis of the created world, *cosmos*. The *forces of chaos* are the dark powers that were thought to be in conflict with the deity and his creation. The motif of the *chaos battle* is found in descriptions of God's struggle with and victory over these powers.

Connotation, a philological term whose opposite idea is *denotation*. By the *connotations* of a word are meant the associations, largely of an emotional and individual nature, which are activated by the word. In contrast, *denotation* signifies the relationship between a linguistic expression and that to which it refers in the extralinguistic world. See *Reference*.

D-circles, see *D-literature*.

D-literature or **Deuteronomistic literature**, a term applied to the literature that emerged in conjunction with the reformation of Josiah in 622 B.C.E. (2 Kings 22—23). The law book that was found in the temple, and that is said to have triggered the reform, is generally held to have consisted of the nucleus (chaps. 12—26) of the present Book of Deuteronomy, whose Latinized name is **Deuteronomium**. This book serves as the prologue of a great historical work that appeared around the time of the destruction of Jerusalem in 587 or 586 B.C.E., and which scholars usually call the *Deuteronomistic Historical Work* or *D-Work*. This work is composed of the Books of Deuteronomy, Joshua, Judges, Samuel, and Kings. The people behind this work are called either the *Deuteronomists* or the *D-circles*.

Deism, the belief that while God did indeed create the world he has not since then intervened in worldly affairs.

Denotation, see *Connotation; Reference.*

Deuteronomistic, see *D-literature.*

Dualism, any religious or metaphysical system which maintains that existence is predicated upon two opposing tendencies, such as the conflict between the forces of good and evil. *Monism* designates the contrary view, according to which a single cause is the ultimate ground of both good and evil.

Elohistic tradition, a designation used by students of the Pentateuch in which they indicate one of the layers of tradition in the corpus on the basis of such things as, among others, the use of the divine name Elohim in the texts in question. Another of these layers is called the Yahwistic stratum (employing the name YHWH).

Eschatology, usually signifies the "last things," but in works on the OT it has the wider sense of "conceptions of the future."

Etymology, a philological term signifying the linguistic origin of a word.

Exegesis (noun), **exegetical** (adj.), used to refer to the scholarly study of the biblical texts. A practitioner of the discipline is called an *exegete.*

Exile, the Babylonian captivity, that began in 587/586 B.C.E.

Immanence, see *Transcendence.*

Ketib, lit. "what is written," the term referring to the consonants of a certain word in the Hebrew text of the Old Testament. When the *masoretes* used to read a word in a different way they did not change the text but vocalized it according to what they read. This reading, which is also noted in the margin of the Hebrew Bible, is called the *Qere,* "what is read".

LXX, see *Septuagint.*

Masoretes, lit. "transmitters," the custodians of the sacred text from about 500 C.E. to about 1000 C.E. Among other things, they introduced a complete system of vowel signs for the Hebrew text.

Metaphor, "that figure of speech whereby we speak about one thing in terms which are seen to be suggestive of another" (J. Martin Soskice).

Mishna, the tradition of the elders, the Jewish oral law laid down in writing at the end of the second century C.E.

Monism, see *Dualism.*

Pantheism, see *Transcendence*.

Parallelismus membrorum, the term used for the phenomenon in which two parts of a verse correspond one to the other. In short, it is a sort of "conceptual rhyme." Consider: "Who shall ascend the hill of the Lord? And who shall stand in his holy place?" (Ps 24:3).

Pericope, a short passage read in public worship.

Priestly traditions, a layer of tradition in the Pentateuch that is especially concerned with the tabernacle and with ritual matters.

Protology, the opposite of *eschatology*, that is, conceptions of the creation and the primeval history.

Reference, the philological term that designates the extralinguistic quantity to which an expression refers. For example, the *reference* of the word "table" is to the *thing* "table." The term is approximately equivalent to *denotation*.

Root metaphor, the basic analogy or model, used to describe the nature of the world, a way of seeing "all that is" through a specific key concept. A root metaphor can organize partial metaphors into a network. It can generate new metaphors. And it has a capacity to survive, while other metaphors often weaken and become clichés. During a certain period the idea of the warring God (above, Chapter 6) was the *root metaphor* of ancient Israel.

Septuagint, usually represented as "LXX," the earliest Greek translation of the Hebrew Bible plus the Apocrypha (ca. 285–247 B.C.E.).

Soteriology, the doctrine of salvation.

Symbol, a visible sign or image (a thing, an action, or a linguistic act) that stands for, represents, and expresses something not observable. A religious *symbol* may be something that was originally profane; it need have no necessary likeness with its "primeval image." Cf. *Metaphor*.

Targum, (from Aramaic *targēm*, "to translate"), the term for the Aramaic paraphrase added to the Hebrew text read in the Synagogue. Such a translation became necessary when the majority of Jews no longer understood Hebrew.

Theophany, a term that really refers to situations in which God manifests himself visibly. In Old Testament exegesis the term refers to the main motif in texts that describe the arrival of God, accompanied by diverse natural phenomena. These natural phenomena are described by a variety of terms (fire, cloud, etc.), but God's countenance is never described.

Transcendence, a term that refers to that which is "wholly other" than the phenomena of the perceptual world or the realm of human knowledge. A *transcendent* concept of God emphasizes God's otherness, his exaltation above this world, and the absolute incommensurability of him and man. An *immanent* conception of God emphasizes God's presence in the world, his *immanence*. This is sometimes developed in the direction of *pantheism*, in which God and the world are identified.

Vulgate, the official translation of the Bible into Latin. This translation was carried out by Jerome, who was entrusted with the task by the Pope in 382 C.E.

Abbreviations

ANET	Ancient Near Eastern Texts Relating to the Old Testament, ed. by J.B. Pritchard. Princeton [3]1969 (Princeton Univ. Press)
AOAT	Alter Orient und Altes Testament
BA	Biblical Archaeologist
BASOR	Bulletin of the American Schools of Oriental Research
BBB	Bonner Biblische Beiträge
BKAT	Biblischer Kommentar: Altes Testament
BN	Biblische Notizen
BZAW	Beihefte zur ZAW
CBQ	Catholic Biblical Quarterly
ConB OT Series	Coniectanea Biblica, Old Testament Series
DBSup	Dictionnaire de la Bible, Supplément
EA	J.A. Knudtzon, Die El-Amarna-Tafeln. Leipzig 1907–15
FRLANT	Forschungen zur Religion und Literatur des Alten und Neuen Testaments
Fs	Festschrift
HAL	W. Baumgartner et al., ed., Hebräisches und aramäisches Lexikon zum Alten Testament. Leiden 1967– (Brill)
HSM	Harvard Semitic Monographs
HTR	Harvard Theological Review
HTS	Harvard Theological Studies
IDB	G.A. Buttrick, ed., Interpreter's Dictionary of the Bible. Nashville 1962 (Abingdon)
IDBSup	Supplementary volume to IDB, 1976
JBL	Journal of Biblical Literature

JR	Journal of Religion
JSS	Journal of Semitic Studies
KAI	H. Donner—W. Röllig, Kanaanäische und aramäische Inschriften, 3 vols. Wiesbaden 1962–64 (Harrassowitz)
KTU	M. Dietrich—O. Loretz—J. Sanmartín, eds., Die Keilalphabetischen Texte aus Ugarit (AOAT 24). Kevelaer and Neukirchen 1976
NERT	Near Eastern Religious Texts Relating to the Old Testament, ed. by W. Beyerlin. London 1978 (SCM)
SBLMS	Society of Biblical Literature Monograph Series
SBS	Stuttgarter Bibelstudien
SEÅ	Svensk exegetisk årsbok
STK	Svensk teologisk kvartalskrift
TBü	Theologische Bücherei
TDOT	Theological Dictionary of the Old Testament; translation of TWAT
THAT	Theologisches Handwörterbuch zum Alten Testament, ed. by E. Jenni—C. Westermann. 2 volumes. Munich 1971–76 (Kaiser)
TWAT	Theologisches Wörterbuch zum Alten Testament, ed. by G.J. Botterweck—H. Ringgren—H.-J. Fabry. Stuttgart 1973– (Kohlhammer)
UF	Ugarit-Forschungen
WMANT	Wissenschaftliche Monographien zum Alten und Neuen Testament
VT	Vetus Testamentum
VTSup	Vetus Testamentum, Supplements
ZAW	Zeitschrift für die alttestamentliche Wissenschaft
ZTK	Zeitschrift für Theologie und Kirche

Bibliography

Abba, R., 1962. "Name." IDB 3, 500–508.

Ahlström, G.W., 1984. An archaeological picture of iron age religions in ancient Palestine. Studia Orientalia (edited by the Finnish Oriental Society, Helsinki) 55, 3.

———, 1986. Who were the Israelites? Winona Lake, Ind. (Eisenbrauns).

Albertz, R., 1974. Weltschöpfung und Menschenschöpfung. Untersucht bei Deuterojesaja, Hiob und in den Psalmen. Stuttgart (Calwer).

———, 1978. Persönliche Frömmigkeit und offizielle Religion. Stuttgart (Calwer).

Albrektson, B., 1967. History and the gods (ConB OT Series 1). Lund (Gleerup).

———, 1968. "On the syntax of 'ehyeh 'ăšer 'ehyeh in Exodus 3:14." In: P.R. Ackroyd—B. Lindars, eds., Words and meanings (Fs D. Winton Thomas). Cambridge (Cambridge Univ. Press), pp. 15–28.

Alt, A., 1953. Kleine Schriften vol. 1. Munich (Beck).

———, 1966. Essays on Old Testament history and religion. Oxford (Blackwell).

Anderson, B.W., 1962 A. "Exodus typology in Second Isaiah." In: B.W. Anderson—W. Harrelson, eds., Israel's prophetic heritage (Fs Muilenburg). New York (Harper), pp. 177–95.

———, 1962 B. "God, names of." IDB 2, 407–17.

———, 1962 C. "God, OT view of." IDB 2, 417–30.

———, 1967. Creation versus chaos. The reinterpretation of mythical symbolism in the Bible. New York (Association). [Philadelphia 1987 (Fortress).]

———, ed., 1984. Creation in the Old Testament. Philadelphia and London (Fortress and SPCK).

Arnold, W.R., 1917. Ephod and Ark (HTS 3). Cambridge (Harvard Univ. Press).

Astour, M.C., 1979. "Yahweh in Egyptian topographic lists." In: M. Görg—E. Pusch, eds., Festschrift Elmar Edel (Ägypten und Altes Testament 1). Bamberg, pp. 17–34.

Attridge, H.W.—R.A. Oden, 1976. The Syrian goddess (De Dea Syria) attributed to Lucian (Texts and translations 9). Missoula, Mont. (Scholars).

Axelsson, L.-E., 1987. The Lord rose up from Seir. Studies in the religious and historical traditions of the Negev and Southern Judah (ConB OT Series 25). Stockholm (Almqvist).

226

Bibliography

Bach, R., 1971. ". . . , der Bogen zerbricht, Spiesse zerschlägt und Wagen mit Feuer verbrennt." In: H.W. Wolff, ed., Probleme biblischer Theologie (Fs G. von Rad). Munich (Kaiser), pp. 13–26.

Bailey, L.R., 1968. "Israelite ʾĒl Šadday and Amorite Bêl Šadê." JBL 87, 434–38.

Barr, J., 1969. "The symbolism of names in the Old Testament." Bulletin of the John Rylands Library 52, 11–29.

Barstad, H.M., 1984. The religious polemics of Amos (VTSup 34). Leiden (Brill).

Bertram, G., 1959. "Zur Prägung der biblischen Gottesvorstellung in der griechischen Übersetzung des Alten Testaments. Die Wiedergabe von schadad und schaddaj im Griechischen." Die Welt des Orients 2, 502–13.

Beskow, P., 1962. Rex Gloriae. The kingship of Christ in the early church. Stockholm (Almqvist).

Bettenzoli, G., 1979. Geist der Heiligkeit. Traditionsgeschichtliche Untersuchungen des QDŠ-Begriffes im Buch Ezechiel. Florence.

Bird, Ph.A., 1981. "'Male and female he created them': Gen 1:27b in the context of the Priestly account of creation." HTR 74, 129–59.

Bjørndalen, A.J., 1986. Untersuchungen zur allegorischen Rede der Propheten Amos und Jesaja (BZAW 165). Berlin (de Gruyter).

Black, M., 1962. Models and metaphors. Ithaca, N.Y. (Cornell Univ. Press).

Blank, S.H., 1951. "An effective literary device in Job xxxi." Journal of Jewish Studies 2, 105–7.

Blenkinsopp, J., 1983. Wisdom and Law in the Old Testament. Oxford (Oxford Univ. Press).

Blum, E., 1984. Die Komposition der Vätergeschichte (WMANT 57). Neukirchen-Vluyn (Neukirchener).

Boecker, H.J., 1964. Redeformen des Rechtslebens im Alten Testament (WMANT 14). Neukirchen-Vluyn (Neukirchener).

Bonnard, P.-E., 1972. Le Second Isaïe. Son disciple et leurs éditeurs. Isaïe 40–66 (Études Bibliques). Paris (Gabalda).

Börker-Klähn, J., 1982. Altvorderasiatische Bildstelen und vergleichbare Felsreliefs (Baghdader Forschungen 4). Mainz am Rhein (Philip v. Zabern).

Brenner, A., 1981. "God's answer to Job." VT 31, 129–37.

Bright, J., 1977. Covenant and promise. London (SCM).

Brueggemann, W., 1979. "Trajectories in Old Testament literature and the sociology of ancient Israel." JBL 98, 161–85.

Budde, K., 1905. Die Religion des Volkes Israel bis zur Verbannung. Giessen.

Caquot, A., 1977. "gāʿar." TWAT 2, 51–56.

———, 1978. "Les énigmes d'un hémistiche biblique." In: Dieu et l'être. Paris 1978 (Études Augustiniennes), pp. 17–26.

Carlson, R.A., 1977. "Den levande Guden—i gammaltestamentligt perspektiv." Religion och Bibel 36, 3–9.

Cazelles, H., 1960. "Le nouvel an en Israel." DBSup 6, 620–45.

———, 1966. "Patriarches." DBSup 7, 81–156.

Bibliography

———, 1978. "Pour une exégèse de Ex. 3:14." In: Dieu et l'être. Paris 1978 (Études Augustiniennes), pp. 27–44.

Childs, B.S., 1974. Exodus. A commentary (Old Testament Library). London and Philadelphia (SCM and Westminster).

Clifford, R.J., 1972. The cosmic mountain in Canaan and the Old Testament (HSM 4). Cambridge (Harvard Univ. Press).

Cody, A., 1968. "Exodus 18:12: Jethro accepts a covenant with the Israelites." Biblica 49, 153–66.

Cross, F.M., 1973. Canaanite myth and Hebrew epic. Cambridge (Harvard Univ. Press).

———, 1976. "The 'olden gods' in ancient Near Eastern creation myths." In: F.M. Cross et al., eds., Magnalia Dei (Fs G.E. Wright). Garden City, N.Y. (Doubleday), pp. 329–38.

Cullmann, O., 1959. The christology of the New Testament. London and Philadelphia (SCM and Westminster).

Dalman, G., 1898. Die Worte Jesu. Leipzig (Hinrichs'sche).

Day, J., 1985. God's conflict with the dragon and the sea. Echoes of a Canaanite myth in the Old Testament (University of Cambridge Oriental Publications 35). Cambridge (Cambridge Univ. Press).

Delekat, L., 1971. "Yáho—Yahwáe und die alttestamentlichen Gottesnamenkorrekturen." In: G. Jeremias et al., eds., Tradition und Glaube (Fs K.G. Kuhn). Göttingen, pp. 23–75.

Delitzsch, Friedrich, 1905. Babel und Bibel. Erster Vortrag. Leipzig, 5th ed.

Dever, W.G., 1984. "Ashera, consort of Yahweh? New evidence from Kuntillet 'Ajrud." BASOR 255, 21–37.

Dick, M.B., 1979. "The legal metaphor in Job 31." CBQ 41, 37–50.

———, 1983. "Job 31, the oath of innocence, and the sage." ZAW 95, 31–53.

Dietrich, W., 1976. Jesaja und die Politik. Munich (Kaiser).

———, 1980. "Gott als König." ZTK 77, 251–68.

Dijkstra, M., 1980. Gods voorstelling. Predikatieve expressie van zelfopenbaring in oudoosterse teksten en Deutero-Jesaja. Kampen (Kok).

Dohmen, Chr., 1985. Das Bilderverbot (BBB 62). Bonn (Hanstein).

Edzard, D.O., 1976. "Il." Reallexikon der Assyriologie 5, 46–48.

Eissfeldt, O., 1928. "Jahwe als König." ZAW 46, 81–105 = Eissfeldt, Kleine Schriften 1, Tübingen 1962 (Mohr), pp. 172–93.

———, 1950. "Jahwe Zebaoth" = Eissfeldt, Kleine Schriften 3, Tübingen 1966 (Mohr), pp. 103–23.

———, 1973. "'ādôn, 'ădōnāy." TWAT 1, 62–78.

———, 1962–1979. Kleine Schriften 1–6. Ed. R. Sellheim—F. Maass. Tübingen (Mohr). Vol. 1 (1962), 2 (1963), 3 (1966), 4 (1968), 5 (1973), 6 (1979).

Emerton, J.A., 1982 A. "New light on Israelite religion." ZAW 94, 2–20.

———, 1982 B. "Leviathan and LTN. The vocalization of the Ugaritic word for the dragon." VT 32, 327–31.

———, 1982 C. "The origin of the promises to the patriarchs in the older sources of the Book of Genesis." VT 32, 14–32.

Euting, J., 1891. Sinaitische Inschriften. Berlin.

Fichtner, J., 1951. "Jahwes Plan in der Botschaft des Jesaja." ZAW 63, 16–33.

Bibliography

————, 1956. "Die etymologische Ätiologie in den Namengebungen der geschichtlichen Bücher des Alten Testaments." VT 6, 372–96.

Fishbane, M., 1971. "Jeremiah iv 23–26 and Job iii 3–13: a recovered use of the creation pattern." VT 21, 151–67.

Fitzmyer, J.A., 1979. A wandering Aramean. Collected Aramaic essays (SBLMS 25) Missoula, Mont. (Scholars).

————, 1981. To advance the gospel. New Testament Studies. New York (Crossroad).

Freedman, D.N., 1976. "Divine names and titles in early Hebrew poetry." In: F.M. Cross et al., eds., Magnalia Dei (Fs G.E. Wright). Garden City, N.Y. (Doubleday), pp. 55–107.

Freedman, D.N.—O'Connor, M., 1982. "JHWH." TWAT 3, 533–54.

Fritz, V., 1987. "Conquest or settlement? The early iron age in Palestine." BA 50, 84–100.

Galling, K., 1928. Die Erwählungstraditionen Israels (BZAW 48). Giessen (Töpelmann).

————, 1956. "Die Ausrufung des Namens als Rechtsakt in Israel." Theologische Literaturzeitung 81, 65–70.

Gammie, J.G., 1978. "Behemoth and Leviathan: on the didactic and theological significance of Job 40:15—41:26." In: J.G. Gammie et al., eds., Israelite Wisdom (Fs Terrien). Missoula, Mont. (Scholars), pp. 217–31.

Gerhardsson, B., 1958. The good Samaritan—the good shepherd? (Coniectanea Neotestamentica 16). Lund (Gleerup).

————, 1985. "Den äldsta kristna bekännelsen och dess rötter." In: B. Gerhardsson—P.E. Persson, Kyrkans bekännelsefråga. Malmö (Liber), pp. 11–106.

Gese, H., 1970. "Die Religionen Altsyriens." In: Die Religionen der Menschheit 10:2. Stuttgart (Kohlhammer), pp. 3–232.

Gibson, J.C.L., 1978. Canaanite myths and legends. Edinburgh (Clark).

————, 1982. Textbook of Syrian Semitic Inscriptions. Vol. 3 Phoenician Inscriptions. Oxford (Clarendon).

————, 1984. "The theology of the Ugaritic Baal cycle." Orientalia 53, 202–19.

Giveon, R., 1971. Les bédouins Shosou des documents égyptiens. Leiden (Brill).

Görg, M., 1976. "Jahwe—ein Toponym?" BN 1, 7–14.

Gordis, R., 1978 A. The book of God and man. [1965] Chicago (Chicago Univ. Press).

————, 1978 B. The Book of Job. Commentary, new translation and special studies. New York (The Jewish Theological Seminary of America).

Gottwald, N.K., 1979. The tribes of Yahweh. A sociology of the religion of liberated Israel 1250–1050 B.C. Maryknoll, N.Y. (Orbis).

Gray, J., 1956. "The Hebrew conception of the kingship of God: its origin and development." VT 6, 268–85.

————, 1961. "The kingship of God in the prophets and Psalms." VT 11, 1–29.

————, 1974. "The day of Yahweh in cultic experience and eschatological prospect." SEÅ 39, 5–37.

————, 1979. The biblical doctrine of the reign of God. Edinburgh (Clark).

Bibliography

Greenspoon, L.J., 1981. "The origin of the idea of resurrection." In: B. Halpern—J.D. Levenson, eds., Traditions in transformation (Fs F.M. Cross). Winona Lake, Ind. (Eisenbrauns), pp. 247–321.

Grether, O., 1934. Name und Wort Gottes im Alten Testament (BZAW 64). Giessen.

Grønbæk, J.H., 1985. "Baal's battle with Yam—a Canaanite Creation fight." Journal for the Study of the Old Testament 33, 27–44.

Habel, N.C., 1976. "Appeal to ancient tradition as a literary form." ZAW 88, 253–72.

———, 1985. The Book of Job. A commentary (Old Testament Library). London and Philadelphia (SCM and Westminster).

Hackett, J.A., 1984. The Balaam text from Deir ʿAllā (HSM 31). Chico, Calif. (Scholars).

Hahn, F., 1974. Christologische Hoheitstitel. 4 Auflage. Göttingen (Vandenhoeck). Translation: The Titles of Jesus in Christology. London and Cleveland (Lutterworth and World).

Halpern, B., 1983. The emergence of Israel in Canaan (SBLMS 29). Chico, Calif. (Scholars).

Hammond, P.C., 1980. "New Evidence for the 4th-century A.D. destruction of Petra." BASOR 238, 65–67.

Hanson, P.D., 1982. The diversity of scripture. Philadelphia (Fortress).

———, 1983. The dawn of apocalyptic. [1975] revised edition 1979. Philadelphia (Fortress).

Hartman, L., 1973. "Into the name of Jesus." Journal of New Testament Studies 20, 432–40.

Hehn, J., 1913. Die biblische und die babylonische Gottesidee. Die israelitische Gottesauffassung im Lichte der altorientalischen Religionsgeschichte. Leipzig (Hinrichs'sche).

Hermisson, H.-J., 1978. "Observations on the creation theology in Wisdom." In: J.G. Gammie et al., eds., Israelite Wisdom (Fs Terrien). Missoula, Mont. (Scholars), pp. 43–57.

———, 1985. "Gottes Freiheit—Spielraum des Menschen." ZTK 82, 129–52.

Hidal, S., 1985. "Israel och Hellas—två världar eller en enda verklighet?" STK 61, 49–58.

Hillers, D.R., 1972. "Paḥad yiṣḥāq." JBL 91, 90–92.

Hirsch, H., 1966. "Gott der Väter." Archiv für Orientforschung 21, 56–58.

Hoftijzer, J., 1956. Die Verheissungen an die drei Erzväter. Leiden (Brill).

Holmqvist, L., 1971. Degeneration of trade marks (Rätts- och samhällsvetenskapliga biblioteket 3). Sine loco. (Jurist- och samhällsvetarförbundets Förlags AB).

Howard, G., 1977. "The tetragram and the New Testament." JBL 96, 63–83.

Huffmon, H.B., 1965. Amorite personal names in the Mari texts. Baltimore (Johns Hopkins).

Hyatt, J.P., 1955. "Yahweh as 'the God of my father.'" VT 5, 130–36.

———, 1967. "Was Yahweh originally a creator deity?" JBL 86, 369–77.

Irwin, W.A., 1939. "Exod. 3:14." The American Journal of Semitic Languages and Literatures 56, 297–98.

Bibliography

Jacobsen, Th., 1976. The treasures of darkness. A history of Mesopotamian religion. New Haven and London (Yale University Press).

Janzen, J.G., 1985. Job (Interpretation. A Bible commentary for teaching and preaching). Atlanta (John Knox).

Jaroš, K., 1982. "Zur Inschrift No. 3 von Chirbet el-Qōm." BN 19, 31–40.

Jeremias, J., 1976. "Theophany in the OT." IDBSup 896–98.

———, 1987. Das Königtum Gottes in den Psalmen. Israels Begegnung mit dem kanaanäischen Mythos in den Jahwe-König-Psalmen (FRLANT 141). Göttingen (Vandenhoeck).

Johnson, B., 1972. "Profetia och uppfyllelse i Gamla testamentet." In: M. Sæbø, ed., Israel, kirken og verden. Oslo (Forlaget Land og Kirke), pp. 39–50.

———, 1985. Rättfärdigheten i Bibeln. Göteborg (Gothia).

Kapelrud, A.S., 1960. "Ba'als kamp med havets fyrste i Ras-Sjamra-tekstene." Norsk Teologisk Tidsskrift 61, 241–51.

———, 1977. "Guden som sviktet?" SEÅ 41–42, 138–46.

Kee, H.C., 1968. "The terminology of Mark's exorcism stories." New Testament Studies 14, 232–46.

Keel, O., 1977. Jahwe-Visionen und Siegelkunst (SBS 84–85). Stuttgart (Katholisches Bibelwerk).

———, 1978 A. The symbolism of the biblical world. New York (Seabury).

———, 1978 B. Jahwes Entgegnung an Ijob. Eine Deutung von Ijob 38—41 vor dem Hintergrund der zeitgenössischen Bildkunst (FRLANT 121). Göttingen (Vandenhoeck).

Kelly, J.N.D., 1960. Early Christian creeds. London (Longmans).

Kilwing, N., 1979. "Noch einmal zur Syntax von Ex 3:14." BN 10, 70–79.

Kinet, D., 1981. Ugarit—Geschichte und Kultur einer Stadt in der Umwelt des Alten Testamentes (SBS 104). Stuttgart (Katholisches Bibelwerk).

Kinyongo, J., 1970. Origine et signification du nom divin Yahvé à la lumière de récents travaux et de traditions sémitico-bibliques (BBB 35). Bonn (Hanstein).

Kjær-Hansen, K., 1982. Studier i navnet Jesus. Århus.

Klein, G., 1902. Schem Ha-mephorasch (Det förborgade gudsnamnet). Stockholm.

Klein, R.W., 1978. "A theology for exiles—the kingship of Yahweh." Dialog 17, 128–34.

———, 1979. Israel in exile. A theological interpretation. Philadelphia (Fortress).

Kloos, C., 1986. Yhwh's combat with the sea. A Canaanite tradition in the religion of ancient Israel. Amsterdam and Leiden (van Oorschot and Brill).

Knauf, E.A., 1984. "Eine nabatäische Parallele zum hebräischen Gottesnamen." BN 23, 21–28.

———, 1985. El Šaddai—der Gott Abrahams? Biblische Zeitschrift 29, 97–103.

Koch, K., 1976. "Šaddaj." VT 26, 299–332.

———, 1979. "Zur Entstehung der Ba'al-Verehrung." UF 11, 465–75.

———, 1988. Studien zur alttestamentlichen und altorientalischen Religionsgeschichte. Ed. E. Otto. Göttingen (Vandenhoeck).

Bibliography

Kraus, H.-J., 1961. Psalmen (BKAT 15:1–2). 2d ed., Neukirchen (Neukirchener).

———, 1966. Worship in Israel. Translated by G. Buswell. Oxford (Blackwell).

———, 1967. "Der lebendige Gott." Evangelische Theologie 27, 169–200.

———, 1979. Theologie der Psalmen (BKAT 15:3). Neukirchen (Neukirchener).

Kreuzer, S., 1983. Der lebendige Gott. Bedeutung, Herkunft und Entwicklung einer alttestamentlichen Gottesbezeichnung (Beiträge zur Wissenschaft vom Alten und Neuen Testament 116). Stuttgart (Kohlhammer).

Kubina, V., 1979. Die Gottesreden im Buche Hiob. Freiburg (Herder).

Lack, R., 1962. "Les origines de Elyon, Le très-haut, dans la tradition cultuelle d'Israel." CBQ 44, 44–64.

Lambert, W.G., 1963. "The great battle in the Mesopotamian religious year. The conflict in the akītu house." Iraq 25, 189–90.

Lang, B., 1981. "Die Jahwe-allein-Bewegung." In B. Lang, ed., Der Einzige Gott. Die Geburt des biblischen Monotheismus. Munich (Kösel), pp. 47–83. Translation: "The Yahweh-alone movement and the making of Jewish monotheism." In: B. Lang, Monotheism and the prophetic movement: an essay in biblical history and sociology. Sheffield 1981 (Almond), pp. 13–59.

Lemche, N.P., 1985. Early Israel. Anthropological and historical studies on the Israelite society before the monarchy (VTSup 37). Leiden (Brill).

Levenson, J.D., 1984. "The temple and the world." JR 64, 275–98.

———, 1985. Sinai and Zion. An entry into the Jewish Bible. Minneapolis (Winston).

———, 1988. Creation and the persistence of evil. The Jewish drama of divine omnipotence. San Francisco (Harper).

Lévêque, J., 1970. Job et son Dieu. Paris (Gabalda).

Lewy, J., 1934. "Les textes paléo-assyriens et l'Ancien Testament." Revue de l'Histoire des Religions vol. 5. 109–10, 29–65.

Lindblom, J., 1964. "Noch einmal die Deutung des Jahwe-Namens." Annual of the Swedish Theological Institute 3, 4–15.

Lindström, F., 1983. God and the origin of evil (ConB OT Series 21). Lund (Gleerup).

Lipiński, E., 1965. La royauté de Yahwé dans la poésie et le culte de l'ancien Israël. Brussels (Palais der academiën).

Loretz, O., 1980 A. "Vom Baal-Epitheton adn zur Adonis und Adonaj." UF 12, 287–92.

———, 1980 B. "Der kanaanäische Ursprung des biblischen Gottesnamens El Šaddaj." UF 12, 420–21.

Ludwig, Th.M., 1973. "The traditions of the establishing of the earth in Deutero-Isaiah." JBL 92, 345–57.

Lundbom, J.R., 1978. "God's use of the idem per idem to terminate debate." HTR 71, 193–201.

Lyons, J., 1977. Semantics 1–2. Cambridge (Cambridge Univ. Press).

Maag, V., 1980. Kultur, Kulturkontakt und Religion. Gesammelte Studien . . . Göttingen (Vandenhoeck).

McBride, S.D., 1969. "The Deuteronomic Name Theology." PhD. diss. Harvard.

Bibliography

McCarter, P.K., 1980. "The Balaam texts from Deir 'Allā: the first combination." BASOR 239, 49–60.

McCarthy, D., 1967. "'Creation' motifs in ancient Hebrew poetry." CBQ 29, 393–406. [See the revised and updated version in B. Anderson, ed., Creation in the Old Testament (Issues in Religion and Theology). London and Philadelphia 1984 (SPCK and Fortress).]

———, 1978. "Exod 3:14: History, philology and theology." CBQ 40, 311–21.

McCurley, F., 1983. Ancient myths and biblical faith. Scriptural transformations. Philadelphia (Fortress).

McFague, S., 1983. Metaphorical theology. Models of God in religious language. London (SCM). Fortress edition 1982.

McKane, W., 1979. Studies in the patriarchal narratives. Edinburgh (Handsel).

Marmorstein, A., 1968. The doctrine of merits in old rabbinical literature; and the old rabbinic doctrine of God: 1. The names and attributes of God. [1920] New York (Ktav).

Martin Soskice, J., 1987. Metaphor and religious language. Oxford (Clarendon).

Mayer, R., 1958. "Der Gottesname Jahwe im Lichte der neuesten Forschung." Biblische Zeitschrift 2, 26–53.

Melugin, R.F., 1976. The formation of Isaiah 40—55 (BZAW 141). Berlin (de Gruyter).

Mendenhall, G.E., 1962. "The Hebrew conquest of Palestine." BA 25, 66–87.

Mettinger, T., 1974. "Abbild oder Urbild? 'Imago Dei' in traditionsgeschichtlicher Sicht." ZAW 86, 403–24.

———, 1976. King and Messiah. The civil and sacral legitimation of the Israelite kings (ConB OT Series 8). Lund (Gleerup).

———, 1978. "Eva och revbenet. Manligt och kvinnligt i exegetisk belysning." STK 1978, 55–64.

———, 1979. "The veto on images and the aniconic God in ancient Israel." In: H. Biezais, ed., Religious symbols and their functions (Scripta Instituti Donneriani Aboensis 10). Stockholm (Almqvist), pp. 15–29.

———, 1982 A. "YHWH SABAOTH—the heavenly king on the cherubim throne." In: T. Ishida, ed., Studies in the period of David and Solomon. Papers read at the International Symposium for Biblical Studies, Tokyo, 5–7 December 1979. Tokyo (Yamakawa Shuppansha), pp. 109–38.

———, 1982 B. The dethronement of Sabaoth. Studies in the Shem and Kabod theologies (ConB OT Series 18). Lund (Gleerup).

———, 1983. A farewell to the Servant Songs. A critical examination of an exegetical axiom (Scripta Minora 1982–1983:3). Lund (Gleerup).

———, 1985. "Fighting the powers of chaos and hell—towards the biblical portrait of God." Studia Theologica 39, 21–38.

———, 1986. "In search of the hidden structure: YHWH as king in Isaiah 40—55." SEÅ 51–52, 148–57.

Metzger, M., 1984. "Eigentumsdeklaration und Schöpfungsaussage." In: H.-G. Geyer, ed., "Wenn nicht jetzt, wann dann?" (Fs H.-J. Kraus). Neukirchen 1984 (Neukirchener), pp. 37–51.

———, 1985. Königsthron und Gottesthron (AOAT 15:1–2). Kevelaer and Neukirchen (Butzon & Bercker and Neukirchener).

Miller, P.D., 1975. The divine warrior in early Israel (HSM 5). Cambridge (Harvard Univ. Press).

———, 1984. "Syntax and theology in Genesis xii 3a." VT 34, 472–76.

———, 1985. "Israelite religion." In: D.A. Knight—G.M. Tucker, eds., The Hebrew Bible and its modern interpreters. Philadelphia and Chico (Fortress and Scholars), pp. 201–37.

Moor, J.C. de, 1971. The seasonal pattern in the Ugaritic myth of Baʿlu (AOAT 16). Kevelaer and Neukirchen (Butzon & Bercker and Neukirchener).

———, 1976. "Ugarit." IDBSup 928–31.

Motyer, J.A., 1959. The revelation of the divine name. London (Tyndale).

Mowinckel, S., 1922. Psalmenstudien II. Das Thronbesteigungsfest Jahwäs und der Ursprung der Eschatologie. Kristiania (Jacob Dybwad). Reprint Amsterdam 1966 (P. Schippers and Br. Grüner).

Mullen, E.Th., 1980. The divine council in Canaanite and early Hebrew literature (HSM 24). Chico, Calif. (Scholars).

Müller, H.-P., 1976. "qdš heilig." THAT 2, 589–609.

———, 1980. "Gott und die Götter in den Anfängen der biblischen Religion. Zur Vorgeschichte des Monotheismus." In: O. Keel, ed., Monotheismus im Alten Israel und seiner Umwelt. Stuttgart (Schweizerisches Katholisches Bibelwerk), pp. 99–142.

———, 1981. "Der Jahwename und seine Deutung, Ex 3:14 im Licht der Textpublikationen aus Ebla." Biblica 62, 305–27.

Norin, S., 1977. Er spaltete das Meer. Die Auszugsüberlieferung in Psalmen und Kult des alten Israel (ConB OT Series 9). Lund (Gleerup).

———, 1986. Sein Name allein ist hoch. Das Jhw-haltige Suffix althebräischer Personennamen untersucht mit besonderer Berücksichtigung der alttestamentlichen Redaktionsgeschichte (ConB OT Series 24). Lund (Gleerup).

Noth, M., 1928. Die Israelitischen Personennamen im Rahmen der gemeinsemitischen Namengebung. Stuttgart [1928]. Reprint Hildesheim 1980 (Olms).

Olsson, T., 1983. "Gudsbild, talsituation och litterär genre." Föreningen Lärare i Religionskunskap Årsbok, pp. 91–109.

Otto, E., 1986. "Kultus und Ethos in Jerusalemer Theologie." ZAW 98, 161–79.

Otzen, B., 1977. Israeliterne i Palæstina. Copenhagen (Gad).

Ouellette, J., 1969. "More on ʾĒl Šadday and Bēl Šadê." JBL 88, 470–71.

Pepper, S.C., 1942. World hypotheses. Berkeley (Univ. of California Press).

Perrin, N., "The interpretation of a biblical symbol." JR 55, 348–70.

Phillips, A., 1977. God B.C. Oxford (Oxford Univ. Press).

Pietersma, A., 1984. "Kyrios or tetragram: A renewed request for the original LXX." In: A. Pietersma—C. Cox, eds., De Septuaginta (Fs J.W. Wevers). Mississanga (Benben), pp. 85–101.

Pope, M., 1974. Job (Anchor Bible). Garden City, N.Y. (Doubleday).

Preuss, H.D., 1968. ". . . ich will mit dir sein!" ZAW 80, 139–73.

————, 1976. Deuterojesaja. Eine Einführung in seine Botschaft. Neukirchen (Neukirchener).

————, 1977. Jahwes Antwort an Hiob und die sogenannte Hiobliteratur des alten Vorderen Orients." In: H. Donner et al., eds., Beiträge zur alttestamentlichen Theologie (Fs Zimmerli). Göttingen (Vandenhoeck), pp. 323–43.

Rad, G. von, 1961. Gesammelte Studien zum Alten Testament (TBü 8). 2d ed. Munich (Kaiser).

————, 1962. Theologie des Alten Testaments. Vol. 1, 4th ed.; vol. 2, 3d ed. Munich (Kaiser).

————, 1966. The problem of the Hexateuch and other essays. Translation of (1961) by E.W. Trueman Dicken. Edinburgh and London (Oliver & Boyd) [SCM 1984].

————, 1975. Old Testament theology. 2 vols. Translation of (1962) by D.M.G. Stalker. London (SCM). [New York 1975 (Harper).]

Raitt, Th.M., 1977. A theology of exile. Judgment/deliverance in Jeremiah and Ezekiel. Philadelphia (Fortress).

Rankin, O.S., 1936. Israel's wisdom literature. Edinburgh and New York (Clark and Schocken).

Rendtorff, R., 1954. "Die theologische Stellung des Schöpfungsglaubens bei Deuterojesaja." ZTK 51, 3–13.

————, 1975. Gesammelte Studien zum Alten Testament (TBü 57). Munich (Kaiser).

————, 1977. Das Überlieferungsgeschichtliche Problem des Pentateuch (BZAW 147). Berlin (de Gruyter).

Reventlow, H.G., 1982. Hauptprobleme der alttestamentlichen Theologie im 20. Jahrhundert (Erträge der Forschung 173). Darmstadt (Wissenschaftliche).

————, 1985. Problems of Old Testament theology in the twentieth century. Translation of (1982). London and Philadelphia (SCM and Fortress).

Ringgren, H., 1969. Israelite religion. Translated by D. Green. London and Philadelphia [1966] (SPCK and Fortress).

————, 1973. Religions of the ancient Near East. Translated by John Sturdy. London and Philadelphia (SPCK and Westminster).

————, 1977. "Att vara eller icke vara . . . Verbet hajā i Gamla Testamentet." Teologisk Tidskrift (Helsinki) 82, 229–37.

————, 1981. "Yahvé et Rahab-Leviatan." In: A. Caquot—M. Delcor, eds., Mélanges bibliques et orientaux . . . M. Henri Cazelles (AOAT 212). Kevelaer and Neukirchen (Butzon & Bercker and Neukirchener), pp. 387–93.

Roberts, J.J.M., 1972. The earliest Semitic pantheon. A study of the Semitic deities attested in Mesopotamia before Ur III. Baltimore (Johns Hopkins Univ. Press).

————, 1973. "The Davidic origin of the Zion tradition." JBL 92, 329–44.

————, 1976 A. "El." IDBSup 255–58.

————, 1976 B. "The religio-political setting of Psalm 47." BASOR 221, 129–32.

Bibliography

————, 1982. "Zion in the theology of the Davidic-Solomonic empire." In: T. Ishida, ed., Studies (see above, Mettinger 1982 A), pp. 93–108.

Rose, M., 1978. Jahwe (Theologische Studien 122). Zürich (Theologischer Verlag).

Rosenberg, R.A., 1966. "Yahweh becomes king." JBL 85, 297–307.

Ross, J.P., 1967. "Jahweh Seba'ot in Samuel and Psalms." VT 17, 76–92.

Rost, L., 1960. "Köningsherrschaft Jahwes in vorköniglicher Zeit." Theologische Literaturzeitung 85, 721–24.

Ruether, R.R., 1983. Sexism and God-talk. Boston (Beacon).

Ruprecht, E., 1971. "Das Nilpferd im Hiobbuch." VT 21, 209–31.

Sæbø, M., 1971. "Creator et Redemptor. Om skapelsens teologiske plass og funksjon i Det gamle testamente." In: Deus Creator (Fs Seierstad). Oslo (Universitetsforlaget), pp. 1–28.

————, 1977. "Hvem var Israels teologer? Om struktureringen av 'den gammelstestamentlige teologi'." SEÅ vols. 41–42, 189–205.

————, 1981. "Offenbarung oder Verhüllung. Bemerkungen zum Charakter des Gottesnamens in Ex 3, 13–15." In: Die Botschaft und die Boten (Fs H.W. Wolff). Neukirchen (Neukirchener), pp. 43–55.

Saggs, H.W.F. 1978. The encounter with the divine in Mesopotamia and Israel. London (Athlone).

Samuelsson, S., 1984. Review article on Lindström (1983), STK 60, 71–77.

Sawyer, J.F.A., 1967. "Root-meanings in Hebrew." JSS 12, 37–50.

Scharbert, J., 1981. "Das 'Schilfmeerwunder' in den Texten des Alten Testaments." In: Fs Cazelles (see above, Ringgren 1981), pp. 395–417.

Schmidt, W.H., 1961. Königtum Gottes in Ugarit und Israel (BZAW 80). Berlin (de Gruyter).

————, 1962. "Wo hat die Aussage: Jahwe 'der Heilige' ihren Ursprung?" ZAW 74, 62–66.

————, 1963. "Baals Tod und Auferstehung." Zeitschrift f. Religions- und Geistesgeschichte 15, 1–13.

————, 1974, 1977. Exodus (BKAT 2: fascicles 1ff.). Neukirchen (Neukirchener).

————, 1983. The faith of the Old Testament. A history. Translated by John Sturdy. Oxford and Philadelphia (Blackwell and Westminster).

Schmitt, R., 1972. Zelt und Lade als Thema alttestamentlicher Wissenschaft. Gütersloh (Gerd Mohn).

Schoneveld, J., 1976. "Proeve van een nieuwe vertaling van 'èhjè ašèr èhjè' in Exodus 3:14." Nederlands Theologisch Tijdschrift 30, 89–98.

Schreiner, J., 1963. Sion-Jerusalem. Jahwes Königssitz. Munich (Kösel).

Seters, J. van, 1975. Abraham in history and tradition. New Haven (Yale Univ. Press).

————, 1980. "The religion of the patriarchs in Genesis." Biblica 61, 220–33.

————, 1983. In search of history. Historiography in the ancient world and the origins of biblical history. New Haven (Yale Univ. Press).

Shild, E., 1954. "On Exodus iii 14—'I am that I am'." VT 4, 296–302.

Soden, W. von., 1964. "Jahwe 'Er ist, Er erweist sich'." Die Welt des Orients 3, 177–87.

Bibliography

Soskice, see Martin Soskice, J.

Stamm, J.J., 1940. Erlösen und Vergeben im Alten Testament. Bern (Francke).

——, 1980. Beiträge zur hebräischen und altorientalischen Namenkunde (Orbis Biblicus et Orientalis 30). Freiburg and Göttingen (Vandenhoeck).

Stauffer, E., 1957. Jesus. Gestalt und Geschichte (Dalp 332). Bern (Francke).

Stolz, F., 1970. Strukturen und Figuren im Kult von Jerusalem (BZAW 118). Berlin (de Gruyter).

——, 1982. "Funktionen und Bedeutungsbereiche des ugaritischen Ba'alsmythos." In: Jan Assmann et al., eds., Funktionen und Leistungen des Mythos (Orbis Biblicus et Orientalis 48). Göttingen (Vandenhoeck), pp. 83–118.

Stuhlmueller, C., 1970 A. Creative redemption in Deutero-Isaiah (Analecta Biblica 43). Rome (Biblical Institute).

——, 1970 B. "Yahweh-King and Deutero-Isaiah." In: Biblical Research = Papers of the Chicago Society of Biblical Research 15, 32–45.

Tadmor, M., 1982. "Female cult figurines in late-Canaan and early Israel: archaeological evidence." In: T. Ishida, ed., Studies (see above, Mettinger 1982 A), pp. 139–73.

Tengström, S., 1976. Die Hexateucherzählung. Eine Literaturgeschichtliche Studie (ConB OT Series 7). Lund (Gleerup).

Terrien, S., 1978. The elusive Presence. Toward a new biblical theology (Religious Perspectives 26). New York (Harper).

Thompson, Th.L., 1974. The historicity of the patriarchal narratives (BZAW 133). Berlin (de Gruyter).

Towner, W.S., 1976. "Retribution." IDBSup 742–44.

Trible, Ph., 1978. God and the rhetoric of sexuality. Philadelphia (Fortress).

Tsevat, M., 1966. "The meaning of the Book of Job." Hebrew Union College Annual 37, 73–106.

Tsumura, T.T., 1980. "The literary structure of Psalm 46, 2–8." Annual of the Japanese Biblical Institute 6, 29–55.

Ulrichsen, J.H., 1977. "JHWH mālāk: einige sprachliche Beobachtungen." VT 27, 361–74.

Vaux, R. de, 1967. Bible et Orient. Paris and New York (Les Editions du Cerf and McGraw-Hill).

——, 1978. The early history of Israel. London (Darton).

Veijola, T., 1982. Verheissung in der Krise. Studien zur Literatur und Theologie der Exilszeit anhand des 89. Psalms. Helsinki (Suomalainen Tiedeakatemia).

——, 1983. "Finns det en gammaltestamntlig teologi?" SEÅ 48, 10–30.

Vetter, D., 1971. Jahwes Mit-Sein, ein Ausdruck des Segens. Stuttgart (Calwer).

Vorländer, H., 1975. Mein Gott. Die Vorstellungen vom persönlichen Gott im Alten Orient und im Alten Testament (AOAT 23). Kevelaer and Neukirchen (Butzon & Bercker and Neukirchener).

Vosberg, L., 1975. Studien zum Reden vom Schöpfer in den Psalmen (Beiträge zur evangelischen Theologie 69). Munich (Kaiser).

Bibliography

Vriezen, Th.C., 1950. "'Ehje 'ašer 'ehje." In: W. Baumgartner et al., eds., Festschrift Alfred Bertholet. Tübingen (Mohr), pp. 498–512.

———, 1956. Theologie des Alten Testaments in Grundzügen. Vageningen (Veenman).

Wambacq, B.N., 1947. L'épithète divine Jahvé Seba'ôt. Brügge (Desclée de Brouwer).

———, 1978. "'Eh^eyeh '^ašer 'eh^eyeh." Biblica 59, 317–38.

Wehmeier, G., 1976. "'lh hinaufgehen." THAT 2, 272–90.

Weidmann, H., 1968. Die Patriarchen und ihre Religion im Licht der Forschung seit Julius Wellhausen. Göttingen (Vandenhoeck).

Weinfeld, M., 1982. "Instructions for temple visitors in the Bible and in ancient Egypt." Scripta Hierosolymitana 28, 224–50.

Weippert, M., 1976 A. "Šaddaj (Gottesname)." THAT 2, 873–81.

———, 1976 B. Review of P.D. Miller (1975). Biblica 57, 126–32.

———, 1980. "Jahwe." Reallexikon der Assyriologie 5, 246–53.

Weiser, A., 1950. "Die Frage nach den Beziehungen der Psalmen zum Kult: Die Darstellung der Theophanie . . ." Fs A. Bertholet. Tübingen (Mohr), pp. 513–31.

Welten, P., 1982. "Königsherrschaft Jahwes und Thronbesteigung." VT 32, 297–310.

Wenham, G., 1980. "The religion of the patriarchs." In: A.R. Millard—D.J. Wiseman, eds., Essays on the patriarchal narratives. Leicester (Inter-Varsity), pp. 157–88.

Westermann, C., 1966. Das Buch Jesaia, 40—66 (Old Testament Library). Göttingen (Vandenhoeck).

———, 1969. Isaiah 40—66. A commentary. Translated by D.M.G. Stalker. London (SCM).

———, 1975. Genesis 12—50 (Erträge der Forschung 48). Darmstadt (Wissenschaftliche).

———, 1976 A. Die Verheissungen an die Väter (FRLANT 116). Göttingen (Vandenhoeck).

———, 1976 B. "Promises to the patriarchs." IDBSup 690–93.

———, 1978. Der Aufbau des Buches Hiob. Stuttgart (Calwer). Translation: The structure of the Book of Job. Philadelphia 1981 (Fortress).

———, 1979. What does the Old Testament say about God? London (SPCK).

———, 1980. The promises to the fathers: studies on the patriarchal narratives. Translation of (1976 A) by D.E. Green. Philadelphia (Fortress).

———, 1981. Genesis (BKAT 1:2). Genesis 12—36. Neukirchen (Neukirchener). Translation: Genesis 12—36. Minneapolis 1985 (Augsburg).

Whybray, R.N., 1983. The Second Isaiah (Old Testament Guides). Sheffield (JSOT).

Widengren, G., 1955. Sakrales Königtum im Alten Testament und im Judentum. Stuttgart (Kohlhammer).

Wifall, W., 1980. "El Shaddai or El of the Fields." ZAW 92, 24–32.

Wiklander, B., "Material för diskussionen om tolkningen av JHWH ṣebā'ôt." Report to the Swedish Bible Commission. Unpublished. No date.

Bibliography

Wildberger, H., 1963. "Jesajas Verständnis der Geschichte." VTSup 9, 83–117.

——, 1972, 1978, 1982. Jesaja (BKAT 10:1–3). Neukirchen (Neukirchener).

——, 1979. Jahwe und sein Volk. Gesammelte Aufsätze zum Alten Testament (TBü 66). Munich (Kaiser).

Winter, U., 1983. Frau und Göttin. Exegetische und ikonographische Studien zum weiblichen Gottesbild im Alten Israel und in dessen Umwelt (Orbis Biblicus et Orientalis 53). Freiburg and Göttingen (Universitätsverlag and Vandenhoeck).

Woude, A.S. van der, 1976. "šēm Name." THAT 2, 935–63.

Würthwein, E., 1954. "Jesaja 7, 1–9. Ein Beitrag zu dem Thema: Prophetie und Politik." In: Theologie als Glaubenszeugnis (Fs Karl Heim). Hamburg (Furche), pp. 47–63.

Wyatt, N., 1983. "The stela of the seated god from Ugarit." UF 15, 271–77.

Zenger, E., 1981. Der Gott der Bibel. Sachbuch zu den Anfängen des alttestamentlichen Gottesglaubens. Stuttgart (Katholishches Bibelwerk).

Zevit, Z., 1984. "The Khirbet el-Qôm inscription mentioning a goddess." BASOR 255, 39–47.

Zimmerli, W., 1969. Gottes Offenbarung. Gesammelte Aufsätze (TBü 19). 2d ed., Munich (Kaiser).

——, 1982. "Jahwes Wort bei Deuterojesaja." VT 32, 104–24.

Zimmerman, H., 1960. "Das absolute egō eimí als die neutestamentliche Offenbarungsformel." Biblische Zeitschrift 4, 54–69, 266–76.

ABSTRACT

In the present monograph the major Old Testament names of the God of Israel are analyzed from the viewpoints of philology and ideology as a means to examine the historical development of the various Israelite conceptions of God. New ways of designating God are taken to be key witnesses to this historical process. Throughout, the Israelite notions of God are seen as emerging from the confrontations of individuals and groups with the new challenges arising from new existential situations. The linguistic status of proper names in Hebrew is discussed, as is the role played by names in mythopoetic thinking of ancient Semitic cultures. The background and significance of "the God of the Fathers" and "YHWH" are submitted to analysis. The names and metaphors used to express the monarchical understanding of God are studied with particular reference to the Canaanite background provided by the literature dealing with Baal and El. Baal and El are compared from both a mythological and an iconographical point of view, and the results of these studies are utilized in the interpretations here offered of such Israelite designations as "the living God," "king," and "YHWH Sabaoth." The latter two designations are understood to express two different aspects of a view of God which employs royal symbolism; they refer to YHWH as a battling God (cf. the Baal type) and to YHWH as a regnant God (cf. the El type). The participial characterizations of God in the Prophet of Consolation open up a new access to the theology of this prophet, and in particular to his conceptions of God. The notions of God in the Book of Job are discussed in a final chapter.

Keywords: Bible, Old Testament, God, God-language, Names of God, Baal, El, Yahweh, "YHWH," "the God of the Fathers," "the living God," God as "King," "the Lord of Hosts," "Sabaoth," "Redeemer," "Creator," "the Holy One," "the Most High," "the jealous God."

INDEXES

Index of
Selected Biblical Passages

Index of Selected Biblical Passages

Index of
Names and Subjects

Index of
Hebrew Words

251